Beyond Punishment

Recent Titles in
Contributions in Criminology and Penology

Bandidos: The Varieties of Latin American Banditry
Richard W. Slatta, editor

America's Correctional Crisis: Prison Populations and Public Policy
Stephen D. Gottfredson and Sean McConville, editors

The Structure of Criminal Procedure: Laws and Practice of France,
the Soviet Union, China, and the United States
Barton L. Ingraham

Women and Criminality: The Woman as Victim, Offender, and Practitioner
Ronald Barri Flowers

Police Administration and Progressive Reform: Theodore Roosevelt
as Police Commissioner of New York
Jay Stuart Berman

Policing Multi-Ethnic Neighborhoods: The Miami Study and Findings
for Law Enforcement in the United States
Geoffrey P. Alpert and Roger G. Dunham

Minorities and Criminality
Ronald Barri Flowers

Marijuana: Costs of Abuse, Costs of Control
Mark Kleiman

Doing Time in American Prisons: A Study of Modern Novels
Dennis Massey

Demographics and Criminality: The Characteristics of Crime in America
Ronald Barri Flowers

Taking Charge: Crisis Intervention in Criminal Justice
Anne T. Romano

Intervention Strategies for Chronic Juvenile Offenders: Some New Perspectives
Peter W. Greenwood, editor

BEYOND PUNISHMENT

A New View
on the Rehabilitation
of Criminal Offenders

EDGARDO ROTMAN

*Contributions in Criminology
and Penology, Number 26*
MARVIN WOLFGANG, SERIES ADVISER

GREENWOOD PRESS
New York • *Westport, Connecticut* • *London*

Library of Congress Cataloging-in-Publication Data

Rotman, Edgardo.
    Beyond punishment : a new view on the rehabilitation of criminal
offenders / Edgardo Rotman.
       p.   cm. — (Contributions in criminology and penology, ISSN
0732–4464 ; no. 26)
    Includes bibliographical references.
    ISBN 0–313–26493–7 (lib. bdg. : alk. paper)
    1. Rehabilitation of criminals. I. Title. II. Series.
HV9275.R64   1990
364.6—dc20   89–37996

British Library Cataloging in Publication Data is available.

Library of Congress Catalog Card Number: 89–37996
ISBN: 0–313–26493–7
ISSN: 0732–4464

First published in 1990

Greenwood Press, Inc.
88 Post Road West, Westport, Connecticut 06881

Printed in the United States of America

The paper used in this book complies with the
Permanent Paper Standard issued by the National
Information Standards Organization (Z39.48–1984).

10 9 8 7 6 5 4 3 2 1

Parts of the present work appeared in a slightly different version in *Journal of Criminal
Law and Criminology* 77, no. 4 (1986): 1023–68. © 1986 by Northwestern University.

To my sister, Viviana, for her unwavering faith in this book.
To my parents, Rosita and Julio, who inspired my concern for
justice. And to my children, Josephine, Maggie, and Fred, who
I hope will maintain it.

Contents

Preface   ix

Acknowledgments   xiii

1.   Introduction   1

2.   From the Stones of Repentance
to the Therapeutic Community   21

3.   The Search for a Formula   59

4.   Against Rehabilitation   101

5.   Rehabilitation: How It Works   143

6.   Conclusions   183

Appendix: The Dr. van der Hoeven Clinic
in Utrecht, the Netherlands   189

Select Bibliography   197

Index   205

Preface

This book is the product of more than a decade of research in Europe and the United States. The project began in Freiburg, Germany, in 1975, at a very special time in the history of rehabilitation. In that year, the long process of reforming the sanctioning system of the German penal code was completed, and Douglas Lipton, Robert Martinson, and Judith Wilks's influential survey, *The Effectiveness of Correctional Treatment*, was published after a long delay. These two events illustrate some of the powerful tensions and contradictions between lawmaking and correctional science in the field of rehabilitation of criminal offenders.

The reform of the German penal code assigned a preeminent position to rehabilitation, following an international legislative trend of the 1970s, that was also reflected in Austrian, French, Spanish, and Swiss legislation. The unprecedented recognition of rehabilitation owed much to the doctrines of the new social defense, the influential crime-policy movement inspired and formulated in France by Marc Ancel, and the 1966 German Alternative Draft for a penal code. The draft emphatically proclaimed that criminal sanctions aimed not only to protect legal values, but also to reintegrate the offender in the community; it entirely restructured the penal code's general part on the basis of such postulates. Among the new measures, the most conspicuous was the intensive rehabilitative treatment for mentally disturbed offenders.

Paradoxically, just as rehabilitation was finally recognized by penal codes and in prison acts, a number of prominent scholars were arguing against it and predicting its demise. The wave of skepticism, initiated in Scandinavia and the United States, had already reached most European intellectual centers. The 1975 Lipton, Martinson, and Wilks survey promised to confirm the famous apothegm "nothing works," derived from an influential article that Martinson published the year before. Although the survey included evidence of the effectiveness of many programs, it was used instead to reinforce Martinson's negative conclusion.

When I began my research at the Max Planck Institute for Criminal Law, I was aware that my arguments went against the main current of penal thought. The criminological section of the institute was about to undertake its own long-term research on the effectiveness of rehabilitative experiments, but its encouraging results did not become known until years later. In the beginning, the road was difficult and the prospects discouraging. Yet I remained convinced that the rehabilitative alternative was not dead, although it needed a comprehensive rethinking and renewal at the conceptual and theoretical level. Without such a renewal, it seemed clear that the tide would turn away from rehabilitation back to worn-out forms of exemplary punishment. It was thus urgent to analyze the crisis of rehabilitative policies.

After some initial research, I realized that rehabilitation was being scapegoated for the failures of two other elements of the criminal justice system: the prison system and indeterminate sentencing. The overcrowded and violence-ridden megaprisons and the abuses of discretion in indeterminate sentencing systems bore no necessary relation to rehabilitative policies. Yet rehabilitation was persistently blamed for the problems arising from these other sources.

My investigation led me to distinguish between two opposing concepts of rehabilitation, one used to bolster oppressive, brainwashing interventions and the other to enhance human dignity and restoration to freedom. The humanistic concept viewed rehabilitation from the offender's perspective and led to the conception of rehabilitation as an individual right.

Years later, as I continued my work at the International Legal Studies program of the Harvard Law School, research findings of several social scientists led to the renewal of rehabilitative policies. Paul Gendreau and Robert Ross overturned the earlier conclusions that rehabilitation is ineffective. Elliot Currie underscored the role of rehabilitation in his global and constructive proposals for crime policy, and Frank Cullen and Karen Gilbert forcefully demanded a reaffirmation of rehabilitation. These and many other efforts were echoed in the extremely successful 1986 conference on reaffirming rehabilitation organized in Alexandria, Virginia, by the National Institute on Institutions and Alternatives directed by Jerome Miller. As my quest continued, I found myself in exceptionally good company. Indeed, in 1987, after an extensive review of the literature, Gendreau and Ross demonstrated ''the revivification of rehabilitation in the 1980s.''

Despite scientific vindication, the central values underlying genuine rehabilitative policies remain threatened in the late 1980s. Deep feelings of uncertainty, fear, and distrust are still pressing toward rigid repressive formulas. The search for security in a world of mounting problems explains, but certainly does not justify, the regression to anachronistic responses to crime. True, certain costs and calculated risks are involved in giving a second chance to criminal offenders. But our shortsighted unwillingness to face that reality is making our society more dangerous. Many offenders are daily discharged back into society with minimal or no preparation to face the momentous social problems and handicaps reserved for ex-convicts. A criminal justice system that creates and then ignores imperative individual needs for assistance and reeducation is bound to generate more crime. A new concept of rehabilitation based on the tradition of individual rights is needed to break this vicious circle and make law abidance a real possibility for ex-offenders. The purpose of this book is to establish a theoretical rationale for this new and workable approach to rehabilitation.

Acknowledgments

Many individuals and institutions generously supported and encouraged my work. I am particularly grateful to Hans-Heinrich Jescheck and Philip Heymann, who were my sponsors in Germany and the United States, respectively, and to Lloyd Ohlin and the Greenwood Press reviewer, who read the manuscript and gave me important advice. I also want to acknowledge Marc Ancel's writings as a constant source of inspiration for my book. My sister, Viviana Zelizer, provided invaluable encouragement and advice through the many years in which, on and off, I pursued this project. Nancy Jackson enriched this work by her intelligent editorial suggestions. I am thankful to the Alexander von Humboldt Foundation, the Max Planck Institute for Criminal Law, and the Harvard Law School, which made the research possible.

I am also grateful to the following colleagues and friends who cooperated in many ways in the realization of this book: Kurt Madlener, Günther Kaiser, Klaus Tiedemann, Frieder Dünkel, Karl-Peter Rotthaus, Barbara Huber, Thomas Würtenberger, Carlos François, Leandro Rotman, Günter Blau, Julie Feldbrugge, J. R. Niemantsverdriet, David Smith, Frederick Snyder, Harold Berman, Alan Stone, Stephen Hicks, Craig Parker, Aviam Soifer, John Pottenger, Jr., Elaine McGrath, Charles and Pauline Sullivan, Gary Marx, Ronald Corbett, Richard Fraher, Fred Chapman, Tom Potter, Gretchen Friesinger, Jeannette Yackle, Heda Kovaly, and the library staffs at the Max Planck Institute, the Harvard Law School, and the Suffolk University Law School.

1

Introduction

SIGNIFICANCE OF REHABILITATION

The rehabilitation of criminal offenders offers the criminal justice system a unique avenue of improvement. Despite the failures and abuses of the past, a revitalized concept of rehabilitation represents a creative opening in the repetitive mechanisms of a merely punitive system. Rehabilitation has enormous potential for humanizing and civilizing social reaction against crime.

Modern rehabilitative policies challenge the fantasy that the dark side of society can be forgotten and that deviants can be simply packed off to prisons. They propose instead to offer inmates a sound and trustworthy opportunity to remake their lives. Advocating the use of imprisonment only as a sanction of last resort, rehabilitation-oriented policies seek more effective channels of social reentry.

Whereas the traditional punitive reaction enforces conformity to law on the basis of fear or pure calculation, rehabilitation creates in the offender the capacity for social participation and responsibility.[1] Because it aims to offer opportunities that will make crime-free life a practicable option, rehabilitation is linked indissolubly with the reorganization of the community.[2]

Rehabilitation is not incompatible with fair punishment. But rehabilitative policies rest on an assumption that it is self-defeating to try to prevent crime by using the very means one is trying to eradicate. Instead of violence and coercion, rehabilitation proceeds through purposeful constructive action. In fact, the rehabilitative idea emerged as an innovative force opposing a purely retributive justice system. But while seeking to counteract its noxious effects, rehabilitative policies recognize that criminal punishment is unlikely to be abolished in the foreseeable future. By counteracting its excesses or compensating for them, rehabilitation helps make punishment more fair. Rehabilitation is in turn enhanced by fairness in sentencing[3] and at every other stage of the criminal justice process. How fairly the offender is treated at early procedural stages has strong bearing on the ultimate success or failure of the correctional phase.

The rehabilitative aim demands a consideration of the offender's entire life, including his or her future. It thus incorporates a concept of justice that goes beyond the symmetrical reaction of retribution and inquires into the subjective reality of the offender. Moreover, the realization of the rehabilitative aim enriches the idea of justice with the element of compassion.[4]

Rehabilitation not only enriches the notion of justice, but improves the law. The quality of law can be measured by its ability to comprehend the largest possible number of facts, and to cover in its generalizations as many situations as possible. By incorporating rehabilitation, a perfected law takes subjectivity into consideration, which would otherwise remain largely excluded from the criminal process. In a purely retributive and deterrent criminolegal system, the individual is only an abstract means to fulfill overriding social goals. Subjective aspects are considered only when relevant to establish the existence of the offense or the degree of responsibility. In contrast, the rehabilitative aim demands that the scope of the legal system be enlarged so that the future life of the offender in the community is considered in sentencing and during the correctional phases. Once the predicament of the individual human being is acknowledged as relevant, rehabilitation becomes an unavoidable humanitarian concern in the legal regulation of imprisonment. ''A prison that houses long-term offenders who have little hope of early release and no sense of usefulness to sustain their future visions cannot be anything but a jungle.''[5]

In recent times, the incorporation of the rehabilitative aim has been a major impulse for progressive reform of many European sanctioning systems. Legal developments impelled by the rehabilitative concern culminate in the recognition of rehabilitation as a right—one that in some countries has received constitutional sanction. It has become increasingly clear that a modern rehabilitative concept not only serves the social interest by preventing recidivism, but also the personal interest of the offender, who benefits from the opportunities of a crime-free life.

The rehabilitative idea introduces broader social issues into the criminal justice system, creating an area of convergence with the social welfare, public health, and educational systems. True rehabilitative action opens the apparatus of criminal justice to other fields concerned with the plight of individual human beings and their needs for solidarity and assistance. Modern rehabilitation has been seen as an extension of far-reaching social planning and reform in the area of criminal justice.[6] Moreover, the performance of the rehabilitative task has mobilized specialists from the most diverse fields of human endeavor. Anthropology, medicine, religion, psychology, history, sports, sociology, and law have all contributed to this effort to reintegrate stranded human beings into the community as valued members.

DEFINING REHABILITATION

Rehabilitation needs to be redefined in a way that avoids conceptual errors made in the past—errors that will be examined in detail in subsequent chapters exploring the historical, sociological, and legal meaning of rehabilitation. For now, it is enough to emphasize that an evolved rehabilitative concept includes the perspective of the offender as well as the state. In its most advanced formulations, rehabilitation has attained the status of a right. In this way, rehabilitation clearly cannot be used as a pretext to extend punishment or coercion beyond their legal limits.

Rehabilitation, according to modern standards, can be defined tentatively and broadly as a right to an opportunity to return to (or remain in) society with an improved chance of being a useful citizen and staying out of prison; the term may also be used to denote the actions of the state or private institutions in extending this opportunity. The definition thus embraces both the offender's rights and the government's policies. Rehabilitation in prisons comprises educational opportunities; vocational training; justly remunerated work; medical, psychological, and psychiatric treatment in an adequate environment; maintenance of family and community links; a safe, fair, and healthy prison environment; postrelease support; elimination of hindrances to reinstatement in the community; and the various services directed to meeting the imprisoned offender's physical, intellectual, social, and spiritual needs, as compatible with incarceration. As this list suggests, a broad concept of rehabilitation is not limited to specific programs but includes an adequate prison environment. Alternatively rehabilitation may take place in noninstitutional settings, allowing the offender to remain in society. In fact, rehabilitation is most fully realized in the community.

Historically, older terms such as *reform*, *regeneration*, and *correction* as well as more modern expressions such as *reentry*, *social reintegration*, *reeducation*, and *resocialization* have all been used to refer to the rehabilitative idea. There have been some differential nuances. For example, *reform* has been used to designate moral transformations as a consequence of punishment and *reintegration* is usually applied to the postrelease stage, but these are of relatively little importance. Following a widespread consensus in the Anglo-American penal literature on the subject, this study will adopt the term *rehabilitation* and regard other expressions as synonymous.

The literal criminolegal meaning of the word can be found in the dictionary under the sociological sense of the word *rehabilitate*. The *Webster's* definition is "to restore (a dependent, defective, or criminal) to a state of physical, mental, or moral health." The *Oxford English Dictionary* also includes among the meanings of *rehabilitation* the "restoration to a higher moral state." One should be careful, however, not to confine the concept to the sense of restoration to a preexisting condition of adequacy. Such use would not cover the achievement of totally new social or psychological developments or the acquisition of new skills. The word *rehabilitation* should therefore be used in the technical field of penology and criminal law with a meaning broader than its dictionary definitions.

Viewed from another perspective, the dictionary definition of *rehabilitation* throws light on its conceptual structure. The term is defined as both "the act of rehabilitation" and "the state of being rehabilitated," thus drawing a useful distinction between the rehabilitative action and the state it produces, actual or ideal. Recognizing the dual components of the conceptual field, instrumental and teleological, facilitates the analysis and transformation of available rehabilitative models. But one should keep in mind that the division between action and goal, the means and the end, is only an artificial analytic device. In fact, the two elements remain inextricably interlinked in a dynamic and unitary process of mutual interaction.

A good way to comprehend the variety of immediate aims or outcomes pursued in rehabilitative programs is to consult the program evaluation literature. For example, Lipton, Martinson, and Wilks listed a number of dependent variables used to measure the effectiveness of rehabilitative outcomes: recidivism, institutional adjustment, vocational adjustment, educational achievement, drug and alcohol readdiction, personality and attitude change, and community adjustment.[7] At the instrumental level, an ever-expanding list of rehabilitative methods includes various forms of psychotherapies, guided group interaction, wilderness training, alternative schools and foster care for juveniles, family therapy, day treatment programs, pretrial release and diversion programs, work-release and prerelease programs, restitution programs, and various community assistance programs.

Besides the positive concept of rehabilitation, there is also a negative one: the avoidance of harm and deterioration. This goal is attained mainly through non-institutional sanctions. Even sanctions that are not specifically rehabilitative, such as fines or professional bannings, accomplish an indirect rehabilitative function insofar as they replace incarceration.

HISTORICAL MODELS

The history of rehabilitation can be represented by four successive models: penitentiary, therapeutic, social learning, and rights oriented. The adoption of each new model did not necessarily exclude its predecessors, which simply became less prevalent. Past models were generally retained in a modified way, coexisting or blending with the new ones. All these models belong to the same family; that is, they are composed of similar elements and respond to similar needs of social systems. They differ in the means used to achieve social goals and in the roles and powers of the members of the rehabilitative relationship. The earlier models granted unrestricted power to the penal authorities, as in the disciplinarian penitentiary regime, somewhat mitigated by the consideration of the health of the inmate in the therapeutic model. The participation of the inmate becomes a central element of the rehabilitative system in the social-learning model and gains legal status in the rights model.

The basic elements of the penitentiary model are work, discipline, and moral education. Different concepts of psychological transformation led to two variations of the model, one approximating the monastic ideal of penance, the other associated with the individualist nineteenth-century ideal of progress through industry and personal effort. Both variations relied heavily on imprisonment to mold the character of the offender. The walls of the cellular prison not only isolated the offender from the contaminating influence of society, but supported the reformative action of religious discipline and indoctrination. Later, penitentiary confinement was the baseline of a gradual liberalization that provided a unique system of incentives and deterrents. These carrot-and-stick reformative schemes were meant to promote habits of self-discipline and industriousness. This new disciplinary approach culminated in the adoption of the indeterminate sentence.

The same indeterminate sentencing structure was later adopted in the emergent therapeutic model. The new model assumed that offenders were sick and attempted to "cure" them of their criminality. Most of the modern debate about rehabilitation revolves around the medical model. Criticism of its flaws precipitated the intellectual crisis of the rehabilitative concept.

Thanks to the medical analogy, the term *treatment* (formerly applied to the administrative handling of prisoners,[8] began to be used in a medical sense. In principle, the therapeutic model can mitigate the harshness of the disciplinarian penitentiary model with the element of care. But its potential for coercion tends to overshadow its positive aspects. In fact, it has lent itself to violations of individual rights under the cloak of therapeutic intervention, what Kittrie characterized as the abuses of the "therapeutic state."[9] At a conceptual level, the model failed to describe a specific pathology that could help to distinguish the average type of offender from law-abiding citizens. In addition, the therapeutic model created a social stigma in the inmate, the internalization of which was bound to create a self-fulfilling prophecy. Eventually an evolved therapeutic model, aware of the social and psychological aspects of disease, paved the way to the social-learning model of rehabilitation.

Sociopsychological theory helped to correct the theoretical flaws of a unilateral therapeutic model that characterized crime as individual pathology. The resulting social-learning model views crime as the product of learned behavior and rehabilitation as a compensation for early socialization flaws resulting, for example, from family breakup or neglect. The rehabilitative purpose is attained by transforming the traditional prison environment into a problem-solving community. The new model assumes that the capacity for law abidance can be learned through a process of human interaction, which includes participation, sharing information and feelings, and preparation for the postconfinement world. Modern European social-therapeutic experiments attempt to create social-learning environments in prisons, but community-based programs are essential to full realization of this model's goals. It finds its most refined expression in a pedagogy of self-determination,[10] which works to emancipate the offender from compulsive criminal behavior without adding further conditioning.

Growing respect for the dignity of offenders and for their rights led to a consideration of rehabilitation from the offenders' perspective. No longer seen exclusively as a state policy, rehabilitation became a right of the offenders to certain minimum services from the correctional authorities. The purpose of such a right is to offer each offender an opportunity to reintegrate into society as a useful human being. It includes both positive aspects, such as the provision of education and vocational training, and negative ones, related to the freedom from substandard conditions of incarceration, that is, from physical or mental deterioration incompatible with social readaptation.

THE MORAL CONTENT OF THE REHABILITATIVE PROCESS

Should rehabilitation be defined to include efforts to produce a moral change in offenders, or should it rather be confined to the acquisition of the capacity to abstain from future crimes? In other words, does the rehabilitative process aim toward inculcation of moral values or mere external conformity?

Over time, the gradual adoption of terms such as *resocialization* or *rehabilitation*, instead of *reform*, marked a shift in emphasis from the moral transformation of offenders toward their social readaptation. This new conception of the rehabilitative aim is not universally accepted. In fact, the advocates of an ethically based rehabilitation predict the failure of any efforts disconnected from a definite order of moral values.[11]

The morally oriented position disregards the fact that individual rights in modern pluralistic democracies may be violated by forced compliance with a given value system. This is an especially sensitive issue in countries where several cultural systems coexist within the same social system, as in the case of large immigrant populations. The moral approach may also lead the rehabilitating agent to a self-defeating attitude of self-righteousness and moral superiority, which will impede a genuine rehabilitative task.

The transformation of state officials into moral agents carries in itself another risk: the overextension of criminal law to moral issues irrelevant to its specific function. This function consists exclusively in protecting vital individual and social interests, embodied in the most basic prohibitions and commands of a particular legal system. Thus, the attempt to moralize the offender beyond those fundamental values necessarily transforms crime control into a paternalistic undertaking. When the coercive methods of criminal law fail to force compliance to that minimum of morality that forms the core of the criminolegal systems, rehabilitation has to seek such compliance through a learning process, rather than by becoming a subtler and more intrusive form of coercion.

Similar difficulties arise when the rehabilitative agent also holds the power of the medical doctor. The pretense of acting on a disease to obtain compliance to social patterns can be as dangerous for individual freedom as is religious or ideological indoctrination. In both cases psychological authority is used for the subtle imposition of a certain value system, contradicting the basic freedoms of modern pluralistic societies. But while the imposition of morality or of a given idea of health should be avoided, rehabilitation may well include the offer of necessary medical assistance or of religious support and practices.

A related problem is that many offenders are members of marginal subcultural groups, affirming some values opposed to those of the larger society. The attempt to transform these people morally, without a keen understanding of the social and cultural factors of their deviance, betrays an ineffective ethnocentric approach. The implied challenge is to find a rehabilitative model capable of coping with situations in which the offender does not share the value system of the agent. Such a model should take into account the fact that deviance may result, not from disease, but from the internalization of subcultural norms. On the other hand, deviance can also be the result of an unquestioning acceptance of social values shared by the law-abiding citizen, such as the possession of certain goods or the use of aggression to reach goals. As Merton pointed out in his seminal work on the subject, the lure of socially accepted values may lead some people to abandon the institutionalized ways to attain them.[12] Past rehabilitative models tried to induce conformity to the value patterns of a given cultural system, using methods that ranged from friendly forms of persuasion to the most intrusive brainwashing procedures. Such value-loaded rehabilitative concepts have been most prevalent in times of high social consensus and cohesion.[13]

If there are grave risks in efforts to inculcate moral values, the limited goal of law abidance is also an imperfect expression of the rehabilitative aim. Mere outer conformity to the law, dictated by cunning calculation or resulting from sheer deterrence, is fragile and transient. The content of the rehabilitative enterprise cannot be so radically restricted without rendering it ineffective.

The answer to the dilemma lies in a rehabilitative action that enhances human freedom instead of narrowing it through the imposition of limiting patterns. Such an alternative model of rehabilitation excludes from its goals any imposition of moral systems based on particular religious or political ideologies. A freedom-oriented model includes an educational action directed toward self-determination and responsibility. Autonomous and responsible social conduct presupposes a certain degree of freedom from psychological and environmental determinism. Thus, an education for responsibility does not infringe the basis of a pluralistic society because it is structured in the direction of the inner freedom of the individual. Such an attitude of respect toward individual freedom generates its own methodology, which at the psychological level means the furthering of self-knowledge and deliverance from mechanically accepted patterns. Although its outcome is no longer the morality based on compulsion and normative imperatives, this procedure is by no means unrelated to morality. It generates a new morality based on the understanding and dissolution of those psychological processes of conflict and isolation that are the substance of immorality. Moral awareness in this deep sense includes responsibility and compassion.

Rehabilitative programs are always dependent on their particular social and cultural context. Significant changes in historical models of rehabilitation reflect not only new policy-making formulas, but changes of attitudes and social practices. Today, at a time of desacralization and dissolution of social normative systems, it is futile to dream of returning to an idyllic past of uniformity. Instead, a new rehabilitative model should aim toward awakening the personal experience of social responsibility.

ANTHROPOCENTRIC AND AUTHORITARIAN MODELS

To resolve the dilemma posed by the moral content of rehabilitative action, it is useful to distinguish between two general prospective models of rehabilitation: one, authoritarian and oppressive in nature, the other liberty centered and humanist.[14] The authoritarian model of rehabilitation is really only a subtler version of the old repressive model, seeking compliance by means of intimidation and coercion. Rehabilitation in this sense is essentially a technical device to mold the offender and ensure conformity to a predesigned pattern of thought and behavior. Stultifying discipline, drugs, and even psychosurgery have been applied as part of this methodology of compulsory adjustment, which deals with the human being fundamentally as a set of reflexes. Although the distinction has typically not been made explicit, recent criticism of rehabilitation has been directed to the authoritarian model, unjustly discrediting other genuine forms of rehabilitation.

The anthropocentric or humanistic model of rehabilitation, on the other hand, grants primacy to the actual human being rather than metaphysical fixations or ideologies, which long served to justify the oppressive intervention of the state. Client centered and basically voluntary, such rehabilitation is conceived more as a right of the citizen than as a privilege of the state. A humanistic public policy regarding crime implies the idea of human perfectibility, which at the level of rehabilitation includes not only the offenders themselves, but also the society that bred them and the institutions and persons involved in their treatment.

The humanistic model of rehabilitation puts no faith whatsoever in individual change obtained through subtly imposed patterns or paradigms. Rather, it assumes that no valid transformation of the offender can be brought about merely by the action of an outside agency. Significant change will come only from the individual's own insight, which alone can dissolve the antisocial influences that conditioned his or her mind. Dialogue is essential, not to issue authoritative statements but to encourage the process of self-discovery. The social control agent needs to understand the psychological determinants leading to antisocial acts, so as to provide the key that will unlock the offender's own conscience.

The humanistic model of rehabilitation excludes all manipulative schemes to alter the offender's personality or behavior and demands fully informed consent and willing intelligent participation. Therapy should be used only when absolutely necessary and should scrupulously respect the individual's private sphere. Therapeutic intervention should not become a further conditioning, but an intensification of inner freedom and an encouragement of self-discovery. Instead of stamping the mind of the offender with a predetermined constellation of behavioral patterns, it should become a guide toward the creative possibilities of thought and new channels of action.

The psychotherapeutic perspective of the humanistic rehabilitative model goes hand in hand with the offer of practical assistance. It rejects the naive hope that idealistic preaching will return offenders to constructive life in a hostile society, which would accept them only on painful and abusive terms. Quite the contrary, it provides the offender with a renewed opportunity to live a crime-free life and become a useful citizen. Such a positive rehabilitative action helps create in criminal offenders a sense of social responsibility by arousing an awareness of their relationship with the rest of society.

A humanistic model of rehabilitation also includes a legal component. Not only are offenders protected against the abusive interference of the state in their rights to liberty and privacy, but a due process style is imposed on the correctional activity, which is geared toward intensifying individual freedom and self-determination. Thus the humanistic model leads to the idea of rehabilitation as a right of the offender: the state has a duty to offer him or her a rehabilitative opportunity. But while the state's rehabilitative initiatives must respect individual rights, they may nevertheless represent a significant element of governmental policies to combat crime.

REHABILITATION AND SPECIFIC DETERRENCE DISTINGUISHED

Rehabilitation must be carefully distinguished from *specific deterrence*, the technical term for the intimidating effect of punishment on convicted individuals. At one time the two concepts may have been blurred together; in historical notions of reformative punishment, its supposed "salutary" effects were hardly distinguishable from its intimidative value.[15] But a modern notion of rehabilitation, dissociated from the goals of punishment, goes far beyond what a behaviorist would call negative reinforcement. It encompasses a broad spectrum of constructive interventions, positive human services and opportunities that tend to reduce offenders' involvement in further criminal activity. Thus it is helpful to free the new definition of rehabilitation from such foreign bodies as specific deterrence.[16]

In its historical forms, rehabilitation encompasses various types of behavioral change through rewards and incentives for constructive action. Although admitting the legitimacy of such methods, especially significant for the treatment of certain mental disorders and insufficiencies, a liberty-centered notion of rehabilitation goes beyond positive reinforcement through immediate or even distant rewards. A true pedagogy of freedom cannot be reduced to environmentally induced change or to subtle forms of persuasion. Genuine change consists in freedom from conditioning, not in exchanging one conditioning for another, thus creating new psychological automatisms.[17] Psychotherapy in its highest sense clarifies antisocial psychological determinisms, thus facilitating a task that must be ultimately undertaken by each individual. In this way, rehabilitation becomes the product of a personal decision and not a subtle imposition.

In institutional environments it is, of course, easier to reduce change to the modification of behavioral patterns, but the limited, short-term results of behavior modification cannot substitute for change through the intelligent apprenticeship of responsibility. Although both methods may coexist in practice, it is important to distinguish between a process of subtle imposition, influence, and conditioning and meaningful change achieved through insight into antisocial psychological determinisms. A humanistic concept of rehabilitation includes forms of psychotherapy that transcend manipulation or coercive persuasion. It also offers many opportunities for self-realization without appealing to reward or punishment. In addition to education, vocational training, and external intervention to improve work opportunities, liberty-centered rehabilitation also includes the transformation of the institutional environment and its replacement, as far as possible, by community-based alternatives. This approach culminates in the notion of rehabilitation as a right, which would preclude intrusive forms of influence and the curtailment of individual autonomy.

REHABILITATION AND THE PURPOSE OF IMPRISONMENT

Traditionally, rehabilitation has been considered to be one of the purposes of imprisonment, on the mistaken assumption that incarceration itself could be rehabilitative. This fallacy arose from a misapplication of the notion of monastic penance to the first penitentiaries. Isolation, relieved only by labor and prayer, proved to have disastrous consequences for the inmates of early nineteenth-century penitentiaries. The identification of imprisonment and rehabilitation survived this failure, however. Moreover, rehabilitation was unfairly judged to share in responsibility for the notorious shortcomings of imprisonment, becoming thus an easy prey of criticism. It was obvious that the rhetoric of rehabilitation masked a grim reality of human deterioration, which increased the ranks of criminals instead of reforming them. This distortion contributed to the crisis of rehabilitative policies in the 1970s.

In fact, rehabilitation has today a totally different nature than imprisonment.[18] A humanist notion of rehabilitation has rid itself of any punitive ingredient. Its relationship with imprisonment is only to counteract the latter's harmful effects or to find ways to avoid it altogether. It is true that in some exceptional cases the prison may act as a ''respite''[19] from the inmate's involvement in criminal social webs. Moreover, rehabilitative efforts can transform the punishment of imprisonment into an occasion to discover new existential perspectives. But imprisonment has to be justified on retributive or incapacitative grounds, never assuming a rehabilitative purpose. Interrupting a criminal career has little benefit without the creation of a purposeful rehabilitative environment, which includes the offer of meaningful opportunities. Today, rehabilitation seeks not only to transform the desocializing prison environment, but also to replace institutional confinement with noncustodial alternatives as far as possible.

Halleck and Witte denied that it is possible to create a benign prison environment without trying to rehabilitate offenders. To endure the restrictions of prison life without bitterness or aggressiveness, they explained, the offender must have hope and a sense of significance.[20] Correctional workers share this psychological need. In this context, Irwin emphasized that dismantling the rehabilitative idea will hurt the morale of correctional officers by depriving them of a justifying philosophy that gives their work purpose and dignity.[21] In modern American megaprisons, meaningful rehabilitative action to counteract the negative effects of imprisonment should be accompanied by action at the social and cultural levels to eradicate institutional violence, neutralize the action of organized gangs, avoid the formation of prison subcultures, and overcome racial conflict.[22] Rehabilitation also requires a sentencing policy that relieves the present inhuman overcrowding of prisons.

Although rehabilitation is not the purpose of imprisonment, it is an overriding goal of a correctional system that seeks to minimize the harms of incarceration. In order to neutralize the desocializing potential of prisons, a civilized society is forced into rehabilitative undertakings. These become an essential ingredient of its correctional system taken as a whole. A correctional system "without socialization offerings nor interest in treatment means, in fact, de-humanization and regression."[23] The recognition that rehabilitation is needed to satisfy the social interest of enlightened crime prevention leads to a further step; its acknowledgement as a legal right of the offender.

REHABILITATION AS A RIGHT AND THE PRINCIPLE "NULLUM CRIMEN, NULLA POENA, SINE LEGE"

To oppose a right to rehabilitation is to ignore the due process limitation to criminal sanctions embodied in the principle *nullum crimen, nulla poena, sine lege*, inherited in substance from the Magna Carta and the post-Enlightenment codification and applied today with few exceptions in all major legal systems of the world. This principle implies not only that conduct cannot be considered criminal unless defined as such by the law before it occurs, but also that no punishment beyond what was prescribed by the preexistent law can be imposed. Although not expressly stated in the U.S. Constitution, this principle is embodied in the prohibition of *ex post facto* laws and bills of attainder and in the Fifth and Fourteenth Amendments.[24] "Just as there must be a declaration of the law's intention to make an act a crime, so its punishment must be promulgated through the same process."[25] The legislative duty to provide fair warning of punishable conduct extends, as an element of due process, to the nature and severity of the prescribed punishment. Due process of law is also violated when imprisonment includes punitive ingredients not specified by statute. This interpretation coincides with the principle established by a district court in Florida that "the courts have the duty to protect prisoners from unlawful and onerous treatment of a nature that, of itself, adds punitive measures to those legally meted out by the court."[26]

According to the *nullum crimen, nulla poena, sine lege* principle, the only valid purpose of imprisonment is to punish according to the law, however tautological this statement may appear. The notion of legal punishment considerably limits the possibility of adding punitive elements, whatever their motivation, to incarceration itself. The deterrent function of criminal law must flow from the normative threat of punishment and may not be left to the discretion of administrative authority. When the law wanted to make imprisonment a particularly excruciating experience, it clearly expressed that intention through the now largely abolished forms of hard labor or penal servitude. In this regard the Select Committee of the House of Lords defined in 1863 the plight of the convicted as "hard labour, hard fare, and hard bed." Rejecting this idea of increasing punishment by adding extra sufferings to imprisonment, later thinkers proclaimed that "offenders are sent to prison as punishment, not for punishment."[27] This view was mirrored in the international movement for the unification of prison sentences, which aimed to abolish the defamatory and afflictive forms of imprisonment and to reduce them to the sole loss of liberty. The question was first introduced during the International Penitentiary Congress of London and further debated in the next congress, which met in Stockholm in 1878.[28] In *Barnes v. Government of Virgin Islands*, the court reflected the viewpoint of enlightened modern penology when it stated that persons "are not sent to penal institutions in order to receive additional punishment; the fact of incarceration itself is the punishment."[29]

The principle *nulla poena, sine lege* has been invoked against an abusive notion of rehabilitation, which led to excessively discretionary sentencing practices.[30] Today, this same principle can be used as a legal pillar to support a constitutional right to rehabilitation. If imprisonment itself is the punishment, the unchecked harmful effects of incarceration on the mental and social health of the inmate represent illegal additional punishment. Institutionalization in an alienating and depersonalizing environment, without opportunities to combat degeneration or foster positive human development, is a source of various harmful effects that play no part in the design of legal sanctions. The law threatens citizens with imprisonment as the consequence of criminal conduct. That is where the deterrent function of the legal norm should stop. The law expects the citizen to foresee the loss of liberty prescribed by statute, but not the additional horrors of incarceration not intended by law. The only way to prevent or compensate for such unjustified deprivations is to carry out a positive program of rehabilitative action.

There is thus no basis for proposing deterrent policies as a novel substitute for rehabilitation, for deterrence has always been the essence of criminal law. A right to rehabilitation does not contradict the deterrent effect of criminal sanctions as long as they do not exceed the limits marked by the due process of law. But it is a basic function of rehabilitation to prevent and counteract such abuses.

SUPERFLUOUS AND IMPRACTICABLE REHABILITATION

Two kinds of offender may seem at first to be outside the scope of meaningful rehabilitative efforts: the socially well-adjusted and the incorrigible offender.

The first category consists mainly of certain white-collar, economic, environmental, or political criminals; civil disobedients; traffic violators; and perpetrators of regulatory offenses in general, who hardly fit into a therapeutic or social-learning model of rehabilitation. As Sutherland observes, for example, the crimes of large corporations cannot credibly be attributed to the emotional instability or complexes of their chief executives.[31] Nevertheless, if rehabilitation is conceived as a counteractive force against unwanted side effects of imprisonment, it may also be necessary for originally well-socialized inmates who in the long run would desocialize without some compensatory intervention. The right to rehabilitation understood as a right not to deteriorate[32] goes beyond a utilitarian rehabilitative policy geared to preventing recidivism, and can be demanded even for so-called socially well-adapted offenders.[33]

Some white-collar criminals suffer from personality troubles, which could neutralize all sense of social responsibility, and would therefore benefit from certain forms of psychological treatment. Other types of reckless conduct arise from sheer lack of technical and professional knowledge. In some specialized areas of the economy governed by extremely complex technical rules, the provision of information on business law, economy, accountancy, cybernetics, or ecology could accomplish a preventive and rehabilitative function. A full awareness of the magnitude of damages caused by illegal behavior in the economic field could conceivably inhibit the commission of further offenses. This would be part of a new approach to moral education, based on the individual awareness of social responsibility and aiming toward self-determination.[34] In the United States, the rehabilitative function has been transferred by analogy to judicial handling of large corporations. Through probation, and also occasionally by resorting to injunctions, judicial authority endeavors to restructure the internal processes of corporations to prevent recidivism.[35] Other legal innovations accomplishing similar functions include the introduction of a public interest director and community service as a corporate sanction.[36]

Incorrigible offenders may also seem beyond the reach of rehabilitative interventions. A number of stubborn recidivists defy all efforts of reincorporation into law-abiding social life. However, this category should be treated with extreme caution because of the relativity of the concept. Perceived incorrigibility may be the result of flaws in the correctional system rather than in the offender's personality. An offender who seems incorrigible within one particular rehabilitative context may be amenable to other treatment approaches. Cases of constant rehabilitative failure are found even in the best treatment-centered institutions and in the most carefully designed community-based programs. But most frequently, stubborn recidivism results from the unchecked negative effects of institutionalization, which include the absorption of criminal values and techniques. Incorrigibility should not lead to incapacitative confinement under the assumption that rehabilitation has failed. Incapacitation, when respecting constitutional safeguards, should be justified in its own right (that is, on the objective demonstration of the offender's dangerousness) and should be carried out within strict legal parameters. Moreover, recidivism is an insufficient criterion to measure dangerousness and does not necessarily mean incorrigibility or the failure of a particular rehabilitative policy.[37] Although a liberty-centered model of rehabilitation can coexist with exceptional incapacitative measures, the absence of tangible rehabilitative results should not be used to justify them. Indeed, when rehabilitation is recognized as a right, independent from its effectiveness,[38] apparent incorrigibility can be no obstacle to the offering of renewed rehabilitative chances. Even when the law prescribes very prolonged confinement, the maintenance of dignity and of the potentialities inherent in being human demand counteractive action and various forms of assistance. The rehabilitative response to cases of apparent incorrigibility associated with some type of mental disorders has given rise to the most conspicuous experiments of this century in "treating the untreatable."[39]

SENTENCING AND REHABILITATION

The traditional belief that rehabilitation was one of the aims of criminal punishment upheld indeterminate sentencing schemes in which rehabilitative considerations played a preponderant role. In fact, the length of imprisonment often depended primarily on the sentencing authorities' judgments on prospective rehabilitation. However, a liberty-centered concept should have no bearing on sentencing decisions. No one should endure a longer sentence in "order to be rehabilitated,"[40] nor should well-adjusted offenders receive shorter or nonincarcerative sentences just because they do not appear to need rehabilitation. In particular, giving milder sentences to white-collar criminals because of their apparent social adjustment would undermine the legitimacy of the sentencing system. Furthermore, if milder sentences are imposed in some cases on the basis of rehabilitative considerations, their denial in other cases could indirectly transform the lack of rehabilitative prospects into an increased punishment.[41]

To separate sentencing decisions from rehabilitative goals does not exclude discretionary sentencing altogether. Retributive justice is better served by individualized punishment than by fixed sentences that disregard the objective and subjective circumstances of each case. Under a rights model of rehabilitation, however, the likelihood of positive rehabilitative results cannot be used as a criterion in meting out punishment. While this model does not preclude benevolence or mercy from sentencing decisions based on other considerations, it does prohibit the use of dubious rehabilitative arguments. Furthermore, the notion of rehabilitation as a right is consistent with the right of the offender to the least-restrictive sentence available, according to conditions predetermined by statute.[42] The options are not determined by rehabilitative prognoses but by explicit legal conditions, with relatively little discretion left to the sentencing authorities.

Although rehabilitative predictions should not figure in the sentencing process, longer sentences may be assigned on the basis of offenders' proven dangerousness. One of the "dangers of dangerousness,"[43] however, is the temptation to use rehabilitative chances or performances as a measure of dangerousness. Such an approach amounts to reintroducing an authoritarian concept of rehabilitation through the back door and using it for repressive purposes instead of enhancing the offender's future chances. Rehabilitation predictions should not play any role in the delicate task of balancing the rights of the individual with the need for societal protection. Recidivism has multiple causes, among which the most serious include institutionalization itself, and the ex-offender's economic and social handicaps created by the legal system.[44] Incapacitative sentences should never be a punishment for failed rehabilitation or a consequence of a poor rehabilitative prognosis. Such sentencing (e.g., for offenders with mental disorders) should be justified in its own right, on the basis of a demonstrated need for social protection and when strict legal conditions are met. Moreover, according to the rights model of rehabilitation, the sentencing authority has an obligation, derived from the basic right to freedom, of choosing the least-restrictive sanction applicable.

Rehabilitative considerations play a central role not only in the design and legislative enactment of sanctions, but also in the creation of the correctional network to which their execution is assigned. Rehabilitation requires sanctions that will favor the later reintegration of offenders into society and help increase their capacity for law abidance. In this regard, the most important policy choice in sentencing reform has to do with the use of noncustodial alternatives to imprisonment and other devices to limit the growth of prison populations. In making this legislative choice a delicate balance must be struck between vital values protected by the criminal statutes and respect for the basic rights of criminal offenders. These rights are currently jeopardized by prison sentences, given the inhuman overcrowding of correctional institutions. Overcrowding not only defeats the basic purpose of fairness, but can make criminal punishment illegal and even unconstitutional when it exceeds the penalty prescribed by the preexisting law.

A fair sentence, essentially based on the offender's degree of culpability, contradicts neither the offender's right to rehabilitation nor governmental rehabilitative policy. Quite the contrary, insofar as a fair sentence favors the process of reconciliation between the lawbreaker and the community, it may have a rehabilitative value in itself. And an unfair sentence is bound to generate anti-social reactions. Unfairness is essentially a disproportion between offense and punitive reaction. Such a disproportion is inevitable when an offender is sentenced to an overcrowded institution. The same corrosive moral effects and prison unrest that result from sentencing disparity are also produced by the current crowding of prisons.[45]

The belief that current punitive practices are not deterrent or incapacitative enough to protect the values violated by a given type of offense cannot be criticized in itself. Outstanding studies have shown that the magnitude of deterrent and incapacitative effects cannot be reliably assessed.[46] Consequently there is little sound basis for either criticizing or defending deterrent or incapacitation-oriented policy. But the deterioration and dehumanization of imprisonment in overcrowded conditions is a glaring fact immediately apparent to any observer. However coherent and balanced a sentencing system may be, it will still be unfair if the end result is unfair punishment, such as imprisonment in overcrowded institutions. In this regard, the right to rehabilitation requires sentencing and correctional policies compatible with rehabilitative prison conditions.

For this purpose, norms for directing offenders to alternative programs should be coordinated with schemes to regulate prison populations directly. The Minnesota sentencing guidelines illustrate how the interaction between the sentencing and correctional systems can be taken into account. The guidelines complied with a legislative mandate to keep in mind the availability of correctional resources. Using a population projection model, the commission adopted a set of guidelines intended to maintain the prison population at about 95 percent of capacity. One motivation for this unique innovation was the sentencing commission's feeling that the state of Minnesota should not operate on an implicit policy that the prisons will be filled beyond capacity.

NOTES

1. Marc Ancel, *La défense sociale nouvelle* (Paris: Cujas, 1981), 253. For Ancel the "pedagogy of responsibility" is a central aspect of a modern humanistic crime policy.

2. On the complementarity of rehabilitation and community reorganization, see Alden D. Miller and Lloyd E. Ohlin, *Delinquency and Community: Creating Opportunities and Controls* (Beverly Hills, Calif.: Sage, 1985), 147–84.

3. On the rehabilitative significance of fair sentencing, see Arthur Kaufmann, "Dogmatische und kriminalpolitische Aspekte des Schuldgedankens im Strafrecht," *Juristenzeitung* 18 (1967): 553.

4. On the relationship between love and justice, see Harold J. Berman, *The Interaction of Law and Religion* (Nashville, Tenn.: Abingdon Press, 1974), 99ff. and Karl Peters, *Grundprobleme der Kriminalpädagogik* (Berlin: De Gruyter, 1960), 141ff.

5. Seymour L. Halleck and Ann D. Witte, "Is Rehabilitation Dead?" *Crime and Delinquency* 23 (Oct. 1977): 379.

6. Wolfang Naucke, *Tendenzen in der Strafrechtsentwicklung* (Karlsruhe: C. F.

Müller, 1975), 36. See also Peter Mrozynski, *Resozialisierung und soziales Betreuungsverhältnis* (Heidelberg: C. F. Müller, 1984).

7. Douglas Lipton, Robert Martinson, and Judith Wilks, *The Effectiveness of Correctional Treatment: A Survey of Treatment Evaluation Studies* (New York: Praeger, 1975), 12.

8. Paul E. Leman, "The Medical Model of Treatment," *Crime and Delinquency* (Apr. 1972): 204.

9. Nicholas N. Kittrie, *The Right to Be Different: Deviance and Enforced Therapy* (New York: Penguin, 1973), 1.

10. See Ancel, *La défense sociale nouvelle*, 253; Albin Eser, "Resozialisierung in der Krise?" in *Festschrift für Karl Peters*, ed. Jürgen Baumann and Klaus Tiedemann (Tübingen: J. C. B. Mohr, 1974), 505; and Edgardo Rotman, "L'évolution de la pensée juridique sur le but de la sanction penale," in *Aspects nouveaux de la pensée juridique (hommage à Marc Ancel)* (Paris: Pedone, 1975), 171.

11. Karl Peters, "Die etischen Voraussetzungen des Resozialisierungs—und Erziehungsvollzuges," in *Festschrift für Ernst Heinitz*, ed. Hans Lütger (Berlin: De Gruyter, 1972).

12. Robert K. Merton, *Social Theory and Social Structure* (London: Free Press, 1964).

13. Francis A. Allen, *The Decline of the Rehabilitative Ideal: Penal Policy and Social Purpose* (New Haven, Conn.: Yale University Press, 1981), 11–22.

14. See statement by Edgardo Rotman, "Latest Trends in Crime Policy and Their Effect on Sentencing," in *New Trends in Criminal Policy* (Proceedings of the Fifth International Colloquium) ed. International Penal and Penitentiary Foundation (Bonn: International Penal and Penitentiary Foundation, 1984), 75–78. A humanistic concept is one that recognizes in human beings their status as persons, "irreducible to more elementary levels," and their unique worth as beings "potentially capable of autonomous judgment and action," Marian Kinget, *On Being Human: A Systematic View* (New York: Harcourt Brace Jovanovich, 1975), v.

15. Karl v. Grolman, *Grundsätze der Criminalrechts-Wissenschaft* (Giessen: Heyer, 1825), 4–5.

16. The National Research Council panel's definition explicitly rules out the effects of specific deterrence as well as those of old age or maturation. See Lee Sechrest, Susan O. White, and Elizabeth D. Brown, eds., *The Rehabilitation of Criminal Offenders: Problems and Prospects* (Washington, D.C.: National Academy of Sciences, 1979), 21–22.

17. Edgardo Rotman, "Las técnicas de individualización judicial frente a un moderno concepto de resocialización," *Revista de derecho penal y criminología* (1972): 114.

18. Norval Morris, *The Future of Imprisonment* (Chicago: University of Chicago Press, 1974) and John Irwin, *Prisons in Turmoil* (Boston: Little, Brown, 1980), 237–38.

19. Irwin, *Prisons in Turmoil*, 240.

20. Halleck and Witte, "Is Rehabilitation Dead?" 372, 378.

21. John Irwin, "The Changing Structure of the Men's Prison," in *Corrections and Punishment*, ed. David Greenberg. (Beverly Hills, Calif.: Sage, 1977), 21, 32.

22. On the possibilities and strategies of neutralizing prison violence, community-based delinquency prevention programs, provision of new opportunity structures, and institutional and community change in general, see Miller and Ohlin, *Delinquency and Community*. On the need to focus on new loci of intervention (e.g., the family, the school,

the workplace, the community), see Susan Martin, Lee Sechrest, and Robin Redner, eds., *New Directions in the Rehabilitation of Criminal Offenders* (Washington, D.C.: National Academy of Sciences, 1981), 135–73 and Elliott Currie, *Confronting Crime* (New York: Pantheon, 1985), 224–78. The need to direct socializing efforts not only to individuals but also to their environment was recognized in "The Revision of the Minimum Program of the International Society of Social Defense," *Bulletin of the International Society of Social Defense*, 26 (English-French ed. 1984). On coping with gangs at the institutional level, see John Conrad, "Who Is in Charge? The Control of Gang Violence in California Prisons," in *Correctional Facility Planning*, ed. Robert Montilla and Nora Marlow (Lexington, Mass.: D. C. Heath, 1979), 135–47.

23. Günther Kaiser, "Resozialisierung und Zeitgeist," in *Festschrift für Thomas Würtenberger*, ed. Rüdiger Herren, Diethelm Kienapfel, and Heinz Müller Dietz (Berlin: Duncker & Humblot, 1977), 371.

24. Cheriff Bassiouni, "The Sources and Limits of Criminal Law in the United States," *Revue internationale de droit pénal* 3/4 (1975) 301, 305.

25. Ibid., 351.

26. Miller v. Carson, 401 F.Supp. 835, 864 (M.D. Fla. 1975), aff'd in part and modified in part, 563 F.2d 741 (5th Cir. 1977). See also Barnes v. Virgin Islands, 415 F.Supp. 1218 (D. V.I. 1976).

27. Alexander Paterson quoted by Marc Ancel, "L'abolition de la peine de mort et le problème de la peine de remplacement," in *Studies in Penology Dedicated to the Memory of Sir Alexander Fox*, ed. M. Lopez-Rey and C. Germain (The Hague: Martinus Nijhoff, 1964), 9.

28. Commission Pénitentiare Internationale, ed., *Le congrès pénitentiaire de Stockholm* (Stockholm: Bureau de la Commission Pénitentiaire Internationale, 1879), 139–70.

29. 415 F.Supp. 1218, 1224 (D. V.I. 1976).

30. Marvin E. Frankel, *Criminal Sentences: Law without Order* (New York: Hill & Wang, 1973), 3.

31. Edwin H. Sutherland, *White Collar Crime* (New York: Holt, Rinehart and Winston, 1967), 257.

32. See pp. 79, 82.

33. For a vivid testimony on the need of rehabilitative support for certain types of white collar offenders, see Brian Breed, *White Collar Bird* (London: John Clare, 1979).

34. See pp. 7, 8.

35. Comment, "Structural Crime and Institutional Rehabilitation: A New Approach," *Yale Law Review* 89 (1979): 353. See also Edgardo Rotman, "La question de la fonction préventive du droit pénal dans la creation et l'application des normes pénales économiques," in *The Sanctions in the Field of Economic Criminal Law* (Proceedings of the Kristiansand Meeting, Sept. 1983), ed. International Penal and Penitentiary Foundation (Bonn: International Penal and Penitentiary Foundation, 1984).

36. See Klaus Tiedemann, "Le système des sanctions en matière de délinquance pénal économique dans les divers ordres juridiques," in *The Sanctions in the Field of Economic Criminal Law*, ed. International Penal and Penitentiary Foundation (Bonn: International Penal and Penitentiary Foundation, 1984), 66.

37. Ancel, *La défense sociale nouvelle*, 325.

38. See pp. 120–22.

39. See pp. 65–68, 174–76.

40. This point has been clearly addressed in Morris, *The Future of Imprisonment*.

41. On the relativity of leniency in sentencing decisions, see James Vorenberg, "Narrowing the Discretion of Criminal Justice Officials," *Duke Law Journal* 4 (1976): 651.

42. See pp. 155–56.

43. Franz Exner, *Die Theorie der Sicherungsmittel* (Berlin: J. Guttentag, 1914), 59.

44. On modern legislative trends favoring the expungement of records after a certain time, see International Penal and Penitentiary Foundation, ed., *Criminal Records and Rehabilitation* (Proceedings of the Meeting of Neuchâtel, 1979) (Neuchâtel, Switz.: Editions Ides et Calendes, 1982), 36, 61, 71. See also Nigel Walker, *Punishment, Danger and Stigma* (Oxford: Blackwell, 1980), 147.

45. See testimony of Edgardo Rotman in U.S. Congress, House Committee on the Judiciary, *Sentencing Guidelines: Hearings before the Subcommittee on Criminal Justice*. 100th Cong., 1st Sess., 1987, 175.

46. See National Academy of Science panel's report in Alfred Blumstein, Jacqueline Cohen, and Daniel Nagin, eds., *Deterrence and Incapacitation: Estimating the Deterrent Effects of Criminal Sanctions on Crime Rates* (Washington, D.C.: National Academy of Sciences, 1978), 3–90.

2

From the Stones of Repentance to the Therapeutic Community

INTRODUCTION TO THE HISTORICAL ANALYSIS OF REHABILITATION

The Divorce between Rehabilitative Ideas and Prison Realities

History enables us to discern the various misleading directions taken in the name of rehabilitation, all of which led ultimately to disenchantment. A historical perspective also reveals the shallow and stereotyped concepts of human transformation at the roots of such failed rehabilitative models, suggesting how the present crisis may be overcome. Abandoning the flawed patterns of the past, rehabilitation should now find its renewal in a deeper and qualitative notion of human change, purged of its association with punishment and appealing to the specifically human capacity for psychological transformation.

Historical scrutiny also throws light on the redemptive contributions of rehabilitation. Despite its failures and distortions, the idea of rehabilitating the criminal offender is related to the faith in the human capacity to change for the better. It is no accident that the idea of rehabilitation came to the fore in periods when the search for excellence dominated the mainstream of human thought, under circumstances marked by inspiration and confidence in the improvement of the human condition.

Although the various expressions of the rehabilitative ideal were shaped by the particular anthropological conceptions prevailing at the time, they all proclaimed the common goal of transforming a purely vindictive penal reaction into a constructive venture. Rehabilitative formulations always claimed to introduce a measure of social or moral improvement to the arid panorama of mere punishment.

The most striking feature of the history of rehabilitation, however, is the abyss between the theoretical aspiration and its factual realization. When the speculations of reformative crime policies left the shelves of penal literature or philosophy to enter into the world of penal reality, they invariably lost their original thrust. The lofty goals of moral or social improvement had to be inserted into a scheme of harsh repressive punishment, also influenced by political and economic interests. The result was a sharp contrast between official declarations and the slight actual role of rehabilitation in the implementation of penal objectives.

However flawed past rehabilitative ventures may have been, they merit some consideration, because many such efforts were considered humanitarian innovations at the time or sprang from genuine philanthropic impulses. One needs to look carefully at the formation of rehabilitative policies, giving adequate attention to the complexity of the many intervening factors.[1] Such analysis may reveal the process of resistance to innovative change through which, in practice, the demands for security and custody displace rehabilitative initiatives.[2]

An important factor to consider in this inquiry is the characterization of rehabilitation as a function of imprisonment throughout much of its history. Because of this confusion, with distant roots in the notion of ecclesiastical penance, the failures of imprisonment were often attributed to rehabilitation.[3] But even when rehabilitative policies were disentangled from imprisonment and embodied in alternative measures, punitive ideologies and bureaucratic interests conspired against their success. David J. Rothman carefully depicted the process through which the pressure of professional or bureaucratic vested interests in America perverted good intentions.[4] Yet, despite obstacles and failures, rehabilitative policies have continued to progress toward the goal of counterbalancing the negative effects of punishment. Today, rehabilitation can be viewed as a distant relative of penal abolitionism, rather than as a variety of punishment.[5]

Revisionist Interpretations

Interpreting the disparities between the reformative ideal and institutional practice, Foucault did not find any failure in the design or application of the reform model. Rather, he argued, the disparity reflects a deliberate scheme to produce delinquency in a highly supervised milieu. The goal of punishment is not to eliminate offenses, but to manage them according to a strategy of class domination. "Prison," declared Foucault, "has succeeded extremely well in producing delinquency, a specific type, a politically or economically less dangerous—and, on occasion, usable—form of illegality."[6] Prison reform has been part of the very functioning of prison since its beginning. Prison's "failure" and its more or less successful reform are not seen as consecutive stages, but as a simultaneous system. Together with the disciplinary structure of the prison and the penitentiary techniques, this system combines "programs for correcting delinquents" together with "mechanisms that reinforce delinquency."[7]

There is an undeniable element of truth in the role ascribed to prisons in Foucault's hallucinatory vision of a social order reduced to relations of power, coercion, and subordination. This corresponds precisely to the purely punitive reaction of the state, a function overestimated by Foucault. The underlying anthropological conception is of human beings devoid of all social inclinations or bonds apart from submission to a stultifying discipline of state power. Foucault's interpretation equates rehabilitation with coercive intervention of state power. Its humanistic possibilities are negated, it becomes merely a utopian gear in the mechanism of domination, "isomorphic . . . with the disciplinary function of prison."[8] Rehabilitation is thus reduced to its most authoritarian form.

The very idea of discipline is diminished in the vision of Foucault, where it means only submission to a rigid routine and to mechanical imposition. In fact, the concept of discipline has a pedagogical meaning going beyond this coercive image. The etymological roots of the word *discipline* originate in *discipulus*, which means "a learner." The resulting Latin word *disciplina* encompasses not only discipline in the ordinary sense, but also instruction and training. Learning, and most particularly social learning, is an outstanding element in a modern concept of rehabilitation, free from the rigid determinations of Foucault's disciplinary picture.

The interpretation of penal policies as concealed strategies of power can easily fall in the traps indicated by Allen for sweeping generalizations and tendentious and reductive arguments.[9] He quoted Banner, who denounced the historical error of believing that "reality is always mean, hidden, sordid and that men normally act not out of generosity but from fear and from considerations of status and gain." Allen also quoted Karl Popper's reference to the "dangerous fashion of our times . . . of not taking arguments seriously, and at their face value, at least tentatively, but of seeing in them nothing but a way in which deeper irrational motives express themselves."[10] The state of mind of many penal innovators was appropriately expressed by Prins, as an inner struggle between the contradictory forces of tradition and innovation. "At the moment when I write," he confessed, "I don't know if the opinions I express, or the way I express them, is due to my readings, my personal reflections, my education, my environment, my nature, my spontaneity."[11]

Fear of the politically and economically dangerous classes has often been cited as an explanation of the emergence of total institutions.[12] But, as Ignatieff pointed out, "class fear cannot account for the specific idiosyncrasies of the institutional solution—the faith in silence, solitude, religious indoctrination and hard labour."[13] Sherman and Hawkins observed that a social service purpose has played a larger part in the justification of the postrevolutionary prison than is sometimes acknowledged. They insist that the reform of criminals was its genuine aim; for example, the Quakers expected to make better men through institutions such as the Walnut Street Jail.[14] Ignatieff also emphasized the pitfalls of social reductionism in explaining the institutional movement. He recognized that John Howard's penitentiary schemes preceded the English labor crisis of 1815, an event he himself used to explain the emergence of institutional programs.[15] Quoting Rothman, he pointed out that the fact of the crisis would not explain why authorities chose the particular remedies they did, when less elaborate methods might have been employed in response to the perceived breakdown of social control.

Ignatieff's examination of the content of reformative schemes in themselves, not merely their relationship to external social functions, represents a significant contribution to the historical analysis of rehabilitation. This type of analysis allows a fruitful understanding of the permanent gap between reform rhetoric and institutional reality, in large part due to a deficient rehabilitative formula. Understanding the past formulas provides a specific basis for criticism.

Ignatieff's inquiry penetrates the mind of the penitentiary pioneers, suggesting how they conceived of deviance and its correction through the reform of character. In his view, deviance was understood in irreducibly individual terms, as a highly personal descent into sin and error. Correspondingly, the early penitentiary supporters saw the institution as furthering the triumph of good over evil, in a "drama of suffering, repentance, reflection, and amendment, watched over by the tutelary eye of the chaplain."[16] The chaos that characterized the prisons in the pre-Enlightenment era "compromised the moral legitimacy of the social system in the eyes of the confined."[17] It was important that the penitentiary reconcile the "imperatives of discipline with the imperatives of humanity" in order to convince the offender of the moral legitimacy of law and its custodians.[18] Ignatieff stressed in his interpretation of the reform of character the "Quaker and Evangelical language of conscience epitomized by Elizabeth Fry" as opposed to the purely rationalistic vision of Foucault. He defined his model as one of symbolic persuasion and opposed it to Foucault's model of disciplinary routinization.[19]

A purely disciplinary interpretation of rehabilitation overlooks the significant connection to legal restraint of state power. Humanistic rehabilitation today is not just a gear in the strategy of power, but represents a development of the rights of the individual against the omnipotence of state penal intervention. Such a rehabilitative conception supports the introduction into prisons of legal limitations and individual safeguards similar to those found elsewhere in the criminal process, which derive from the common-law tradition and were developed in the post-Enlightenment codification. The concept of rehabilitation as a right is thus linked with the transformation of the legal status of the prisoner in both national and international legislation, and with the recognition of a network of specific prisoners' rights.[20] This phenomenon corresponds in America to the prisoners' rights movement, a source of major changes in the law and practice of corrections since the 1960s.

Historical Revisionism and the Transformations of Imprisonment

The legal punishment of imprisonment is far from the immutable unitary phenomenon depicted in Foucault's revisionist discourse. Despite all retrogressions and its present dramatic problems of intrainstitutional violence and over-crowding, imprisonment has progressed continually from the chains and penal servitude of its beginnings. Over time, the legal status of the prisoner has been affirmed, prison sentences have been shortened, the afflictive content of im-prisonment has been reduced, and such degrading forms as hard labor or penal servitude have been eliminated. Even if prison has proved not to be the specific instrument to rehabilitate offenders, valid efforts have been made to avoid the various negative and desocializing consequences of incarceration. The strength-ening of prisoners' rights and dignity is a significant step toward their reinte-gration into society.

In England, Garland recently criticized Foucault's theory because of its inabil-ity to capture the historical transformations of imprisonment. He challenged the thesis that the modern penal system originated at the beginnings of industrialized urban society. Rather, he argued that the early decades of imprisonment, includ-ing the Victorian penal system, lack the later concern for individualization that characterizes the modern "epoch of rehabilitation." The Victorian penitentiary followed an extremely detailed disciplinarian regime uniformly applied to all in-dividuals. According to the prevailing "classic" criminology of the time, pris-oners were conceived as legal subjects entitled to equal treatment before the law. Victorian prisons, in consonance with Foucault's thesis, "exhibited a close and detailed form of discipline or dressage,"[21] but did not take account of the individ-ual offender's peculiarities. Garland located the origin of modern individualized forms of penalty in Britain in the "brief period between the Gladstone Committee Report of 1895 and the start of the First World War in 1914."[22] His demarcation of periods thus parallels Rothman's account of similar changes of penal policies in the United States.[23] Garland criticized Foucault for downplaying the shift "from individualism to individualisation"[24] and erroneously identifying the mod-ern form of penalty with "the system constructed a whole century earlier with the development of modern prisons and its disciplinary forms."[25] In his study "of the framework of assumptions, logics and objectives" that supported the life and pol-icies of modern penal institutions, Garland tried to disprove the Foucauldian the-sis that prison was "from the start a technique of transformation and not a 'punishment,' directed at the criminal's nature and not his act."[26]

The strength of Garland's arguments lies in the exposure of Foucault's in-sufficient differentiation between the old prison system and the one resulting from the late nineteenth-century penal policies. Garland showed the social and political relevance of the transformation of a prison dominated by the idea of uniformity of treatment to one based on criminological consideration of the offender's personality. The latter model supposed not only individualized sanc-tions but also the creation of a network of specialized institutions for different categories of offenders. This diversification of sanctions and institutions is ul-timately seen by Garland as a change in the strategies of social control of the burgeoning welfare state.

It would be a mistake to draw too sharp a line between the two periods.

Changes in the form of penalty are less clear-cut in reality than in theory. As Garland himself recognized, many features of Victorian punishment survived the post-Gladstonian transformations; at the same time, the new approach had important precedents in the past. Even in 1796, for example, the warden of New York's Newgate prison, Thomas Eddy, created an individualized treatment program aimed at the reformation of the offender, which was based on a classification that distinguished hardened offenders from criminals who retained some sense of virtue and young persons convicted for the first time.[27] To appraise Garland's account, one must consider the peculiarities of the British history of imprisonment, which was limited until the mid–nineteenth century to minor property offenders; transportation and capital punishment were used for serious crime. In regard to prison rehabilitation, the real turning point was the experiment of Machonochie in Norfolk Island, which generated a new penitentiary technique.[28] Another landmark is the input of behavioral sciences and social psychiatry in the treatment of habitual offenders after World War II and the various experiments aiming toward the model of the therapeutic community.

Rehabilitation and Social Ideology

The following historical overview focuses on the intrinsic features of successive rehabilitative models as a comparative basis for the construction of a new model. Of course the study of rehabilitative models should consider their extrinsic relations with the prevailing social ideology of their time. For example, Rothman's account of the emergence of the penitentiary is exceptionally helpful in understanding the origins of rehabilitation in America.[29] He links the birth of the penitentiary with the general movement toward institutionalization in other areas, such as the poorhouse, the insane asylum, the orphanage, and the reformatory. This trend emerged during the era of President Andrew Jackson, reflecting an acute concern for social order and coherence. According to Rothman, institutionalization was a reaction to the transition from colonial society to more mobile forms of communality, in which the traditional mechanisms of control, mainly the family and the town community, seemed to be losing their grip on individuals. The perception of social decay aroused a desire to return to the social order of prerevolutionary times.

The asylum, in Rothman's interpretation, helped dispel the specter of disorganization and impending social catastrophe. This solution was based on an environmental theory that explained crime, poverty, and insanity on the basis of social flaws that could be corrected through social action. The penitentiary, as a specific kind of asylum, was intended to fulfill a dual purpose: "It would rehabilitate inmates and then, by virtue of its success, set an example of right action for the larger society."[30] The penitentiary was supposed to reconstitute the crumbling social structure, of which crime was only a symptom. It became thus a utopian remedy for all evils in society.

Allen emphasized the need to understand what he calls the rehabilitative ideal

within a cultural context.[31] In his view, rehabilitation is the response of society
to its deviants when the normative and value system is strong enough to reabsorb
them. Vigorous rehabilitative policies arise in societies where there is "strong
and widespread belief in the malleability of human character and behaviour,"
which in turn presupposes that dominant groups are highly confident in their
definitions of character, in their standards of good behavior and in the capacity
of institutions to transform deviant behavior.[32] In addition, there must be enough
social consensus to define clearly the content of the rehabilitative goal, to make
a "distinction between the malady and the cure." These preconditions have been
met, Allen found, in societies as diverse as nineteenth-century antebellum America and the People's Republic of China.[33] However, the rehabilitative ideal based
on collective acquiescence to exemplary models of conduct seems more akin to
political dictatorships than to democratic modern societies and can hardly be
included in the humanistic model of rehabilitation. Rehabilitation defined as
malleability implies a paternalistic acceptance of manipulative brainwashing
schemes, a danger Allen recognized.[34] This notion leaves no room for the liberal
aspirations of a social ethic based on free individual conscience and intelligent
discovery of true human value.

Most of the experiments that constitute the history of rehabilitation were
isolated, pioneering undertakings at odds with a prevailing repressive system of
punishment. Even the asylums established in the United States at the beginning
of the nineteenth century were isolated phenomena, while the great majority of
the inmates remained in establishments similar to those of colonial times.[35] The
concrete manifestations of the rehabilitative idea thus were only a small factor
in the overall field of crime control. Their importance lies in their qualitative
superiority and their potential, as pilot experiments, to influence the rest of the
correctional system. On the negative side, their existence provided an excuse to
avoid wider reforms, and rehabilitative rhetoric was used to legitimize abusive
state intervention.

The following historical analysis of rehabilitation is organized chronologically
and attempts to draw connections to conceptions of human transformation prevailing in successive historical periods. Its ultimate goal is to understand the
workings and underpinnings of today's rehabilitative experiments, which often
represent a combination of past models, reflecting a considerable historical depth.
Accordingly, after a chronological outline of the principal embodiments of the
rehabilitative idea, four basic historical models will be formulated: penitentiary,
therapeutic, social learning, and rights oriented. These models do not follow a
uniform progression, nor can they be found in their pure form in concrete
rehabilitative systems, which instead typically combine elements of several
models. In what Garland calls the twentieth-century ideology of penal welfarism,
the rehabilitative model comprises elements of paternalism, evangelicism, and
scientism coexisting in an "eclectic and flexible framework of representation."[36]
Moreover, "the penal-welfare strategies never wholly displaced other, more
traditional strategies of sentencing and punishment."[37] The history of rehabili-

tation has the same characteristics Thorsten Sellin observed in the general history of social reaction to crime:

> The history we are studying is not like a ladder, on which each rung marks a clear division between one stage and the one above. It is more like a river, arising from several tributaries, some of which, owing to the operation of changing climatic factors, tend to grow more powerful, while others show signs of drying up, yet, all are adding their respective flow to the main stream.[38]

ANTIQUITY

The idea of the moral transformation of the offender, which is at the root of modern rehabilitative policies, first appeared in antiquity. As early as 1050 B.C. a Chinese book expounded a penal policy based on the idea of amendment. Ancient Chinese law established the institution of the "beautiful stone," a veined stone placed at the entrance of the courtroom. The offender was obliged to contemplate the symmetry of its veins, which was considered to be the image of natural order. After thirteen days of contemplation, he was employed in public works.[39]

Plato, in his astonishingly modern tripartite prison system, envisaged a house of corrections (*sophronisterion*) for offenders against the religious cult who were considered capable of reform. In his conception, imprisonment had to last at least five years and inmates had to be treated gently during that time. Failure to reform led to the death penalty.[40] Although there is no evidence that Plato's reformative ideas were anything more than a theoretical construct, it is unlikely that this system was utterly unrelated to Athenian institutional life. In Plato's days imprisonment was reserved for those awaiting execution and for delinquent debtors, and it has not been demonstrated that it existed as an independent punishment in the Greek justice system of the time.[41] Plato's penal ideas should be assessed in the wider philosophic and educational context of ancient Greek thought, with particular reference to Socrates' appeal to self-knowledge and his instruction in virtue. Socrates' relentless examination of the human mind is a forerunner of modern psychotherapy, one of the most significant ingredients in the current rehabilitative treatment of criminal offenders.

CHRISTIANITY

The Greek ideas on reformative punishment evolved into the Christian notion of *poena medicinalis*, which inspired monastic penance. The Christian contribution to the development of a rehabilitative spirit in the application of criminal sanctions is rooted in various texts of the New Testament, particularly the admonition to love one's enemy. The principle of agape, source of all other ethical prescriptions, implies loving one's neighbor, even one's enemy, as oneself.[42] This means that the criminal, as a neighbor, can no more be avoided than one's own self and is as present and real as one's own ego. The consideration of the offender as a human being is the cornerstone of a humanist crime policy and of its rehabilitative derivations. The parable of the lost sheep, stressing the importance of amendment, was also influential. On the whole, most Gospel texts emphasize forgiveness and reconciliation. Although the *lex talionis* continued to be the prevailing principle, the Gospels had a deep humanizing influence on criminal law, especially during the first centuries of Christianity. The law of the first Christians sharply contrasted with Roman penal practices, which sentenced convicted offenders to work for life in insalubrious mines (*ad metalla*) or threw them to wild beasts in the amphitheaters.

Moral reformation occupies a prominent place in Saint Augustine's penal thought. Although he affirmed the Church's power to punish heresy, coercion had only a subsidiary role in his message. When dealing with heretics, he believed, the Church should use friendly persuasion, kind admonition, and peaceful discussion. Yet, true to his times, Augustine emphasized the curative force of punishment, as a bitter but health-giving medicine.

The most influential embodiment of the Christian rehabilitative conception was the disciplinary punishment practiced within monastic orders. Through solitary confinement and meditation in the cell, the order attempted to combine the pain of imprisonment with the spiritual growth of the transgressor. This blend of punishment and amendment (which modern penology regards as conflicting goals) became the embryo of modern imprisonment and provided the formula for nineteenth-century correctional experiments. In monastic punishment originated both the humanistic and the authoritarian elements that marked future developments of the rehabilitative idea.

Monastic incarceration contrasted with the cruel vindictive practices prevailing in folk law and with vindictive theory exercised by Church courts. A breach of disciplinary rules was sanctioned with a system of penances conceived as a medicine for the soul and providing a variety of forms of atonement.[43] Monks confessed to their offenses and were punished secretly before being reintegrated into the local monastic community.[44] Often the punitive element prevailed over the component of mercy, and monastic imprisonment deteriorated into torture and mutilation.[45] Later canonic law distinguished between penance as coercive atonement and *poena medicinalis*, restricted to the censure or reprimand of deviants. The goal of penance was to protect the public order (*salus publica*) of the Church, while *poena medicinalis* aimed at the personal spiritual welfare of the transgressor (*salus privata*). The two were linked, though, insofar as the Church used coercive punishment when the *poena medicinalis* proved ineffective. *Poena medicinalis* was also used as psychological coercion to obtain the transgressor's compliance with the authority of the Church.[46] The idea of punishment as a cure for the soul was a two-edged sword. It could be accompanied by compassionate care and educational endeavor working toward a positive transformation. But the spiritual health (*salus animae*) of the condemned was also invoked to justify inhuman segregation and even torture. Conceiving punishment as an instrument of spiritual purification can be the first step down a dangerous slope that may lead to the extreme error of considering torture an "act of love" or a means of catharsis.[47] Even the use of torture to seek out the truth in the criminal process (*inquisitio veritatis per tormenta*) has been occasionally credited with penitential value.[48]

Monastic imprisonment became widely known in the late nineteenth century through an essay by Jean Mabillon titled "Reflections on the prisons of the monastic orders," left unpublished at the time of his death in 1707.[49] This Benedictine monk closely studied monastic life and concluded that the four rules of conduct—isolation, work, silence, and prayer—ought to be applied to secular corrections. He advocated a spirit of charity, compassion, and mercy and made critical proposals to improve the conditions of monastic imprisonment. Contemplation and solitary confinement were thought to have a high reformative value, and even before their adoption by the prison reformers of the Enlightenment and the designers of the modern penitentiary, they were occasionally applied to ordinary citizens.[50]

Modern institutional criticism has perceived a correlation between monasticism and the practices of what Foucault called the disciplinary society.[51] According to this hypothesis the regimentation of the cloister provided a paradigm for schemes of social control applied to institutions for the insane, the poor, and the criminal as well as the school, the family, and the barracks. Monastic orders provided an example of extreme visibility of thoughts and behavior, of mind and body. Through detailed regulation of everyday life, procedures of reprimand, self-accusation, and denunciation, they achieved total discipline as well as effective institutional functioning.

Modern total institutions can only be regarded as caricatures of monastic discipline, however. Members of monastic orders were willing to obey those in authority because they shared a common goal that dispelled the risks of arbitrariness and abuse inherent in modern institutionally enforced discipline. At its worst, monastic life was a totalitarian regime, in which all pluralism was excluded by definition. Even so, the monk's initial voluntary decision gave meditation and contemplation as a means to self-transformation a different value from that of the early penitentiary experiments.

Discipline in the religious sense meant not only restraint but also spiritual apprenticeship, a way of learning a life considered exemplary. However, the total withdrawal into a self-contained community is no guarantee of inner transformation. It may result instead from self-delusion, leading to mere conformity and obedience as an escape from individual responsibility. The modern idealization of the community as a panacea to transform the lawbreaker should thus be closely scrutinized. If members are not genuinely involved in the process of their individual transformation and if the community isolates itself from the concern for wider human predicaments, it tends to develop authoritarian and aggressive features, which can eventually become self-destructive, as in the extreme example of the 1978 Guyana mass suicide.

After the Church established itself as an autonomous legal authority in the late eleventh and twelfth centuries, concern for the protection of social order largely displaced the rehabilitation-oriented notion of punishment as a form of spiritual education or medicine for the soul. The Church took over a retributive function that had earlier been left in other hands. New concepts of sin and punishment emerged, based on the prevailing doctrine on atonement introduced by Anselm. This led to a retributive theory, but as Berman explained, the aim was not to avenge the victim but to constitute a "tribute," a price that had to be paid to vindicate the law.[52]

The doctrine of atonement can also be related to a humanist notion of rehabilitation centered on the personal dignity of the offender. Viewing the transgressor as a sinner, rather than a criminal, gave him "a certain dignity, vis-à-vis his accusers, his judges and his fellow Christians,"[53] who were sinners like himself. Although judges cast themselves as instruments (however unworthy) of the divine, the attribution of sin to all members of society freed criminal punishment from the element of self-righteousness and moral superiority on the part of the judge. Even the executioner was obliged to kneel down before the condemned man at the last moment and ask his forgiveness for the blow he was about to strike.[54] This application of the theological concept of sin can be regarded as a precedent of the modern sociopsychological notion of alienation, which includes both the criminal and the noncriminal. Just as sin is seen as alienation from God, psychological alienation estranges the individual from his or her own self, which is replaced by values imposed by the social environment that are not true to the individual's nature. As comprehensive as sin, the notion of alienation is related to the idea that all members of the social body share responsibility for each crime, demanding a broader scope for human transformation, which should include the representatives of the criminal justice system themselves.[55] Today, the sense of forgiveness and of respect for human dignity can no longer depend on a discretionary decision, however enlightened, of the spiritual or state authority. The affirmation of the dignity of criminal offenders has been channeled into a positive recognition of their rights.

SIXTEENTH-CENTURY HOUSES OF CORRECTION

Prison historians differ as to the use of imprisonment as punishment during the Middle Ages. Its primary functions were undoubtedly the safe custody of suspects awaiting trial and of the condemned before execution, as well as the coercion of debtors and the contumacious. Some writers reject the possibility that the overcrowded and pestilent county jails could have served other purposes.[56] However, there is abundant evidence that punitive imprisonment was increasingly used after the thirteenth century for a wide range of nonfelonious offenses.[57] According to McConville, secular punitive imprisonment during the Middle Ages was exclusively retributive and deterrent, and it served no theory of reformative punishment.[58]

The first modern attempts to reform social deviants and misdemeanants were

the houses of correction established in much of western Europe from the mid–
sixteenth century on. Their emergence was essentially a way to control the
alarming increase in the number of beggars, vagrants, and petty offenders.
According to Sharpe, "the house of correction arguably represents early experimentation with the 'modern' idea that the offender is capable of amendment,
and ought to be reformed by society as well as punished."[59] The main rehabilitative instrument of the houses of corrections was labor discipline, which was
supposed to transform the offender into an honest and hard-working citizen.
They began the transition from publicly humiliating punishment toward the new
penal policies that flourished in the nineteenth century.

Although there is no agreement on the origin of the houses of correction,[60]
the Bridewell in England is generally considered the first establishment of the
sort, which served as a model for its Dutch analogues. In Tudor times, the palace
of Bridewell was transformed into a "house of occupations," receiving its first
prisoners in 1556. The original petition to create the institution was based on
the conclusion that thievery and beggary were caused by idleness and that "the
mean and remedy to cure the same must be by its contrary, which is labor."[61]
The London Bridewell was thus devised as a measure to reduce pauperism and
vagrancy through forced labor. It also reflected the abhorrence felt by an industrious society, increasingly Protestant, for idleness and lack of productivity.[62]
The idea was to impose a strict regime of labor and discipline on vagabonds and
prostitutes. Those who did not perform their daily quota of work were physically
punished with the whip and the stocks. Besides work and discipline, the reformative aspect included compulsory attendance at prayers before and after work.
This rudimentary methodology, later applied in other houses of corrections also
called Bridewells, initially seemed to have some success. One century later,
however, Bridewells had so deteriorated that they were indistinguishable from
the common jails.[63]

In the Netherlands, the houses of correction were called *tuchthuisen*, which
literally means "houses of discipline." Men were assigned to *Rasphuis*, women
to *Spinhuis*, referring to the kinds of labor practiced in them: rasping hard wooden
logs and spinning, respectively. The first Rasphuis was inaugurated in Amsterdam in 1596. These institutions were primarily created as reformatories for petty
thieves and professional beggars, but they were also used for juveniles.[64] Whereas
England dealt with its felons through "transportation" (deportation to a colony)
after the seventeenth century, the Dutch houses of correction gradually became
prisons for serious offenders.

An important factor in the creation of the Amsterdam houses of correction
was the need to control professional vagrancy, which threatened to deprive the
rising industrial enterprises of labor.[65] But these institutions also embodied true
reformative aspirations, as reflected in a memorandum written by the magistrate
Jan Laurenszoon Spiegel in 1589 regarding the first house of correction, considered by Sellin to be "one of the greatest documents in the history of penology."[66] The program was based on care for the physical and moral well-being

of the inmates and included vocational training in highly diversified industries. The central role of labor was to a certain degree supported by the Calvinist emphasis on industriousness. Calvinism played an important role in the Reformation in the Netherlands, and its glorification of work, discipline, and communal organization also influenced the emergence of the houses of correction. Spiegel took special care to avoid stigmatization of inmates: They entered the institution only in the dark of night and their stay was kept absolutely secret.

As time went by, the institution deteriorated into a "municipal factory with a captive labor force," enforced through cruel disciplinary penalties.[67] The Amsterdam houses of correction are thus an early example of how quickly reform aspirations become thwarted by institutional realities, anticipating the bureaucratization and deterioration of many later rehabilitative programs. It is precisely this discrepancy between ideal and practice that gave substance to the revisionist theories of rehabilitation.

The same model of reform through work and discipline was employed by mayor Jean Vilain XIV in the creation of the famous prison in Ghent in 1775, anticipating the nineteenth-century Auburn system of working in common and nocturnal solitude. The Ghent prison also set a precedent in the use of architecture—in this case an octagonal building of cellular type—to obtain total control over the inmate's life. Such institutions were praised by prison reformers of the nineteenth century, although their disciplinarian philosophy is criticized today. In contrast, the idea of humane treatment and dialogue as a vehicle to reform offenders was successfully applied by Filippo Franci in late seventeenth-century Florence. He used a section of the Hospice of San Filippo Neri, an institution for mendicant boys, to correct deviant juveniles through preaching and exhortation.[68] During their confinement a regime of total secrecy and anonymity was scrupulously maintained. The germ of modern counseling techniques is already evident in this experiment. A significant application of the reformative idea in the eighteenth century was the Hospice of San Michele in Rome, founded by Pope Clement XI in 1703. This correctional institution for young delinquents was also an asylum for orphans and elderly destitute. Its rehabilitative formula was a strong discipline, cellular isolation during the night and work in common during the day, supplemented by vocational training and elementary and religious education.

THE PENITENTIARY

The construction of a penitentiary annex to the Walnut Street Jail in Philadelphia, inaugurated in 1776, is generally considered to be the beginning of modern imprisonment. It was the result of the Pennsylvania Quakers' struggle against the death penalty and gruesome corporal punishment. Their humanitarian efforts had already had an important influence on early American penal practices.[69] Whereas the death penalty and various forms of cruel corporal punishment were used extensively in Europe and the other colonies, William Penn's Great Law of 1682 specified capital punishment only for premeditated murder, all other offenses carrying punishments of fines or imprisonment. In the same year Penn established the House of Correction in Pennsylvania along the lines of those he had visited in the Netherlands. Unfortunately, his mild and progressive criminal legislation was replaced in 1718 by the extremely severe English criminal code.

Motivated by their religious condemnation of cruel and debasing treatment of human beings, the Quakers conceived the essentials of the modern penitentiary. They advocated the principle of solitary confinement, an idea that had its roots in Platonic thought and in the religious disciplinary model of the monastic orders. The penitentiary methodology was directly inspired by the British experiments of the late eighteenth century, which in turn were a response to John Howard's denunciation of the unhealthy and sordid warehousing of human beings in his famous report "The State of Prisons in England and Wales," published in 1776. Howard's principal proposals were the isolation of inmates during the night and the use of religious education and work as reformative tools. He considered that solitude and silence favored reflection and repentance, but he advised against absolute isolation. The remarkable contribution of Jeremy Bentham to the evolving idea of humane and rational punishment should also be mentioned. He believed reform was based on education, discipline, and hard work. To carry out his idea he designed the Panopticon, an architectural structure that would allow maximum surveillance and control of the inmate. First applied in America in 1826 in the construction of the Pittsburgh Western Penitentiary, Bentham's approach was still used more than a century later in Illinois. It is now criticized for the very reasons that motivated its conception.

In the Walnut Street Jail a block of sixteen single cells was used to confine hardened criminals who would otherwise have been condemned to death. Their regime was one of absolute and solitary segregation, at first tempered only by the visits of the prison staff and later by the admission of selected visitors acting as reformative agents, namely the members of the Philadelphia Society for Alleviating the Miseries of Public Prisons. Solitary hard labor was also part of the reformative scheme; less serious offenders were allowed to work and dine together during the day, but they were to obey a strict rule of silence.

The value of this first American rehabilitative experiment has been contested. According to Rothman, the religiously inspired revulsion against the death penalty prevailed over reformative considerations.[70] Qualitatively, however, the Walnut Street Jail's approach is very similar to the reformative methodology applied after the 1820s, sharing both strengths and weaknesses. This pioneer model was praised by Larochefoucauld-Liancourt, in an account published in 1796.[71]

The first wave of reform gradually lost momentum and received a new impulse only in the 1820s with the construction of penitentiaries in Pennsylvania and New York and later in other states of the Union. According to Rothman, it was only then, with the emergence of the penitentiary, that the reformative ideal actually played a central role.[72] Crime was explained as the result of the corrupting influence of a society in which the old moral codes were cracking and family and Church had lost their grip.[73] The answer was sought in a return to the supposed colonial social order. This ideally entailed a drastic change of environment through strict isolation of the inmates and their submission to edifying influences as well as the creation of habits of work and regularity. Such a task had the utopian undertone of changing society at large, as it was based on the hope of finding a valid model of behavior for all members of society.

The rehabilitative model embodied in the American penitentiary was a continuation of the monastic tradition of solitude, hard labor, and religious indoctrination. Its distinctive feature was its large-scale application to criminal offenders. The penitentiary model put great emphasis on isolating the inmates from the community as well as separating them from one another. This policy was based on a fear of criminal contagion as well as a belief that inmates' successful readjustment into the community after release depended on preserving their anonymity. Modern criminology remains concerned with these same issues, now referred to as the subculture of prisons or the penal stigmatization process. The degree to which the inmates were isolated from one another was the key distinction between the Pennsylvanian and the Auburn penitentiary systems, whose advocates monopolized the early nineteenth-century penological debate.

In the Pennsylvanian system, also known as the separate system, the inmates were completely isolated in their own cells, where they were also forced to work. This approach was first applied without labor in the undersized cells of the Pittsburgh Western Penitentiary, but the single-cell system without labor proved to have devastating effects on the mental and physical health of the inmates. The Pittsburgh penitentiary was rebuilt in order to permit labor within its cells; in the Eastern Penitentiary, at Cherry Hill (inaugurated in 1829), the system was liberalized with the introduction of work and the construction of individual exercise yards.

In the so-called silent system practiced in the New York State prison at Auburn, the prisoners were locked up in their individual cells during the night, but worked and ate together during the day in a regime of strict silence, using the lockstep when marching in groups. This system prevailed, mainly for economic reasons, in the penitentiaries built in the nineteenth century. The debate on the merits of the Pennsylvanian and Auburn systems raged in America, involving prominent personalities of the time, such as Francis Lieber and Dorothea Dix. It was transferred to Europe with equal intensity, especially after the 1832 report of Beaumont and Tocqueville on American prisons, and remained the main topic of the penitentiary reform debate.

The extreme Pennsylvanian system had little success in Europe. It had a precedent in the prison of Gloucester, built in 1785 following the proposals of Howard as well as the Bridewell of Glasgow. Although the Pennsylvanian system was fervently supported by Crawford, who visited the United States in 1834, England resolved the question through the radically different method of transportation. Adult convicts with sentences exceeding one year were transported to the penal colonies in Australia, whereas the system for juveniles involved working together during the day. In Germany, the ideas of Mittermaier, an advocate of the Auburn system, prevailed. Despite the articulate pleas of Ducpetiaux, probably the strongest advocate of the extreme isolation system, it was also rejected in Belgium, Italy, Denmark, and Austria.

In France, the main advocate of penitentiary reform was Charles Lucas, a decided opponent of the Pennsylvanian system. He accepted total isolation only for juveniles or for short periods of time, until the prisoner was transferred to the penitentiary in the prison van, a veritable penitentiary carriage.[74] Lucas strongly opposed the solitary segregation of the long-term sentenced offender, supporting the Auburn or silent system instead.[75] This regime had a European precedent in the Ghent house of correction, where silence had been used in order to avoid corruption and to maintain a regime of obedience, reflection, and work. In support of the Auburn system of labor in common during the day, Lucas quoted the first report of the Boston Society of Prison Discipline, published in 1826, which indicated a considerable increase of mortality and of both physical and mental illness due to the total isolation of the Pennsylvanian system.[76] On the other hand, Lucas considered that the solitary reading of the Bible, advocated by the Quakers of Pennsylvania, did not meet the needs of the Catholic faith.[77] He underlined the importance of worship in common and pointed out that religion should aim first at the senses and emotions, to reach the ignorant masses from which most of the prisoners came. Ducpetiaux replied that Catholicism could adequately respond to the challenge of the separate system. Its ministers could also regenerate prisoners in isolation, carrying out the same enlightened task as the reformed chaplain.[78]

Lucas criticized the American penitentiary movement for having been exclusively preoccupied with the prevention of criminal contagion among prisoners convicted to long-term sentences, to the neglect of earlier stages of the criminal procedure.[79] Focus should shift to the juvenile offender, the pretrial detainee, and the transportation of prisoners to the penitentiary, he argued. Corruption really took place in the houses of correction, in jails, and during the transfer to the prison. By the time the offender reached the penitentiary, criminal know-how had already been transmitted, and efforts to reform such "learned" criminals were doomed to failure.[80] Lucas insisted that penitentiary reform should proceed in the opposite direction to the American experiments, starting where criminal contagion originated in the first place. In this regard, he was not only concerned with the stages of the criminal process previous to conviction, but advocated a preventive pedagogical action on society.[81] In addition to supporting prison education as a means to avoid recidivism, he conceived forms of social pedagogy that would reach the external society, the family, and the factory. In this way he anticipated the most recent trends in modern crime policy, which seek to act on the social environment as well as the individual, instigating social learning within the groups in which the deviant will participate.[82]

From today's perspective, the Auburn silent system seems the more humane of the two systems. Total isolation is now regarded as cruel and unusual punishment, and could have only been supported in good faith as the result of blatant psychological error. Its rather punitive character can be inferred from the reports of the time. Crawford, one of its main supporters, acknowledged that solitude was intended to inspire a permanent terror.[83] And yet he was a firm believer in the eventual improvement of the inmate's moral character and the opening of his hardened heart to kindness and religious values.[84] A more legitimate argument for the Pennsylvanian system appears to be the prevention of extortions from other inmates after their release.[85]

Among supporters of the Pennsylvanian system, punitive and deterrent considerations went hand in hand with reformative aspirations: "the deterrent influence of isolation is more effective than that of any other punishment," Ducpetiaux wrote, quoting Crawford.[86] Nonetheless, Sherman and Hawkins saw a genuine reformative impetus in the Pennsylvanian system, whereas they noted that the reformation of offenders was only a minor consideration in the Auburn system.[87] And furthermore, "with the emergence of Auburn as the dominant model, there came the dominance of crime control and retributivist motives over the hopes for indirect influence through social service."[88]

In fact, both the Pennsylvanian and Auburn systems reflect a basic confusion of rehabilitation with punishment through their common identification with imprisonment. Imprisonment per se was thought not only to rehabilitate, but also to punish and deter. The rehabilitative formula inherent in the early penitentiary movement, discredited today, cemented the link between rehabilitation and imprisonment, to the extent of confusing rehabilitation with punishment. In effect, supporters of both the Pennsylvanian and Auburn systems expected some kind of moral transformation as the result of enforced seclusion. In the separate system this meant a dramatic reduction of external freedom, through strict solitary confinement tempered only by religious preaching, reading of the Bible, and, at best, solitary labor. The silent system is only a mitigated variation of the same formula. A regime that might have worked in the prisons of the monastic orders, given previous religious orientation and vocation, proved to be extremely destructive with ordinary offenders. Instead of encouraging a spiritual awakening, the extreme reduction of the inmates' field of social interaction often resulted in their psychological and physical collapse, and even in madness. Such flaws could also be found within monastic imprisonment, during some periods of cruel abuses denounced by Mabillon in his plea for merciful treatment.[89]

Two misconceptions significantly flawed the early penitentiary experiments. One was the ethnocentric mistake of regarding the criminal as a prospective monk, ignoring his social and cultural background. Bible reading was unlikely to succeed as a rehabilitative tool when most prisoners were illiterate. The second error was to believe that segregating the inmate would be sufficient to remove him from the corrupting influence of society. This naive environmentalist notion of antisociality ignores the fact that the individual carries society in himself or herself, even inside the walls of the penitentiary.[90]

The identification of rehabilitation with imprisonment as punishment was never greater than in these first modern rehabilitative experiments. By revealing the harmful effects of prisons and total institutions, modern sociology helps to detach rehabilitation from imprisonment and allows one to see the former as a force counteracting the desocializing effects of the latter.

INCENTIVE STRATEGIES AFTER THE MID–NINETEENTH CENTURY—THE INDETERMINATE SENTENCE

After the first penitentiary experiments, centered on a belief in spiritual growth through discipline, a new rehabilitative method was elaborated. Its field of action was primarily the institution, but it also gave increasing attention to periods before and after release. The basic idea was that the inmate should earn his advance toward freedom, through stages of progressive liberalization, as the result of his own effort. In fact, this approach manipulated freedom deprivation in a carrot-and-stick scheme of deterrents and incentives. The pressure of imprisonment combined with the hope of gradual liberalizations and shortening of the sentence was deemed to create social and working habits in the inmate that would persist after the release. As in earlier correctional methods, rehabilitation remained indissolubly linked with imprisonment.

The new rehabilitative technique, which had a lasting influence on all modern corrections, first acquired prominence in the mid–nineteenth century with the pioneering efforts of Machonochie and Sir Walter Crofton. Its roots, however, lie in early forms of imprisonment, with labor as its main ingredient. In the Dutch Rasphuis, for example, good behavior enabled the inmates to advance from the rasping of wood to the weaving mill.[91] In the Bridewells too, inmates progressed from painful and difficult tasks to more comfortable work. Progression also played a substantial role in the French *bagnes*, naval-port prisons that replaced the galleys. It later became a pillar of the reformative movement and had lasting influence on the design of prison strategies and sentencing policies through the conception of indeterminate sentencing and the institution of parole.

This new rehabilitative methodology gained momentum in the mid–nineteenth century. The turning point was the bold experiment carried out in 1840 by Captain Machonochie in the Australian penal colony of Norfolk Island, to which hardened long-sentence convicts were transported by Great Britain. In a pamphlet published two years earlier, he had argued that the aim of punishment was to reform the individual by teaching self-discipline.[92] For this purpose, Machonochie advocated sentences of indeterminate duration, allowing the prisoner to acquire such proper self-discipline. Instead of a fixed period of time to be served, the sentence should consist of a specific task to be carried out. Machonochie's first drastic innovation was to suppress to a large extent the use of flogging and chains. He encouraged instead the development of responsibility, allowing prisoners to earn "marks of commendation" through labor and good conduct. Besides the number of marks necessary to pay for their lodging, food, and clothes, inmates could earn extra credits, to be applied toward their eventual release, through austere living, industriousness, and exemplary behavior. Machonochie's revolutionary methods aroused much criticism among supporters of traditional punitive policies, and he was removed from his office in 1842.

Machonochie's methods were further developed in Ireland in 1854, by Crofton, who was also inspired by the humanitarian and reformative approaches of von Obermaier in Bavaria and of Manuel Montesinos in the prison of Valencia. The Irish Progressive System "made the improvement of a prisoner's position in gaol, and his liberation on license, within the period of his sentence, to depend upon his own exertions and well doing.[93] The system involved four stages. At first the inmate was subject to deprivations and strict discipline. He then progressed to labor on fortifications, with the possibility of earning marks rewarding good behavior and educational and working efforts. Crofton's main innovation was in the third or intermediate stage, in which inmates were transferred to an open institution. Nearing a state of freedom, the prisoner lived in a small prison unit, where he worked in conditions of trust similar to those of free labor and attended edifying lectures by speakers from neighboring towns. According to Crofton's own judgment,

this stage was adopted not only for the purpose of more naturally preparing the criminal for free life, and of evincing to him that the prison authorities were so satisfied with his previous test of amendment as to further trust him; but also to better pave the way for his employment in the labor market through the nature of his tests.[94]

The fourth period consisted of aftercare following release; the institution's staff also searched for employment for the prisoner about to reenter society. The release was carried out under tickets of leave, a system of conditional pardon to remit the sentences of transported prisoners.

Although the progressive stage system received wide support, critics at the beginning of this century pointed out serious shortcomings: its potential to instigate hypocrisy and to breed an atmosphere of ill will and envy among the inmates.[95] The rehabilitative formula implied in the progressive stage system lacks genuine, enduring motivation. It can certainly be used as a disciplinary mechanism but it cannot generate true educational initiatives. Furthermore, such coarse patterns of massive behavioral conformity are bound to lead to abuses in the form of psychological or labor exploitation of the inmate. Despite these flaws, the progressive stage formula has remained, openly or covertly, a basic element of most rehabilitative ventures within correctional institutions.

The classification of offenders "based on character and on some well-adjusted mark system" was at the core of the progressive stage system. The National Penitentiary Congress held in Cincinnati in 1870 enthusiastically endorsed this approach. The appeal to what would be called later "positive reinforcement" was expressed in the sixth principle of the declaration adopted by the congress:

Since hope is a more potent agent than fear, it should be made an ever-present force in the mind of the prisoners, by a well-devised and skillfully applied system of rewards for good conduct, industry and attention to learning. Rewards, more than punishments, are essential to every good prison system.[96]

This congress also anticipated crucial reforms that were later included in the program of the Italian Positivist School of Criminology, namely indeterminate sentencing and the institution of parole. The congress's foresight is particularly remarkable because Cesare Lombroso's *L'uomo delinquente*, the first major contribution of the Positivist School, was not published until 1876. But whereas the positivists saw incapacitation as a means to protect society against the dangerous offender, the Cincinnati Penitentiary Congress took a quite different view of indeterminate sentencing, emphasizing reformation. Its declaration of principles proclaimed that sentences should be limited only "by satisfactory proof of reformation."[97] This policy orientation gradually gained acceptance and ultimately prevailed in the United States. Faith in this type of rehabilitation sustained the legitimacy of the penitentiary and allowed the expansion of discretionary indeterminate sentencing.[98]

The ideas discussed at the Cincinnati Congress were soon put into practice by Zebulon Brockway, a leading participant in the meeting. As he pointed out in his presentation, his system was "drawn from experience" and not "deduced from cloistral meditation."[99] The source of his "plan for a true prison" was his actual contact with penal realities through the organization of reformatories. Although deeply inspired by Christian principles of mercy and compassion, his concept of rehabilitation or reformation excluded forcible religious indoctrination.[100] On the contrary, he insisted that "the change sought in the character of criminals, called reformation, is of practical nature, and has to do with daily life in ordinary social relationships."[101]

Brockway implemented the new concepts as superintendent of the Elmira Reformatory (New York), which became a model for other institutions and exerted a worldwide influence on prison reformers of the time. According to McKelvey, Brockway "stands without rival as the greatest warden America has produced." Most of his ideas, however, were borrowed from Machonochie and Crofton; what "was really new about the Elmira system was that labor was not performed for the benefit of the Government but for the good of the inmate."[102] Brockway's system combined indeterminate sentencing, privileges as a reward for good conduct, compulsory and diversified education, and release on parole. He graded the inmates according to their conduct and also considered their educational and work performance. Through a system of marks they could earn eligibility for parole. Conversely, misbehavior would push them back into a lower grade of classification.

The institution was ruled by a bill drawn up by Brockway and passed by the legislature with a single amendment: the addition of a provision limiting an inmate's detention to the maximum sentence established in the criminal code for each crime. Elmira became the cradle of the indeterminate sentence that later dominated American penal legislation. The institution was intended for first offenders between sixteen and thirty-one years of age, but in practice recidivists always constituted one-third of the inmates.[103] Believing that criminals could be reformed on the basis of Christian principles, Brockway advocated a charitable attitude toward them. He occasionally resorted to physical punishment, however, and as an executive investigation revealed in 1894, "discipline at Elmira was not as promised consistently mild and encouraging."[104] Reviewing the extensive inquiries into Brockway's treatment of inmates, Pisciotta recently found "wide discrepancies between the rhetoric of the managers and the practice of the institutions."[105] Although the testimony of witnesses was politicized for or against the management, according to Pisciotta, it reveals unmistakably that "Elmira was, in the final analysis, a prison."[106] Order seemed largely the result of fear of extremely severe corporal punishment, and "the central tenet of 'prison science'—humane, benevolent, individualized care—was certainly not provided."[107]

Rothman explained corporal punishment as inherent in institutional life: Maintenance of order and obedience in penal institutions always requires the threat of one more sanction, whether it is another and harsher prison, solitary confinement, or beating. Katz believed that the brutality at Elmira extended beyond the requirements of institutional order and that pervasive sadism within the institution requires an explanation other than convenience, as in Rothman's account.[108] Ironically, the harshness of its disciplinary punishments may have resulted from the very idealistic nature of Brockway's aspirations. As a general proposition, the higher the goals set by reformers, the greater the frustration and guilt caused by failure. The more hopes are invested in an idealistic, sometimes utopian venture, the more drastic and even uncontrolled the reaction may be if hopes are thwarted. Idealism may lead to self-glorification, authoritarianism, and intolerance, attempting to force events into the ideal mold. Institutional or community leaders may end up feeling aggressive and spiteful toward the outer society or reacting harshly against recalcitrant insiders.

One of Elmira's main assets was its educational offerings, which drew on the contributions of college professors, public-school principals, and lawyers. The program encompassed various general subjects, sports, religion, and military drill. For the less capable, pioneer trade schools were created, where tailor cutting, plumbing, telegraphy, and printing were taught. The creation of a school atmosphere was a major objective in Brockway's rehabilitative concept.

POSITIVISM AND REHABILITATION

The positivist school of criminology transformed both the concept of the criminal offender and the aims and content of penal sanctions. The classic school of criminology had conceived of the offender as being endowed with free will. Now that image was replaced with a new conception of the criminal as an essentially abnormal creature rigidly conditioned through a psychobiological or social causation. This view was the consequence of applying to criminology some concepts of experimental science that by the late nineteenth century had not yet moved beyond an absolute linear determinism. Not until twentieth century discoveries in microphysics and relativity did it become clear that the concept of cause is an abstraction without significance when it is not related to concrete situations. Causal relations are complex, hierarchical, intertwined, and interactive.

The new ideas about the causes of crime necessarily influenced the society's ways of reacting against it. Garofalo, a jurist, was the first to formulate a positivist theory on the penal sanction, which correlated with the notion of dangerousness as the basis for criminal responsibility. In his view, the penal sanction aimed primarily to protect society through special prevention. The foremost goal was the elimination or segregation of the dangerous offender and, when possible, compensation for the harm produced by the offense.[109] Rehabilitation had no place in a deterministic outlook that rejected free will and moral responsibility. Despite Garofalo's acid criticism of the reformative theory, Allen found his proposal of ''enforced reparation'' for certain offenses more in accord with the rehabilitative ideal than even Garofalo suspected.[110] Besides, his objections to ''moral therapy'' and reformation did not extend to programs directed to the very young offender, as at Elmira.[111]

Even the most extreme manifestations of positivism indirectly made a substantial contribution to future rehabilitative policies. Although their rigid determinism is incompatible with any moral therapy or reformation, the positivists' concern for the scientific study of criminal offenders ultimately bolstered sentencing policies directed to their rehabilitation. Another major representative of the positivist school, Enrico Ferri, was less skeptical than Garofalo about the rehabilitative possibilities of criminal sanctions. In describing the ways in which social defense against criminality was carried out, Ferri mentioned both indeterminate segregation of a few incorrigible offenders and reeducation or social readjustment of the large majority of amendable offenders.[112]

THE INFLUENCE OF THE POSITIVIST SCHOOL ON POLICY-MAKING AND LEGISLATION

After positivism's heyday, various penal theories emerged that attempted to integrate the new anthropological and sociological knowledge about the criminal offender with the traditional legal principles of punishment and responsibility. The result was a fragmentation of the legal system. Early twentieth-century penal codes separated punishment, reserved only for those capable of moral responsibility, from security measures, intended for the irresponsible and based on their dangerousness. This duality can be traced in the Norwegian penal code of 1902, in special Swedish acts, in the Argentine penal code of 1921, in the Italian penal code of 1930, in English law through both the Children Act and the

Prevention of Crime Acts of 1908 (later improved by the Criminal Justice Act of 1948), in the Belgian Social Defense Act of 1930, in the Swiss penal code of 1937, in a 1933 amendment to the German penal code, and in the Greek penal code of 1950.

Such security measures were first incorporated in modern legislation by Carl Stooss, who included them in the Swiss preliminary draft penal code of 1893, borrowing that idea from old Swiss cantonal legislation. Unlike many later penal codes, the 1893 draft allowed both types of sanction to be used interchangeably at the discretion of the judge; both were essentially instruments to combat criminality, assigning a significant role to rehabilitation. Although accepting the retributive nature of criminal punishment, Stooss considered that reformation or amendment was its aim. His draft assigned a rehabilitative aim even to indeterminate measures of security for dangerous habitual offenders. Article 40 foresaw a temporary conditional release after five years in the case of a favorable rehabilitative prognosis. This provision contrasts with the dangerous offender legislation of the time, which was much harsher, and inspired later policy trends.

At the policy-making level, the intellectual influence of the positivist school of criminology was felt in the establishment of the International Union of Criminal Law, founded in 1889 by Franz von Liszt (Germany), Gerard van Hamel (the Netherlands), and Adolphe Prins (Belgium). Their purpose was to create an international forum to discuss the new ideas introduced by the positivist movement, which were only partially accepted by the members of the union. Their fundamental principle was that crime and punishment should no longer be treated as a purely legal matter, but also as a sociological phenomenon. The mission of criminal law was precisely to fight against crime conceived as a social phenomenon, by means of the positive knowledge of its causes. Accordingly, all the new anthropological and sociological data had to be taken into account in the design of crime-prevention policies. In this fight against crime, punishment remained one of the most effective weapons, but no longer the only one. While urging that short prison sentences be replaced by suspended sentences and fines, the union argued that the length of medium- and long-term sentences should depend not only on the seriousness of the offense, but also on the results of prison rehabilitation efforts. Besides, incorrigible habitual offenders should remain out of circulation as long as possible.

These ideas were to a great extent the product of von Liszt's proposals. Although he rejected the absolute determinism of the positivists, von Liszt wanted to incorporate the new knowledge derived from social and behavioral sciences in the design of future policies and institutions. In his program, the concern for crime prevention overshadowed the search for an abstract absolute justice, as in Kant or Hegel. This endeavor, however, was limited by the individual safeguards and rights contained in criminal law, which he considered "an insurmountable barrier to crime policy."[113] Von Liszt developed the teachings of Ihering, emphasizing the idea of a goal in criminal law. He suggested a goal-oriented sanction as opposed to purely retributive punishment. Striking a compromise between repression and prevention, he affirmed that criminal punishment consisted of prevention carried out through repression. Its goal was the rehabilitation of the amenable and those in need of such treatment, the deterrence of those who did not need it and the incapacitation of the incorrigible.

Von Liszt was skeptical regarding the possibility of rehabilitating adults, and his proposals for pedagogically oriented corrections were primarily meant for juveniles. Their rehabilitation was conceived in terms of intellectual and physical development, and the acquisition of habits of regularity in life, especially concerning work.[114] In his earlier proposals von Liszt reserved the harshest treatments and extremely hard labor for the antisocial habitual criminal, whom he considered hopelessly incorrigible.[115] He followed the prevailing trend of his time, which favored the segregation or elimination of hardened habitual criminals. Later in life, he adopted a more merciful and benevolent approach toward those deemed incorrigible.[116]

Von Liszt aspired to create a general science of criminal law, encompassing several branches of natural science related to crime and punishment. It was expected to yield a crime policy grounded on biological and sociological realities. He never argued against the traditional retributive principles of classic criminal law, however.

The revolt against the dogmatism of classic criminal law reached the crime policy level through the social defense movement, which took shape in the late nineteenth century and became operant at the beginning of the twentieth. This movement saw crime policy as the rational organization of the society's reaction against crime.[117] Its primary source of knowledge was criminology and the new behavioral sciences. Thus criminal law lost its monopoly in the solution of problems caused by crime. Without identifying with positivism or with its deterministic ideology, social defense policies sought to approach the problems of crime from a multidisciplinary perspective, while they steadfastly upheld the respect for individual rights and the protection of humanistic values. This movement reached its full development only after World War II, when its main demand became the prevention of criminality and the rehabilitation of the offender. Its humanist and universalist commitment soon transformed it into a major source of inspiration and guidance for both modern crime policy and the reform of criminal law.

Prins was the first to formulate an autonomous doctrine of social defense, which he envisaged as a renewed conception of the fight against crime.[118] Going beyond mere legal technique, he based his proposals on criminological data and built a system out of the prevailing crime policies of his time: the substitution of other alternative sanctions for short prison sentences, the individualization of criminal sanctions, and the reform of prisons. Arguing that the state penal reaction should be based on the offender's dangerousness rather than moral responsibility, he emphasized the need to incorporate in positive law special preventive measures of indeterminate duration for both abnormal and habitual offenders. Prins's ideas on the treatment of persistent offenders were tempered by mercy, favoring the incapacitation of incorrigible dangerous criminals rather than their brutal elimination through the death penalty.[119] He underlined the need to distinguish individuals likely to be improved or cured from those who should be merely rendered harmless.[120] In spite of the prevailing eugenic theories of his time, he urged that the feebleminded and the defective offender be protected from inhuman elimination.[121] Furthermore, he favored pedagogical reforms that would help reintegrate the mentally retarded and defective into the community,[122] citing the methods of training and special education then being used in pioneer institutions in England and in the United States.[123]

THE MOVEMENT TOWARD THE INDIVIDUALIZATION OF SANCTIONS

France

Early twentieth-century crime policy in America underwent changes much like those seen in Europe. At the sentencing level, sanctions became individualized, which meant an individual, case-by-case strategy of rehabilitation.[124] This trend was part of a wide international movement whose origins can be traced to France in the early nineteenth century. Analysis of the French precedents is thus particularly useful.

Although the postrevolutionary French penal code of 1791 established fixed penalties for each crime, the trend thereafter was toward greater flexibility. The 1810 penal code extended the range of possible sentences for a particular offense, thus increasing judicial discretionary powers. These were further broadened when laws of 1824 and 1832 made it possible to consider mitigating circumstances for all offenses. The movement toward individualization of penal sanctions culminated in 1898 with the theoretical systematization of Raymond Saleilles.[125]

A leading legal scholar of his time, Saleilles wanted to adapt positivistic policies to the demands of justice. In the idea of individualization he found a way to translate this compromise into positive law. He defined three aspects of individualization—legislative, judicial, and penitentiary—corresponding to the stages at which sanctions were chosen and applied. The legislative level merely consisted of the parameters set by the law to regulate individualization at the judicial and penitentiary levels. Saleilles rejected the idea of the born criminal and emphasized the goal of rehabilitation, made possible by human freedom. Both freedom and determination had their place in human personality, but without freedom "there is no hope of return to virtue." He condemned the "tendency to recognize only criminals by nature, to regard them all as beset with an incurable criminality, as belonging to the lost."[126] This hope of rehabilitation underlay a particularly flexible sentencing system that made it possible to adapt the sanction to the personality of the offender to some extent.

The European movement toward individualization resulted in only a relative increase of discretion, as the penal sanction had to be chosen within ranges predetermined by statute. The indeterminate sentence met only limited acceptance and was viewed primarily as a security measure for multirecidivists or abnormal offenders. A distrust of the state, founded on a past of oppressive abuses, prevented indeterminate sentencing from achieving the sweeping success it attained in America.[127]

Great Britain

The British transformations of late nineteenth-century crime policies have been analyzed by Garland, who found in them the origin of modern welfare state penal strategies with lasting effects throughout the present century. In his view the period between the Gladstone Committee Report of 1895 on penal reform and the beginning of World War I marked the transition from the Victorian system to the new forms of punishment.[128] In Britain, the role played by Saleilles and the members of the International Union of Criminal Law—striking a pragmatic compromise between traditional legalism and positive criminology—was undertaken by Sir Evelyn Ruggles-Brise, chairman of the Prison Commission.[129]

Garland divided the new strategies into three sectors: normalizing, correctional, and segregative. The normalizing sector was represented by community-based sanctions directed to "straighten out characters and reform the personality of their clients in accordance with the requirements of good citizenship."[130] The correctional sector, which came into play after the failure of the normalizing apparatus, was composed of a new series of institutions designed for particular kinds of offender defined in terms of their corrigibility, youth, character, and so on. These institutions were statutorily obliged to provide a regime of corrective training, education and reform.[131] The segregative sector was reserved for those who had refused or been unable to submit to the discipline of the dominant social order. It consisted primarily of preventive detention institutions introduced by the 1908 Act on Detention for Habitual Criminals, which also accomplished rehabilitative functions. Preventive detention was to be terminated when it had been established that the inmate would probably "abstain from crime and lead a useful and industrious life" (¶220). Correctional institutions such as state reformatories for the "inebriate and feeble-minded" and ordinary prisons also performed important segregative functions. Despite official rhetoric, the role of the prison shifted away from correction and toward segregation. Change came about as reformable categories of offenders, such as children, juveniles and first offenders, were removed from prisons, whose population was increasingly restricted to the most serious and stubborn cases. The reformative function became accordingly less practicable.[132]

The segregative sector acted as a safety valve should the penal network fail, just as the penal complex "supplied the coercive back-up for the institutions of the social realm."[133] Penal institutions were assigned important functions consonant with the new eugenic theories and demands. These were mirrored in the "infiltration of eugenic terms into penological discourse," as penal reformers used expressions such as "segregation of the unfit." However, the new policies did not wholly displace the traditional principles of criminal law, and "preventive detention has been little used, because of judicial resistance to its terms."[134]

During the Victorian period, Garland pointed out, "reformation" was officially recognized as a subsidiary or secondary aim of penalty. In practice, however, the dominant objective of British authorities followed Bentham's view that punishment should "grind rogues" in the interest of deterrence and retribution. "If, by doing so, it should grind them honest, then so much the better."[135] The Gladstone report, which Garland considered the starting point of the modern transformation of penalty, established a compromise position, allowing that "some criminals are irreclaimable, just as some diseases are incurable," but that "the great majority of prisoners" can be rehabilitated.[136] New conceptions and methods of corrections based on the idea of the criminal as an abnormal being replaced the old evangelical or utilitarian reformative schemes.[137]

Although the new policies espoused ambitious social-engineering goals, they introduced few supporting techniques. In fact, rehabilitation had to rely on personal influence and on the traditional physical, intellectual, and moral aspects of prison training.[138] As in the corresponding period of extensive state intervention in the United States, the British criminological program offered an effective social defense through eliminative means, "but little in the way of prevention and rehabilitation."[139] In fact, Garland believed that the official recognition of rehabilitation in the twentieth century was not based on the dubious scientific knowledge of the time, but rather on a political and ideological rationale of social control. Rehabilitation was offered as a pawn in the struggle for legitimation of the "complex logic of normalization, correction, and segregation that compose the penal strategies of the welfare state."[140]

The rehabilitative model introduced by the new strategies of penalty aimed to "fortify and build up force of character," whereas the old idea of penal discipline sought "to crush and break."[141] Early twentieth-century rehabilitative techniques rewarded the inmate's "regular habits," "punctuality, orderliness, smartness and obedience," "respect of authority and industrious labor," "temperance, thrift and selfhelp," or other similar formulas cited by Garland, relying on the individual's own will to conform.[142] This rather shallow model of social adjustment and superficial adaptation has been one of the main objects of contemporary criticism of rehabilitation.[143]

United States

During the progressive era in the United States, trust in the state's benevolence allowed an astonishingly quick shift toward the indeterminate sentence with release through parole. Confidence in rehabilitation justified such a change, because the sentencing decision was based to a great extent on a particular offender's potential for rehabilitation. Such faith in individual betterment has been related to the social cohesion of a time in which no divergence between public interest and the well-being of the deviant was suspected. Reformers saw no opposition between the power of the state to help and its power to police.[144] The progressive era illustrates how the rehabilitative ideal, conceived as readaptation to a uniform value system, flourishes in times of consensus on societal values.[145] Faith in rehabilitating the deviant converged with confidence in overcoming the social causes of crime by extending the benefits of the successful social and economic American system to all.

The progressive concept of rehabilitation reflected scientific optimism, not only at the level of the social sciences, but also in the psychiatric individual approach. Such optimism rested basically on the assumption that knowledge of the causes of crime would ultimately lead to their uprooting. Indulging in simplistic medical analogy, reformers erroneously thought that a correct diagnosis would guarantee the effective prescription to cure criminality. This belief legitimated discretionary and flexible sentencing based on fitting the medicine to each individual's special needs. Individualization, however, resulted in a random accumulation of incoherent data without any consistent theory, making it impossible to select the relevant cause of deviance and guide the intervention accordingly.[146] The advent of the medical model during the progressive era, supported by the growing reputation of Freudian doctrines, did not provide practical treatment approaches.

At the level of penitentiary techniques, however, the notion of rehabilitation underwent significant changes that had lasting influence on twentieth-century penal practices. Instead of the isolated and rigid routine of the Jacksonian model, the prison was to be assimilated as far as possible to the community. "Rather than serve as a model to the society, the penitentiary was to model itself on the society."[147] The reformers tried not only to reinforce offenders' bonds with the community, but also to instill in them a sense of responsibility for their own conduct. As in Europe, alternatives to imprisonment became a main ingredient of the progressive rehabilitative scheme. Probation, the Anglo-American counterpart of the Franco-Belgian suspended sentence, represented a basic tool of this flexible strategy.[148]

There was also a growing feeling that the prison should be democratized, to pave the way for the future reintegration of the inmate to a democratic society. This ambition culminated in Thomas Mott Osborne's attempt to introduce the concept of inmate self-government into the penitentiary.[149]

The experiments with self-government in institutions started in 1826 with the Boston House of Reformation, directed by Reverend E. M. P. Wells. Most inmates were juveniles convicted of theft or arrested for vagrancy, remanded by the state of Massachusetts for correctional purposes. The experiment, based on progressive earning of privileges, included a court composed by twelve inmates. Inmates also filled the roles of the chief of police and his deputies.[150] In 1895 William R. George founded the George Junior Republic in Freeville, New York, consisting of 100 delinquent boys and half as many girls between the ages of fourteen and twenty-one years, some of them declared incorrigible. The "republic" was modeled on the United States government, with its three branches:

legislative, executive, and judicial. The inmates lived in small houses scattered over 350 acres of land, supervised by adult employees. Positive results were reported, and in 1908 a number of similar institutions joined together in the National Association of Junior Republics.[151]

Osborne was president of the George Junior Republic's board of trustees for fifteen years before starting his own experiment. In 1913, when he became chairman of a commission for the reform of the New York penal system, he applied the idea of self-government and self-support to adult inmates of the Auburn prison. His motto, borrowed from Gladstone, was It is liberty alone that fits men for liberty.[152] The Mutual Welfare League Osborne established at Auburn included a committee of 49 prisoners appointed by secret ballot among the prison's 1,400 inmates. This committee participated in the planning of treatment and in disciplinary tasks, for which a special grievance court composed entirely of prisoners was created. In 1914 Osborne was appointed warden of Sing Sing prison, where he organized another Mutual Welfare League. He was also a pioneer of the later anti-institutional approach, which replaced rigid and stultifying discipline with prisoners' active participation in their own rehabilitation.[153] Osborne achieved a prison atmosphere in which the inmates could develop a sense of responsibility. His main instrument was trusting inmates to exercise meaningful decision-making powers. Opposition from correctional officers and politicians eventually brought about Osborne's departure and the collapse of his Mutual Welfare League in 1929.[154]

MID–TWENTIETH CENTURY CRIME POLICY: THE NEW SOCIAL DEFENSE, THE ROLE OF THE REHABILITATIVE IDEA IN THE REFORM OF PENAL AND PENITENTIARY LAW

The penal and legal reforms brought about in Continental Europe by late nineteenth-century crime policies, corresponding to the progressive era innovations in America and to the strategies of the welfare state in Britain, have been maintained in substance throughout the twentieth century. After World War II, however, the idea of rehabilitation received new emphasis in penal discourse and was transformed both qualitatively and quantitatively. The optimistic reconstruction that followed the fall of the totalitarian regimes paved the way for an influential movement of humanistic crime policy: the new social defense. This school sought to organize the social reaction against crime rationally, rejecting narrow retributionist schemes that focused only on the abstract infringement of the law and ignored the individual human being. No longer satisfied with a passive defense of society, the new doctrine encouraged a positive action of resocialization. For this purpose, it was argued, criminal law should apprehend the personalities of offenders dynamically, taking into account all their individual and social components.[155]

According to Marc Ancel, to whom the new social defense owes its inspiration and formulation, the resocialization of the criminal offender is the primary aim of penal sanctions. These also have—he recognized—both a retributive function and a general preventive effect derived from the fear of state intervention as a consequence of the crime. The resocialization treatment takes place within a legal framework, respecting the rights of the individual and sternly rejecting brainwashing techniques. In this regard, the main imperative of the new social defense is the recognition of the value of the human being. The humanistic anticriminal reaction is centered in the idea of protection. Protection is extended both to the social group, through a rational criminal law system, and to the individual offender, developing his or her intrinsic capacity to become a valuable member of society. Rehabilitation does not constitute an end in itself, but only a means to protect the basic rights of the human being.[156]

The new social defense has been defined as a "pedagogy of responsibility."[157] It is based "not on a theoretical notion of responsibility, but on the feeling of responsibility that all human beings normally possess. The treatment of resocialization should precisely restore it together with self-command, when this is totally or partially lost."[158] To attain its crime-policy goal, the new social defense integrates penalties and security measures in a unitary sanctioning system that allows "their free utilization, socially oriented and scientifically individualized."[159] Moreover, it constantly seeks to discover more human and effective ways of reacting to criminals with alternatives to institutionalization playing a central role.

The new social defense is deeply intertwined with the humanist tradition, which makes the flesh-and-blood human being preeminent over any dogmatic adherence to rigid formulas.[160] It also remains open to the evolution of criminological thought and to social and legal transformations. Accordingly, the new social defense cannot be reduced to the particular treatment policies in vogue during its first stage of development, which reflected a special atmosphere of optimism and social reconstruction that prevailed during the postwar years. Its main positive contributions were to enhance the rights of prisoners, press for their international recognition, and inspire penitentiary reform as well as a new legal system for juvenile offenders. The new social defense also influenced French legislation regarding the extension of prerelease and aftercare services, the creation of a special judge for the execution of sentences (*juge d'application des peines*), the consideration of the offender's personality in criminal procedure, the introduction of suspended sentences with probation, the judicial control of presentenced offenders, and a series of sentencing alternatives. A 1983 bill created three new alternatives to imprisonment: temporary or permanent prohibition to use one or more vehicles, day fines, and community service orders (*travail d'interet general*).

Without disowning these fruitful developments, Ancel recently submitted the idea of resocialization to a rigorous criticism primarily directed against the abuses of treatment and the arbitrary transformation of the human being into a medicalized object.[161] In many cases the divorce between rehabilitative aspirations and penitentiary reality has discredited the 1950s conception of institutional treatment. It remains indisputably valid, however, in two areas: specific medical or paramedical treatment, which should include a number of mentally disordered offenders, and voluntary treatment. Ancel also underlined the significance of social action on the social environment to which the offender must eventually reintegrate and assigned a larger role to social assistance.

The postwar affirmation of a commitment to rehabilitation had an important impact on the reform of criminal law in the 1960s and 1970s. A principal landmark in this legislative development was the Alternative Draft for a Penal Code (General Part) of 1966, prepared by a group of young German and Swiss law professors, which greatly influenced later reform of the sanctioning system. Countering the more traditional Government's Draft of 1962, they proposed a set of rules based on a modern and progressive crime policy.[162] Penal sanctions are assigned the double function of protecting legal values and reintegrating the offender into the community in §2, ¶1. As the drafters noted, the legal order is certainly better protected when the lawbreaker is persuaded not to infringe the law again. Again, §37 establishes that prison sentences should aim to further the reintegration of the offenders into the legal community, awaken their sense of self-responsibility, and encourage their relationship with the outer world. The custodial function of prison sentences should be reduced to an indispensable minimum. Rehabilitation is assigned a preeminent role in sentencing in ¶59. In contrast to the indeterminate sentencing system, the maximum prison length is determined by a special concept of "culpability for the offense" (Tatschuld), which excludes subjective considerations not strictly linked to the misdeed, thus limiting discretion considerably. Below this ceiling the rehabilitative aim and the protection of legal interests are the chief considerations to be taken into account in the final sentencing decision. Other provisions with rehabilitative significance include the elimination of prison sentences shorter than six months or longer than fifteen years;[163] adoption of a uniform type of imprisonment, eliminating the publicly humiliating forms of penal servitude; extension of suspended sentences with probation; and establishment of institutions of social therapy.

The rehabilitative emphasis, although somewhat compromised, influenced the reforms leading to the new General Part of the Penal Code of the Federal Republic of Germany (FRG), in force since 1975. This code embodied the change from a retributive to a rehabilitation-oriented criminal law.[164] Such a transformation is mirrored in the sentencing rules of ¶46, which require the judge to take into account not only offenders' culpability, but also the effects of penalties on their future life in society. This provision created the need to determine the precise role of culpability and rehabilitation in sentencing. Several theories were mooted for that purpose.

As in most continental legislation, the German penal code sets maximum and minimum ranges of punishment for each offense, which correlate with the degree of culpability. The dominant theory grants consideration to the rehabilitative aim as long as the sentence remains between those ranges. This so-called elbowroom theory (*Spielraumtheorie*) is opposed by the pinpoint theory (*Punktstrafe*), which considers that the degree of culpability is a fixed point between the maximum and minimum penalties, from which a certain elasticity for rehabilitative concerns is allowed. A number of scholars advocated the stepwise model of sentencing (*Stellenwerttheorie*), totally excluding rehabilitation as a consideration in determining the length of sanctions and assigning it a role only on decisions on suspension or deferral of the sentence. Although not entirely abolished, as in the Alternative Draft, prison sentences under six months, considered harmful and too short to be rehabilitative, are considerably restrained. They can be imposed only exceptionally, when essential to influence the offender or protect the legal order. As in the Alternative Draft, fifteen years is the upper limit of prison sentences, with the exception of life sentences, which are mandatory in cases of murder and genocide, and optional for a limited number of very serious crimes. The reform also followed the Alternative Draft in liberalizing the application of suspended sentence with probation, which is of undeniable rehabilitative value. In addition, the new code contained important provisions establishing social therapeutic institutions. These provisions were repealed in 1985. Nonetheless, social-therapeutic institutions are functioning within the legal framework of the Federal Prison Act (§9).

NOTES

1. On an integrated interpretation of correctional history, see Alexander Pisciotta, "Corrections, Society, and Social Control in America: A Metahistorical Review of the Literature," *Criminal Justice History* 2 (1981): 109–30, 122. See also David Garland, *Punishment and Welfare: A History of Penal Strategies* (London: Heinemann, 1985), 78.

2. On resistance to reform, see Hubert Treiber, *Widerstand gegen Reformpolitik* (Düsseldorf: Bertelsmann, 1973). Anthony Allot, *The Limits of Law* (London: Butterworths, 1980), 196–202, dealt with the resistances to social transformation through law, tendency to routine, and search for fixed patterns. Bureaucrats are especially resistant to liberalization. He defined a bureaucratic system as one in which controls are imposed on people's behavior in accordance with patterns devised and operated, not by the people themselves, but by bureaucrats and for the attainment of goals set by bureaucrats. See also A. D. Miller, L. E. Ohlin, and R. B. Coates, *A Theory of Social Reform: Correctional Change Processes in Two States* (Cambridge, Mass.: Ballinger, 1977).

3. See pp. 10–11.

4. David J. Rothman, *Conscience and Convenience: The Asylum and Its Alternatives in Progressive America* (Boston: Little, Brown, 1980).

5. On the concept of abolitionism and its relationship with rehabilitative policies, see Günther Kaiser, "Abolitionismus—Alternative zum Strafrecht?" in *Festschrift für Karl Lackner*, ed. Wilfried Küper (Berlin: De Gruyter, 1987), 1028.

6. Michel Foucault, *Discipline and Punish: The Birth of the Prison* (New York: Vintage Books, 1979), 277.

7. Ibid., 234.

8. Ibid., 271.

9. Francis Allen, *The Decline of the Rehabilitative Ideal: Penal Policy and Social Purpose* (New Haven, Conn.: Yale University Press, 1981), 39.

10. Ibid, 107 n.25.

11. Adolphe Prins, *La défense sociale et les transformations du droit pénal* (Brussels: Misch et Thron, 1910), 37.

12. The term *total institution* was coined by Goffman to designate those institutions whose "encompassing or total character is symbolized by the barrier to social intercourse with the outside and to departure that is often built right into the physical plant, such as locked doors, high walls, barbed wire, cliffs, water, forests, or moors." See Erwin Goffman, *Asylums: Essays on the Social Situation of Mental Patients and Other Inmates* (New York: Doubleday, 1961), 4.

13. Michael Ignatieff, "State, Civil Society, and Total Institutions: A Critique of Recent Social Histories of Punishment," in *Crime and Justice: An Annual Review of Research*, ed. M. Tonry and N. Morris (Chicago: University of Chicago Press, 1981), 3:175.

14. Michael Sherman and Gordon Hawkins, *Imprisonment in America* (Chicago: University of Chicago Press, 1981), 84.

15. Ignatieff, "State, Civil Society, and Total Institutions," 172.

16. Ibid., 175.

17. Ibid., 170.

18. Ibid.

19. Ibid., 171.

20. See pp. 69–71.

21. Garland, *Punishment and Welfare*, 14.

22. Ibid., 5.

23. Rothman, *Conscience and Convenience*, 3.

24. Garland, *Punishment and Welfare*, 28.

25. Ibid., 31.

26. Ibid.

27. Sherman and Hawkins, *Imprisonment in America*, 84.

28. See p. 38.

29. David J. Rothman, *The Discovery of the Asylum: Social Order and Disorder in the New Republic* (Boston: Little, Brown, 1971).

30. Ibid., xix.

31. Allen, *Decline of the Rehabilitative Ideal*, 5.

32. Ibid., 11.

33. Ibid., 14, 16.

34. Ibid., 43.

35. Michael Zuckerman, "Book Review of Rothman's *Discovery of the Asylum*," *University of Pennsylvania Law Review* 121 (1972): 398, 402.

36. Garland, *Punishment and Welfare*, 257.

37. Ibid., 258.

38. Thorsten Sellin, "Correction in Historical Perspective," in *Correctional Institutions*, ed. R. Carter, D. Glaser and L. Wilkins (Philadelphia: J. B. Lippincott, 1972), 9, 10.

39. Jean Escarra, "Introduction," French translation of the Penal Code of the Chinese Republic of 1928 (Bibliothèque de l'Institut de Droit Comparé de Lyon, 1930), xxvi, quoted by Marc Ancel, *La défense sociale nouvelle* (Paris: Cujas, 1981), 41, 42. English

translation by Gertrude R. Browne for Works Progress Administration (WP 2799), *Chinese Law* (Seattle: University of Washington, 1936).

40. Plato, *The Laws*, bk. X, 908, in *The Dialogues of Plato*, trans. B. Jowett (New York: Random House, 1937), 2:649.

41. Thorsten Sellin, *Slavery and the Penal System* (New York: Elsevier, 1976), 15, 16.

42. Joseph Fletcher, *Situation Ethics: The New Morality* (Philadelphia: Westminster Press, 1966), 79.

43. Harold J. Berman, *Law and Revolution: The Formation of the Western Legal Tradition* (Cambridge, Mass.: Harvard University Press, 1983), 71.

44. Ibid.

45. Hans von Hentig, *Die Strafe* (Berlin: Springer, 1955) 2:172, 173.

46. Johannes Nagler, *Die Strafe* (Leipzig: Verlag von Felix Meiner, 1918), 161.

47. See Glauco Giostra, "Tre settori da differenziare nei rapporti tra giuridizione ed esecuzione penale," *Rivista Italiana di diritto e procedura penale* (1981): 1374.

48. Ibid.

49. Thorsten Sellin, "Dom Jean Mabillon—A Prison Reformer of the Seventeenth Century," *Journal of the American Institute of Criminal Law and Criminology* 17 (1926–1927): 581.

50. G. Kaiser, H.-J. Kerner, and H. Schöch, *Strafvollzug: Eine Einführung in die Grundlagen* (Heidelberg: C. F. Müller, 1977), 28.

51. On this correlation, see Hubert Treiber and Hans Steiner *Die Fabrikation des zuverlässigen Menschen* (Munich: Heinz Moos Verlag, 1980); Walter Kargl, *Kritik des Schuldprinzips: Eine rechtssoziologische Studie zum Strafrecht* (Frankfurt: Campus Verlag, 1982), 322–25.

52. Berman, *Law and Revolution*, 183.

53. Ibid., 183.

54. Ibid., 184.

55. Edgardo Rotman, "L'évolution de la pensée juridique sur le but de la sanction penale," in *Aspects nouveaux de la pensée juridique (hommage à Marc Ancel)* (Paris: Pedone, 1975), 163–76.

56. A. V. Judges, quoted by Sean McConville, *A History of English Prison Administration* (London: Routledge & Kegan Paul), 2.

57. R. B. Pugh, *Imprisonment in Medieval England*, quoted by ibid., 2.

58. Ibid., 4.

59. J. A. Sharpe, *Crime in Seventeenth-Century England*, (Cambridge: Cambridge University Press, 1983), 152.

60. McConville, *A History of English Prison Administration* 23.

61. Ibid., 29.

62. Ibid., 25, 26.

63. Sellin, *Slavery and the Penal System*, 74.

64. Thorsten Sellin, *Pioneering in Penology* (Philadelphia, University of Pennsylvania Press, 1944), 9.

65. Ibid., 17.

66. Ibid., 28.

67. Sellin, *Slavery and the Penal System*, 69.

68. Thorsten Sellin, "Filippo Franci—A Precursor of Modern Penology," *Journal of the American Institute of Criminal Law and Criminology* 17 (1926–1927): 104–12.

69. Albert Hess, *Introduction to the Reports of the Prison Discipline Society of Boston* (Montclair, N.J.: Patterson Smith, 1972), viii.

70. Rothman, *Discovery of the Asylum*, 62.

71. Francois Alexandre Larochefoucauld-Liancourt, *On the Prisons of Philadelphia: by a European* (Philadelphia: Moreau de Saint-Mery, 1796).

72. See p. 26.

73. Rothman, *The Discovery of the Asylum*, 82.

74. Foucault, *Discipline and Punish*, 263.

75. Charles Lucas, *Extrait du compte-rendu a la société de la morale Chrétienne du 22 avril 1839*, 11, 12.

76. Académie de Sciences Morales et Politiques, *Communication de M. Charles Lucas sur les prisons d'amérique* (Paris, 1840), 6.

77. Charles Lucas, *Des moyens et des conditions d'une réforme pénitentiaire en France* (Paris: Au Bureau de la Revue de Legislation, 1840), 86.

78. Edmond Ducpetiaux, *Des progrès et de l'état actuel de la réforme pénitentiaire* (Brussels: Societe Belge de Librairie, 1837), xii.

79. Lucas, *Extrait du compte-rendu*, 16.

80. Ibid., 19.

81. Lucas, *Des moyens et des conditions*, 58.

82. See p. 157 and Ancel, *La défense sociale nouvelle*, 576.

83. Quoted by Ducpetiaux, *Des progrès*, 39.

84. Ibid., 125.

85. Ibid., 139, 140.

86. Ibid., 9.

87. Orlando Lewis quoted by Sherman and Hawkins, *Imprisonment in America*, 87–88 n.128.

88. Ibid., 88.

89. Sellin, "Dom Jean Mabillon," 602.

90. Rotman, "L'évolution de la pensée juridique," 168.

91. See p. 32.

92. John Vincent Barry, *Alexander Machonochie of Norfolk Island* (London: Oxford University Press, 1958), 243–61.

93. E. C. Wines, ed., *Transaction of the National Congress on Penitentiary and Reformatory Discipline held at Cincinnati, Ohio, October 12–18, 1870* (Albany: Argus Company, 1871), 66.

94. Ibid., 68.

95. Compare Gabrie Tarde, *Penal Philosophy* (Boston: Little, Brown, 1912), 524 and Moritz Liepmann, "Die Problematik des 'Progressiven Strafvollzugs,' " *Monatschrift für Kriminalpsychiatrie* (1926): 56.

96. Wines, *Transaction of the National Congress*, 541.

97. Ibid.

98. Rothman, *Conscience and Convenience*, 40.

99. Wines, *Transaction of the National Congress*, 65.

100. Ibid., 45.

101. Ibid.

102. Torsten Eriksson, *The Reformers: A Historical Survey of Pioneer Experiments in the Treatment of Criminals* (New York: Elsevier, 1976), 102 and Blake McKelvey,

American Prisons: A History of Good Intentions (Montclair, N.J.: Patterson Smith, 1977), 52.

103. Eriksson, *The Reformers*, 100.

104. Rothman, *Conscience and Convenience*, 36.

105. Pisciotta, "Corrections, Society and Social Control," 123.

106. Alexander W. Pisciotta, "Scientific Reform: The 'New Penology' at Elmira," *Crime and Delinquency* 29 (Jan. 1983): 620.

107. Ibid., 626.

108. Michael B. Katz, *Poverty and Policy in American History* (New York: Academic Press, 1983), 212, 213.

109. Ricardo Garofalo, *La criminología* (Madrid: La España Moderna, n.d.), 338.

110. Francis Allen, *The Borderland of Criminal Justice* (Chicago: University of Chicago Press, 1964), 80, 84.

111. Ibid., 85.

112. Enrico Ferri, *Principios de derecho criminal* (Madrid, 1933), 312.

113. Franz von Liszt, *Strafrechtliche Aufsätze und Vorträge* (Berlin: J. Guttentag, 1905), II:80.

114. Ibid., II:397.

115. Claus Roxin, *Strafrechtliche Grundlagen-Probleme* (Berlin: De Gruyter, 1973), 67.

116. Ibid., 69.

117. Ancel, *La défense sociale nouvelle*, 321.

118. Ibid., 92.

119. Prins, *La défense sociale*, 89.

120. Ibid., 74.

121. Ibid., 155.

122. Ibid., 162.

123. Ibid., 165.

124. See Rothman, *Conscience and Convenience*, 43.

125. Raymond Saleilles, *L'individualisation de la peine; étude de Criminalité Sociale* (Paris: F. Alcan, 1898).

126. Raymond Saleilles, *The Individualization of Punishment* (Boston: Little, Brown, 1911), 192.

127. See Rothman, *Conscience and Convenience*, 70.

128. Garland, *Punishment and Welfare*, 5.

129. Ibid., 173.

130. Ibid., 238.

131. Ibid., 241.

132. Ibid., 242, 243.

133. Ibid., 243.

134. Ibid., 17.

135. Ibid., 266.

136. Ibid., 79.

137. Ibid., 106.

138. Ibid., 107.

139. Ibid., 170.

140. Ibid., 228.

141. Ibid., 234.

142. Ibid., 255.

143. See pp. 7, 113–15.

144. Rothman, *Conscience and Convenience*, 61.

145. Allen, *The Decline of the Rehabilitative Ideal*, 11, 12.

146. Rothman, *Conscience and Convenience*, 93.

147. Ibid., 118.

148. See p. 157.

149. Rothman, *Conscience and Convenience*, 119. See also J. E. Baker, *Prisoners' Participation in Prison Power* (Metuchen, N.J.: Scarecrow Press, 1985).

150. Eriksson, *The Reformers*, 133.

151. Ibid., 134, 139.

152. Ibid., 140.

153. Thomas O. Murton, *The Dilemma of Prison Reform* (New York: Holt, Rinehart and Winston, 1976), 203.

154. Ibid., 17.

155. Ancel, *La défense sociale nouvelle*, 35, 193.

156. Marc Ancel, "La protection des droits de l'homme selon les doctrines de la défense sociale moderne," in *Études en l'honneur de Jean Graven*, ed. Faculte de Droit de Genève (Geneva: Librairie de l'Université, Georg, 1969), 5.

157. Ancel, *La défense sociale nouvelle*, 253.

158. Ibid., 188 n.26.

159. Ibid., 232.

160. "Humanism," Paul Kurtz wrote, "does not represent a fixed program or platform, but rather is a general outlook, a method of inquiry, an ethic of freedom, and it is committed to a limited number of basic values and principles." See Paul Kurtz, "Does Humanism Have an Ethic of Responsibility?" in *Humanist Ethics*, ed. M. B. Storer (Buffalo, N.Y.: Prometheus, 1980), 13.

161. Edgardo Rotman, "La politique du traitement a la lumière de la troisième édition de *La Défense Sociale Nouvelle*," *Revue de science criminelle et de droit pénal comparé* (1984): 573.

162. For a comparison of the two drafts, see Claus Roxin, "Strafzweck und Strafrechtsreform," in *Programm für ein neues Strafgesetzbuch*, ed. Jürgen Baumann (Frankfurt: Fischer, 1968).

163. See p. 147.

164. Günter Blau, "Die Kriminalpolitik der deutschen Strafrechtsreformgesetze," *Zeitschrift für die gesamte Strafrechtswissenschaft* 89 (1977): 520.

3

The Search for a Formula

DISCIPLINING THE OFFENDER: THE PENITENTIARY MODEL

Within the complex historical development of the rehabilitative idea, some dominant patterns can be identified, which can be represented by the penitentiary, therapeutic, social-learning, and rights models.[1] The competition between humanistic and oppressive elements plays a central role in this progression, which must be understood if we are to develop a model that can overcome the abuses and failures of the past.

The penitentiary model of rehabilitation encompasses two basic variations, which developed in the first and second halves of the nineteenth century. The first corresponds to the Jacksonian penitentiary, comprehending in turn the Pennsylvanian and Auburn systems.[2] The second is the progressive-stage system and its various subformulas, beginning with the initiatives of Machonochie and culminating with the indeterminate sentence and the Elmira experiment.[3]

Imprisonment was the main ingredient in both variations. In the early nineteenth-century version the walls of the penitentiary provided the isolation necessary for a reformative concept based on moral preaching, solitary contemplation, and religious readings. Rehabilitative hopes were also vested in disciplined labor, which was carried out either in solitude (separate system) or in the silent presence of other inmates (silent or congregate system). Both systems regimented the life of the inmate totally and maintained a high degree of supervision, in which the prison architecture played a significant role.[4] Separate standardized cells were used as the optimal means of isolation and surveillance. Toward the end of the century, the trend to individualization of prison sentences mitigated an exaggerated disciplinary model in which, following the spirit of the early penitentiary, each individual was treated exactly alike.

The late nineteenth-century variation of the penitentiary model used the pressure of imprisonment to create a system of incentives and deterrents. In this carrot-and-stick scheme, release was the ultimate reward. Conversely, the deterrents were the loss of privileges or demotion to a lower stage of the progression, where deprivation of liberty was stricter. As inmates were given a chance to work toward eventual discharge, the enforced discipline of the original penitentiary forms was transformed into a self-discipline based on habituation to certain patterns of behavior. But although the institution was linked to society, reformers still believed that a highly controlled environment was needed for rehabilitation. Penitentiary confinement was the necessary starting point for an incentive system that would allow the new behavior technologists to mold the character of the inmate according to fixed patterns of labor and discipline.

CURING THE OFFENDER: THE THERAPEUTIC MODEL

At the turn of the century, biological and psychiatric interpretations of social deviance began to assume a central role in criminology and policy-making. A medical, or therapeutic, model of rehabilitation emerged, resting on the assumption that criminal offenders suffered from some physical, mental, or social pathology. Once crime had been diagnosed as illness, it was logical to use the methods and language of medical science to "cure" offenders of their criminality. Indeed, the normal mechanisms of criminal law would be inadequate to prevent recidivism. Thus the doors of criminal justice were opened to psychiatrists and behavioral scientists.

In the first decades of the twentieth century the therapeutic model amounted to a speculation that knowledge of causes would generate the remedy for criminality. The sole tangible consequence of the analogy between corrections and medicine was the expansion of incapacitative custodial policies against dangerous offenders at the expense of their individual rights. However, the sparing introduction of psychiatric services in prisons, more for diagnostic than for therapeutic purposes, did not change this situation substantially.

In the past, therapeutic rehabilitation had been conceived more broadly as the "cure of souls." In early Christian communities the notion took the form of practices of mutual edification and fraternal correction, as well as the reconciliation with the community of the truly penitent offender. In the expression *cure of souls*, the word *cure* stems from the Latin *cura*, whose primary sense is "care" ("healing" is a secondary, specialized meaning).[5] Its disciplinarian form is termed in canonic law *poena medicinalis*.[6]

In contrast with this idea of moral treatment, a biological school of criminology emerged in the last century. Its deterministic connotations precluded any genuine rehabilitative undertaking and fostered a policy of incapacitation or neutralization resulting in the eugenic programs of the early twentieth century.[7] Among other antecedents of modern biological explanations of crime were phrenology, which tied psychological and behavioral traits to various parts of the brain, and craniology, which related psychological traits to the shapes of the skull. Its main representatives were Gall and Spurzheim. This school was influenced by Morel's theory of degeneration, which attributed to heredity various forms of social deviance, including insanity and feeblemindedness.[8] Interest in the somatic aspects of criminals culminated in Lombroso's deterministic theory of the born criminal, in whose original formulation rehabilitation played hardly any role. As the content of the biomedical model evolved toward a criminological model of psychiatric bent, the possibility of rehabilitative treatment began to gain wider consideration in correctional policies.

Psychiatry and corrections had converged during certain periods of history, while developing separately in others. Before the Enlightenment, criminals and the mentally ill were usually confined together, whereas the two categories of inmates were strictly separated in the period of moral treatment.[9] However, the methodology applied to the insane influenced the future treatment of criminals. Psychiatric and criminal justice endeavors reached a new convergence under the concept of social hygiene in the second half of the nineteenth century. Virchow, a prominent medical professor, demanded reforms in the criminal law, making public health care its principal task. He equated the criminal with the mentally ill and thought that the states' responsibility regarding crime was not satisfied merely through criminal law. Furthermore, he assigned criminal law a future pedagogical, psychological, and medical task.[10]

Foucault provided valuable insights into the relationship between social hygiene policies and psychiatry. He traced the first steps toward what he called the "psychiatrization of criminal danger" between 1800 and 1835, in connection with cases of homicidal monomania.[11] Some monstrous crimes were committed without apparent rational explanation, showing none of the traditional symptoms of dementia, furor, or imbecility. Because most of these cases were murders in domestic settings, they were categorized as crimes against nature and not mere violations of social norms. On these grounds the theory of homicidal monomania was developed, which Foucault saw as an entirely fictitious entity, alluding to a derangement that would have no other symptom than the crime itself.[12] In this way psychiatry made inroads on criminal punishment and began to incorporate medical knowledge into the rules of criminal law.

Foucault views this phenomenon as a mechanism of power directed to the unsettling social problems raised by the new industrial societies. The target of both criminal law and psychiatry was an amorphous mass of dangerous classes that included the criminal and the insane. The emergent public hygiene medical model justified their prolonged confinement. In the second half of the nineteenth century, after the decline of moral treatment and the asylum, the treatment of the mentally ill was predominantly custodial in nature. Psychiatry became important in the nineteenth century, according to Foucault, "not simply because it applied a new medical rationality to mental or behavioral disorders," but also "because it functioned as a sort of public hygiene."[13]

The psychiatric invasion of criminal law gained momentum toward the end of last century, and the advent of Freudian thought brought new life to the therapeutic model of rehabilitation. This model, although enriched with substantial psychoanalytical and sociological contributions, remained during the first decades of the twentieth century a diagnostic instrument, rather than reaching a truly therapeutic level. The meagerness of this criminal therapy did not prevent the emergence of a "medical myth," which encouraged a lavish application of the vocabulary of medical science to situations of a purely punitive nature.[14]

The terminological transformation within criminology can be clearly seen in a 1911 brochure describing the Instituto de Criminologia, a psychiatric annex to the National Buenos Aires Penitentiary, conceived by Jose Ingenieros as the first of its kind and inaugurated in 1907.[15] According to its brochure, the institute was "a laboratory and a clinic to gather the basic elements to prepare the future transformations of criminal law." The medical terminology is striking. The three components of what Ingenieros called "the application of the positive method to the study of social and individual pathology" were "criminal etiology," "clinical criminology," and "criminal therapy." These correspond, in a perfect analogy with the vocabulary of medicine, to the search for causes, the diagnosis, and the "social or individual measures of prevention and repression of criminality."

Psychoanalysis gave a new impulse to the nineteenth-century view of the criminal offender as diseased. Some of its representatives, going beyond strict Freudian doctrine, claimed that they could treat ordinary criminals. A new medical model of psychological bent gradually replaced the old biomedical deterministic approach. The application of this psychoanalytically oriented medical model to the criminal justice system extended the grounds for excusing offenders from criminal responsibility and supported a new rehabilitative optimism, especially after World War II. Even at the beginning of the century, the advent of psychoanalysis broadened psychiatric power, opening the door of prisons to the experts, even when they did not adhere to the Freudian doctrine. In the 1920s and 1930s, however, some of Freud's followers, focusing on the very early child-mother relationships, at the pre-oedipal stage, claimed it was possible to treat behavior disorders leading to juvenile delinquency. August Aichorn, Karl Abraham, Hans Zulger, Franz Alexander, and William Healey were some of the principal representatives of psychoanalysis in the field of criminology during that period.[16]

Traditional criminal justice has often been criticized for its lack of concern for the person of the offender.[17] Aiming to transform society's attitude and behavior toward criminals, psychoanalytic criticism played a key role in opening the law to the inner realities of human beings. By demanding that the retributive vindictive mentality should be ruled out, it paved the way to a humanist rehabilitation.[18] Although its premises may not have been scientifically watertight and its practical achievements were slight, it enlarged the horizon of criminal science. Besides the offense and the offender, criminal law itself and the punitive social reaction fell under psychological scrutiny. Alexander, Staub, Eric Fromm, and Paul Reiwald were pioneers in psychoanalyzing the "punitive society."

THE SOCIAL LEARNING MODEL

Meaning

The crisis of the medical model is a consequence not merely of its abuses but of defects in the model itself. In its traditional form, the biomedical model has proved to be inadequate even for medicine, and still less suitable for psychiatry and its correctional derivations. It is based on the classic scientific notion of "the body as a machine, of disease as the consequence of breakdown of the machine, and of the doctor's task as repair of the machine."[19] Modern medicine has reacted against such concepts, taking into consideration the psychological and social variables in the definition and treatment of disease. "A medical model must also take into account the patient, the social context in which he lives, and the complementary system devised by society to deal with the disruptive effects of illness, that is, the physician role and the health care system. This requires a biopsychosocial model."[20] Even within medicine, disease is no longer seen as an exclusively biochemical or neurophysiological process. Rather, it is considered as a problem of living, and therapy today means a concern with the totality of human life. Moreover psychiatry is currently moving toward a more integrated approach to the patient in which biological and social, as well as analytical, concepts are considered. It tries to understand the patient as a total person.[21]

Similarly in corrections, a biopsychosocial medical model emerged as the psychomedical model of the 1920s and 1930s was influenced by social psychiatry. This combination gave rise to the most important rehabilitative experiments of the twentieth century.[22] As the therapy of mentally disordered offenders evolved toward a social-learning model, valuable implications were drawn out for corrections as a whole. These innovations were derived from the newly conceived experiments on the therapeutic community in psychiatry as well as the growing awareness of the need to counteract the negative effects of total institutions.[23]

The evolved medical model overlaps to a certain extent with the social-learning model. The increasing role of social learning in psychotherapy today has made "therapy" and "social learning" somewhat interchangeable.[24] However, the shift toward the social and environmental element as the core of rehabilitative strategies deprives the medical model of the defining element of "sickness." From the social-learning perspective criminal behavior is seen rather as a learning disorder in the socialization process.[25] It is more accurate to use the terminology of social learning to refer to group and environmental strategies of an educational rather than therapeutic nature. Rehabilitation is no longer an individualized treatment of particular individuals, but a generalized process of social apprenticeship. It is at this level that the notion of rehabilitation as opportunity surmounts the narrow limits of medical treatment and encompasses the offering of a broad range of social experiences aimed at developing skills, motivation, knowledge, and interactive capacity.

Rehabilitation as Surrogate for Socialization

By the middle of this century the socialization theory had become highly developed, especially in America, as the result of the convergent interest of a wide range of disciplines led by psychology, anthropology, and sociology.[26] Both criminology and penology followed this challenging scientific concern. Many forms of criminality were explained as flaws in the early socialization process, and the idea of compensatory socialization provided a new rehabilitative model to the correctional system.

Socialization is essentially the process through which an individual becomes a participant in the social system. It can be considered from both the individual's and society's viewpoint. From the perspective of individual psychology, socialization is basically a process of communication and learning, which includes norms, values, skills, knowledge, motivations, and feelings. In regard to criminal rehabilitation the most relevant of these elements are moral norms or values that underlie the provisions of criminal law. From society's viewpoint the socialization process is the attainment of the degree of consensus needed to maintain the viability of a social system. The internalization of basic cultural norms creates the necessary degree of social cohesion. Stability is achieved by making human behavior relatively predictable.

Except in totalitarian dictatorships, the integrative function of the socialization process does not imply that the interests of society and those of the individual are exactly the same. In a pluralistic and democratic society such convergence is highly limited. Furthermore, in democratically evolved societies, the acceptance of social norms tends to be a voluntary act by which individuals understand the meaning of the transmitted values while retaining their critical capacity.

Modern socialization theory has moved beyond mechanistic conceptions of social adjustment. Wurzbacher distinguished between socialization, enculturation, and personalization as three different forms of interaction between the person, culture, and society.[27] He saw socialization as a process of social coinage through which the individual is incorporated in the social group. Socialization does not mean a mechanical assumption of roles, for it includes a critical insight into the incorporation of ideas and behavioral patterns. Enculturation is the transmission and internalization of culture, which is defined as an abstract system of patterns and symbols through which the individual interprets and assigns significance to individual and social existence. Personalization is characterized by Wurzbacher as the development of the individual through self-determination. It also involves a responsible two-way exchange between the individual and culture.

The socialization process starts in the family, school, church, and other community groups in which the young are brought to conform to certain forms of behavior expected by society. In the modern world, family dissolution and the neglect of children conspire against such early socialization. These problems are aggravated by the lack of enculturation, which keeps juveniles from perceiving the basic values protected by criminal law. The general dissolution of values in modern society and the confusion brought about by wars and social conflicts hamper the transmission of a value system opposed to crime.

The lack of personalization, in Wurzbacher's conception, leads to an inability to judge, select, and coordinate the influence of natural, cultural, and social environmental factors. This failure is the main cause of recidivism and habitual crime. Thus immaturity and a lack of capacity for responsible decisions and self-determination became a prevalent etiological explanation of chronic criminality and of a considerable portion of juvenile delinquency. A new image of the criminal resulted, in which he was seen as childish or immature. This image had far-reaching influence, not only on etiological theories on crime, but also on the structuring of rehabilitative techniques and the treatment of mentally abnormal offenders.

The rich spectrum of theory and research generated in various scientific disciplines around the idea of socialization created a significant conceptual framework to guide rehabilitative endeavors. With some insight into human development from early childhood on, it became possible to design surrogate forms of socialization to be applied in correctional and community-based programs. The ambitious aspiration of compensating for a faulty socialization process was supported by theoretical trends that deemphasized the early stages of development and considered socialization to be a process stretching over an individual's entire life. The concept of adult socialization favored the conception of corrections as a social learning and educational undertaking.[28] In addition, socialization theory clarified the relationship between socialization agents and those with whom they communicate. Moreover, the focus on secondary socialization processes allowed for an evaluation of the influence of the legislature, judiciary, police, and mass media on the formation of the individual.

Social Therapy—Lessons from the Treatment of Mentally Disordered Offenders

The social-therapeutic response focuses on the transformation of the institutional environment, creating a network of compensatory social interaction. At first social-therapeutic experiments were designed as mere supplements to the traditional prison routine. The subsequent evolution has been toward the transformation of the whole institutional structure. Environmental and organizational modification has thus become the core of the modern social-therapeutic experiments. This broad scheme of social learning is complemented with various specific forms of psychotherapy.

The transformation of the institutional structure aims to create what the German

Alternative Draft of a Code for Execution of Sentences (1976) called "a problem solving community." The generic nature of such an approach makes it potentially applicable to all institutionalized offenders, including those in regular correctional institutions. The traditional therapeutic model, confined to those labeled as sick or abnormal, is thus transcended by the broader social-learning techniques. The risks of stigmatization are also considerably diminished.

Modern social therapy creates other social-learning fields outside the institution's walls. The opening to the community is an aspiration of most social-therapeutic efforts, although their activities are still largely carried out within institutional settings. The importance of extra-institutional intervention in modern social therapy is mirrored in aftercare services. Their quality and extent has become a decisive factor in the effectiveness of social therapy. It has become clear that inmates need to be offered support during a gradual release period. Among inmates of social-therapeutic institutions, those who undergo a prerelease period of preparation through furloughs and leaves of absence recidivate less than those directly released from a closed regime.[29] The integration of rehabilitative treatment with community cooperation should become a central aspect of future social therapeutic developments. Progress in this area is thus intimately linked with the ideal of community-based corrections.

The term *social therapy* was coined in 1947 by Viktor von Weizaecker in the field of mental health. He characterized it as a psychotherapeutic method of helping the mental patient by influencing his social environment. The term mirrors a momentous change in psychiatric science: the discovery of the social dimension of the mental patient. This perspective found its realization in the therapeutic community, conceived by Maxwell Jones after World War II.

The therapeutic community essentially replaces the hierarchical structure of the institution with a horizontal association of mutually responsible human beings who resolve their common problems through a process of intensive human interaction. The vehicles of this process are the frequent meetings and group discussions where decisions are reached through the participation of both inmates and staff. Meetings and group sessions are also the occasion for scrutinizing and clarifying a variety of psychological problems arising from the complex network of human interrelations peculiar to total institutions. Such notorious negative effects as depersonalization, dependency, and loss of initiative are counteracted by the demand for active interaction and dynamic participation in decision making.

This idea of the therapeutic community has guided the European social therapeutic institutions for criminal offenders, but it has been modified to suit the requirements of the criminal justice system. Practiced either as a security measure or as a variation of prison sentences, social therapy remains, broadly speaking, a criminal sanction. Although a far more constructive alternative than plain punishment, it still belongs to a legal system of consequences to the commission of criminal offenses. As such, it has to comply in some measure with the deterrent and incapacitative demands of the system.

The social-therapeutic establishments have not entirely lost the character of penal institutions, despite their predominantly rehabilitative orientation and the relaxation of many constraints. An early experiment in the Netherlands, which entirely removed the barriers between the inmates and staff, was discontinued due to public resistance.[30] A much milder attempt to liberalize the conditions of imprisonment in a German social-therapeutic institution was also rejected by the public.[31] A negative press campaign ultimately forced modifications in the program. Clearly, advanced rehabilitative experiments may become very sensitive political issues, creating negative overreactions. They are not altogether incompatible with the administration of criminal justice, however. A certain distance has to be maintained between inmates and staff even in the leading avant-garde experiments. However, the coercive structure of the traditional prison has been reduced to a minimum consistent with the rehabilitative quality of the institution.

In the traditional prison communication between staff and inmates is based exclusively on authority and subordination, a one-way vertical relationship. A main goal of the social-therapeutic institutions is to change the authoritarian pattern of communication. In contrast to the limited, rigid, and formal contacts of the average prison, there is room for spontaneity and for overcoming authoritarian isolation. Inmates participate in decision making enough to develop a sense of mature responsibility. Even the usual activities of work and recreation are organized so as to generate self-esteem, psychological autonomy, and self-determination. This approach requires extending considerable trust to the inmates. In this regard, the social-therapeutic institution can act as a model for the overall correctional system, that is, as "a living proof that relinquishing many of the hallowed principles of security and order does not necessarily mean the end of the world."[32]

Problems arising from institutional life are discussed and solved in common during the frequent conferences of the therapeutic community. Negative psychological phenomena—derived from freedom deprivation, distrust, and persecutory attitudes in both the guardians and the guarded—are identified and explored in meetings of a therapeutic nature.[33] The transformation of the institutional communication structure requires coordination between the therapeutic staff and security personnel. Their harmonious involvement is necessary for the creation of a true field of social learning within the institution.

Intensive communication makes possible greater role flexibility. This helps security officers overcome their resistance to participation in the therapeutic venture, and encourages therapists to abandon their theoretical rigidity for the sake of treatment practicability. Overcoming the distrust between prison officers and the therapeutic staff paves the way for genuine cooperation and effective teamwork in the basic therapeutic task. In some units, trained prison officers accomplish significant therapeutic functions. Their intervention tends to reduce social distance from the inmates, most of whom belong to a lower social class than the professional therapists.

Besides the generic environmental approach directed toward social learning, social therapy encompasses the application of various specific psychotherapeutic techniques. Group therapy is favored because of its practical advantages, particularly in large institutions. There are some exceptions to this rule, as at the Mesdag Kliniek of Groningen.[34] Following psychoanalytical tenets, this institution admits only patients of specific type for whom only individual therapy is thought appropriate, because they cannot maintain anything but a one-to-one relationship.

Many psychotherapeutic techniques and schools compete in different social-therapeutic institutions, where they are sometimes applied simultaneously or combined, usually following eclectic criteria. Client-centered, gestalt, psychoanalytic, and behavioral therapies may all be involved. Candidates for social therapy generally suffer from personality disorders with a tendency toward acting out that makes treatment in closed institutions necessary. However, the opening of institutions to outside society and the expansion of the social learning thrust beyond its walls remain preeminent goals of social therapy.

A main point of contention is the motivation for treatment. The original social-therapeutic theory, adapted to the legal framework of security measures of indeterminate duration, held that it was the pressure of the psychological ailment itself (*Leidensdruck*) that drove the inmate to seek treatment. It was in fact imprisonment, and not a preexisting psychological ailment, that created the need for therapy. This dangerous theory, which leads to justifying incarceration on therapeutic grounds, was abandoned in the more modern social-therapeutic institutions. In practice, most offenders suffering personality disturbances, as social therapy candidates do, tend to reject any further therapeutic offer once they are released.[35]

The present trend toward voluntary treatment within the legal framework of determinate sentencing makes it difficult to arouse therapeutic motivation. Therapists need considerable imagination and skill to make the patient aware of his need for sociopsychological transformation. The only possible means are dialogue and personal involvement, because the stress of prolonged incarceration and the reward of anticipated release are no longer available. A recent proposal would permit involuntary commitment in the social-therapeutic institution, but limited to a five-month period. During this time inmates would have the chance to reach a truly informed decision on the continuation of their own treatment in this special type of institution.[36]

The experimental side of social therapy is highly significant. Besides serving as intensive rehabilitative experiments, social-therapeutic establishments often support research into the causes of repetitive crime and the treatment methods used against it. Instead of dogmatically applying rigid theoretical principles, they generally function with an inquisitive spirit. Recent evaluative studies of various social-therapeutic programs have yielded encouraging results.[37] In the future, experimental research should help to solve basic problems such as the possibilities of expanding social therapy from a restricted number of offenders to larger portions of the correctional system.

THE RIGHTS MODEL

Rehabilitation and Individual Rights

In modern pluralistic democracies, public policies are limited by individual rights. This moral and legal phenomenon is the result of a long process that began with the natural law theorists of the seventeenth century and the philosophers of the Enlightenment, developed through the nineteenth- and twentieth-century constitutions and culminated in far-reaching conceptions of human rights, widely recognized today in most civilized countries and incorporated into international law.

For a long time, individual rights provided a basis for criticizing abusive rehabilitative policies. Rehabilitation was then regarded as a threat to individual rights, jeopardizing freedom and privacy. Individual rights thus restrained public policies in which rehabilitation was conceived as exclusively a governmental interest or as a collective goal. Critics showed that policies were used to justify paternalistic state intervention in which the life of the inmate or probationer was shaped by public officials according to their own value systems. The threat to individual autonomy became all the more alarming with the adoption of intrusive therapies, brainwashing techniques and chemically controlled behavior modification programs. The more blatant abuses, however, were those perpetrated against the right to freedom, as the supposed rehabilitative effects of incarceration were used to justify its extension within the legal framework of indeterminate sentencing.

Recognition of the prisoner as a possessor of rights eventually reconciled the apparent conflict between the idea of rehabilitation and the rights of the individual. A vast network of prisoners' rights emerged in various national and international legal bodies, most conspicuously in the 1955 United Nations Minimum Rules for the Treatment of Prisoners and in the years after the 1950s. Provisions of new laws affirmed an actual right to rehabilitation, already proclaimed at the crime-policy level.[38] A renewed liberal concept of rehabilitation ultimately discovered solid support and justification in the very concept of rights. Individual rights were found to be at stake not only in cases of abusive rehabilitative intervention, but also when there was no rehabilitation at all. Even a writer whose proposals rely mostly on deterrent policies had to recognize that "it is not what is done but what is not done that makes our prisons inhumane and produces recidivism."[39]

The right to rehabilitation presupposes a series of prisoners' rights as its indispensable basis. These rights, which have emerged in prison rules, penitentiary laws, and special provisions of broader codes, and as the result of the court's intervention, create the basis for a broader right to rehabilitation that extends to the situation of offenders after their release, and have a rehabilitative value in themselves. The recognition of prisoners as possessors of rights should bolster their development and strengthen their social personalities. Unless elementary human rights (such as decent lodging, food, safety, and avoidance of tortures exceeding liberty deprivation) are honored, more elaborate rehabilitative undertakings would be meaningless. In fact, the right to rehabilitation includes all the others. As a global right, it encompasses the protection of the prisoner in the areas of health, education, training, and work. These rights are components of an integral system directed toward the rehabilitative goal. The first step in such an undertaking is to ensure that elementary human needs are satisfied. From there begins a continuum of rights that extends to the offer of specific rehabilitative means, such as voluntary psychotherapy.

The prisoners' rights movement thus generated "positive" rights, requiring affirmative care or positive contribution to the inmates' welfare, as well as negative ones.[40] The movement not only protected imprisoned individuals against overly intrusive state intervention, but included in embryo form a right to develop their human potentialities as the most effective way to counteract the harms of imprisonment. Although rehabilitation is included in the realm of rights, it nevertheless continues to play a role in state penal policies, within the limits marked by the rights of the individual offender. Moreover, an enforceable right to rehabilitation transforms benevolent initiatives to provide for the prisoners' human need into administrative legal obligations.

The denial of rehabilitation and the consequent lack of concern for the future life of the offender amounts to a passive and indifferent acceptance of the inevitable deterioration brought about by life in prison. Imprisonment in itself jeopardizes other rights different from those forfeited through the commission of the crime and the consequent criminal punishment. Moreover, a large majority of inmates are socially handicapped offenders, who need basic support in education, job training, and fundamental social learning. Because their social handicap is considerably aggravated by the stigma of a criminal record, social agencies must make special efforts to support their social reintegration.

These basic human needs create the moral basis to institute a legal duty of the state to counteract the effects of disabling criminal punishment, particularly when applied to offenders with a flawed socialization process, and to establish a correlative right of the criminal offender to rehabilitation. This right demands from the state an affirmative care and a positive contribution to inmates' welfare as ways to counteract the harms of imprisonment. Rehabilitation in this sense means a state effort to prevent and neutralize the unwanted harmful side effects of its own punitive intervention,[41] and to respond to the human challenge posed by the extremely socially deprived offender.

In the past, rehabilitation strengthened the power of the state, either as a form of oppressive paternalism or by increasing the discretion of judicial or administrative sentencing authorities. The new approach, in contrast, implies an affirmation of the individual against the state, without denying the social interest in rehabilitation. Under the rights model rehabilitation is no longer a matter of the state's largess, subject to the vicissitudes of policy change. Instead, rehabilitation is the culmination of a continuum of the offenders' rights, guaranteeing the dignity of human beings confronted with criminal pursuit and conviction.[42]

Legally, the rehabilitative aim is expressed in penal codes as well as penitentiary laws and prison ordinances. Article 37 of the Swiss penal code, for example, provides that prison sentences "should act on the offender in an educational way and prepare him for the reentry into civil life." Rehabilitation became an overriding goal of the sanctioning system in the German Alternative Draft for a Penal Code of 1966. Its Article 2 established that penal sanctions and security measures "serve the protection of the legal values and the reintegration of the offender in the legal community." In some countries rehabilitation attained constitutional status, as in Italy, Germany, Spain, and a number of state constitutions in the United States.

Rehabilitation as a Constitutional Mandate: A Comparative Analysis

Italy. Article 27 of the Italian constitution (in force since 1948) provides that "criminal sanctions should never consist in a treatment imposed against the sense of humanity and should conversely be directed toward the reeducation of the convicted offender." A decision of the Constitutional Court (February 12, 1966, No. 12) established the coherence of the two parts of the provision: a treatment inspired by humanitarian criteria is the necessary precondition for reeducational action.

In this interpretation the constitutional norm requires legislators to consider the aim of reeducation in formulating any penal law and to use all available means to carry it out. Nevertheless, sanctions in which that aim is absent or minimal are not precluded. The Constitutional Court expressly decided that fines do not contradict the educational function enjoined on the penal system (July 19, 1968, No. 113).

Giostra observes that Article 27 is a logical consequence of Article 2 of the Italian constitution, which proclaims a state based on social solidarity. Article 27 lends a social dimension to criminal punishment and favors the reintegration of the offender into society, while fully respecting his moral freedom.[43] In his analysis of the Italian constitution, Dolcini finds nothing that would justify a view of reeducation as the acquisition of a "new morality."[44] He explains that the concept of reeducation has a general meaning of "acquisition of the capacity to live in society respecting criminal laws" and that prison sentences are no excuse to manipulate the offender's personality or to transform him into a sort of "model citizen."[45] Giostra defines "the reeducated citizen" on the basis of specific constitutional provisions; he is

the one who accomplishes the duties of political, economic and social solidarity and has recovered the capacity to participate in the political, economic and social organization of the country, in a critical way, freely associating, respecting criminal law and securing the respect of his own rights, through the political and legal instruments authorized by the legal system.[46]

Some authors interpreted Article 27 of the 1948 constitution as a mere programmatic principle, whereas others claimed it was immediately enforceable.[47] Despite the constitutional provision, the rigorist system of the 1930 penal code and of the penitentiary ordinance of 1931 prevailed for thirty years, and all attempts at reform met obstacles and opposition.[48] The conditional release of those condemned to life imprisonment (*ergastolo*) was sanctioned only in 1962 for offenders who served twenty-eight years. But the discussion was really settled with the sanction of a penitentiary law in 1975[49] that cleared the way for a cautious introduction of probation, community service orders, semiliberty, and parole.[50] Article 27 ¶3 of the Italian constitution thus achieved concrete application in the new law, whose Article 1, ¶5 calls for giving convicts and inmates reeducational treatment "tending to their social reintegration, also through the contact with the external environment."

This norm became the guiding principle of penitentiary reform and was incorporated in the 1976 regulations, where the goal of reeducation is understood as a "process of modification of those attitudes that are an obstacle to constructive social participation."[51] Reeducation is interpreted as a synonym for "social reentry," "social reintegration," and "resocialization."[52] This idea contradicts the constitutionality of life sentences without conditional release and is also incompatible with the death penalty.[53] The Constitutional Court recently declared Article 54 of the 1975 Prison Act unconstitutional, inasmuch as it does not foresee the possibility of shortening the life sentences of prisoners who participate in rehabilitative programs, as foreseen for other prisoners.[54]

The constitutional provision shapes not only penal and penitentiary functions, but also social welfare agencies and services with jurisdictions in areas connected with the control of criminal behavior. Article 27 also plays a decisive role in the execution of nonpunitive security measures for certain types of dangerous offenders.[55]

The new penitentiary law seeks to mitigate the noxious effects of imprisonment. Through various measures it protects the inmates from depersonalization. Its provisions require prison officials to give inmates a certain degree of autonomy in the handling of money and to protect their privacy against excessive intrusion. Links with the external world are to be developed, including access to the mass media without censure and visits of outsiders, especially family members, to the institution. Regulation of furloughs and leaves was liberalized, but then limited by a 1977 law. Moreover, with the institution of semiliberty, the penitentiary law encourages a gradual reintegration of the offender into the community. Conditions in Italian prisons do not allow a full realization of the new prescriptions, which have nevertheless taken the right direction and supported the educational goal assigned to prison sentences by the constitution.[56] A recent statute (October 10, 1986, No. 663) provides that those convicted to life sentences are eligible for furloughs after having served ten years and for semiliberty after twenty. They can also gain "good-time" benefits to reduce the time needed for the above-mentioned benefits and also to the minimum time needed for parole.

The constitution allows the legislator to choose the techniques of reeducational treatment, so that the most advanced methods, according to the latest scientific developments, may be employed. The new penitentiary law foresees that prison staff will work with experts in psychology, social work, education, psychiatry, and clinical criminology to develop approaches to observation and treatment.[57] The basic rehabilitative techniques are the traditional devices of work, with strong emphasis on job training, and education. A remarkable innovation is the possibility of granting work furloughs.

Federal Republic of Germany. A constitutional right to rehabilitation of criminal offenders was advocated in the FRG on the basis of Article 20, ¶1 of the Fundamental Law, which proclaims the principle of social responsibility of the state (*Sozialstaatsprinzip*). Scholars construed this provision as prescribing a rehabilitation-oriented prison legislation.[58] According to this interpretation, the constitutional provision mandated assistance to the prisoner in his or her social reintegration, but without specifying how the rehabilitative services should be provided.[59] This scholarly affirmation was endorsed in 1973 by the Federal Constitutional Court in the *Lehbach* case.[60]

In 1970, the same court had already recognized rehabilitation among other components of "just punishment," such as the protection of society, the condemnation of the crime as infringing social values, atonement, and retribution of culpability.[61] Another landmark is the 1972 decision, in which the whole area of corrections was given a public law status, with direct constitutional relevance.[62] But it was the *Lehbach* decision that made rehabilitation a preeminent correctional goal, calling for the creation of the "capacity and will to lead a responsible life, learning to live with self-determination in free society without breaking the law, while taking its chances and enduring its risks."[63]

This decision of the Constitutional Court quashed a resolution of a lower court allowing the showing of a documentary television film about a murder that had caught the public attention at the time. Suit had been brought by a man who was serving time for aiding and abetting the crime. He argued that broadcasting the program, which included references to him, would make his prospective reintegration into the community more difficult. The producers based their defense on Article 5 of the Fundamental Law, which protects the freedom of broadcasting. The decision of the Federal Constitutional Court, however, gave preeminence to the rehabilitation of the offender and forbade the showing of the film.

The Constitutional Court based its decision on Article 2, ¶2 of the Fundamental Law, which foresees a right to free personality development, in combination with Article 1, protecting human dignity. The court did not limit itself to recognizing the passive right of the claimant to resist an action harming his future resocialization, but reached out beyond the terms of the lawsuit and held that the state had an active duty to seek the resocialization of the criminal offender. The court found that the principle of the state's social responsibility mandates active assistance to convicts in their rehabilitation. Prisoners and ex-convicts were considered handicapped in their personal and social development, and thus entitled to social welfare, including provisions for their aftercare. In this way the court accepted the arguments affirming the right to rehabilitation as an essential element within the social welfare state.

The underlying constitutional doctrine of rehabilitation is based on the need to compensate for an insufficient socialization process, not through a repressive, intimidating discipline, but through internalization of the values embodied in the prohibitions and commands of the Fundamental Law.[64] Moreover, the freedom of conscience guaranteed by Article 4, ¶1 of the constitution excludes a brainwashing coercive rehabilitation and restricts its goal to ensuring compliance with the minimal demands of the basic system of social values.

Another element in the German constitution that may be used to justify a right to rehabilitation is explored by Müller-Emmert.[65] The principle of proportionality, a derivation of Article 20, ¶1 of the Fundamental Law[66] holds that basic constitutional rights can be legislatively restricted only when such restriction is indispensable to attain a social goal covered by the value system of the Fundamental Law.[67] Imprisonment entails a series of unwanted side effects, the most serious of which is the desocializing influence of institutional life. The pressure of criminogenic prison subcultures aggravates this influence. These harmful effects exceed the scope of criminal punishment, whose goals should be attained through the mere deprivation of liberty and not with the additional deterioration brought about by "prisonization."[68] Failure to counteract such phenomena with a rehabilitation-oriented correctional system amounts to the infliction of restrictions and pains inimical to "the indispensable social goals covered by the value-system of the Fundamental Law." Consequently, according to Müller-Emmert, passive toleration of their occurrence without any resocialization effort infringes the constitutional principle of proportionality. To avoid such infringement, correctional rules must give preeminence to the rehabilitative aim and make possible its practical application.

An important and often misinterpreted decision of the Federal Constitutional Court determined that "the state has not the task to 'better' its citizens and thereupon lacks the power to deprive them of their freedom in order to 'better' them, provided that they represent no danger for themselves or others while remaining in freedom."[69] This decision prompted many discussions about the supposed legal impossibility of rehabilitating criminal offenders altogether.[70] In fact the decision was meant to apply to abandoned persons or those in danger of neglect, such as vagrants or derelicts in need of help. Criminal offenders, in contrast, are not deprived of their liberty because they need to be rehabilitated but because they have committed a crime. Rehabilitation in their case is not only admissible but made mandatory by the *Lehbach* decision.

Treatment-centered corrections were organized in the FRG through the Federal Prison Act of 1976. A treatment orientation is reflected in §2 of the act, establishing that the aim of prison sentences is to enable the inmate to lead a socially responsible crime-free life in the future. The act provides for a detailed regulation of imprisonment basically directed to help the inmate reintegrate into the community.[71] The constitutional mandate of rehabilitation is mirrored in the principle that life in penal institutions should resemble the general conditions of life in the free society as far as possible.[72] It is also reflected in the dictum that utmost efforts should be made to counteract detrimental effects of imprisonment.[73] The word *treatment* is used in a very broad way, encompassing not only specific rehabilitative means such as social therapy, but also education, vocational training, counseling, various forms of participation in the life of the institution and even simple human interaction. Treatment in this very general sense is the basic methodology of imprisonment; it permeates the whole legal and institutional system of corrections.

Spain. In Spain, the rehabilitative aim attained constitutional rank in 1978. Article 25,2 ¶1 of the new constitution determined that "prison sentences and security measures shall be directed toward the reeducation and the social reintegration of the offender and shall not consist of forced labor." De la Cuesta recognized that resocialization or rehabilitation of the criminal offender is the central aim of imprisonment, although not necessarily the only one, and he emphasized its significance for the building of a penitentiary system more consonant with humanist principles and less harmful to the individual rights of the inmates than the present one.[74] Furthermore, Article 23,2 ¶2 and ¶3 of the constitution states that

convicted offenders shall be entitled to the basic rights included in this chapter [bill of rights], with the exception of those expressly curtailed by the content of the sentencing decision, the nature of the penal sanction and the penitentiary law. In all cases they will have the right to a remunerated work and to social security benefits, as well as the right to have access to culture and to the integral development of their personality.

Article 1 of the General Organic Penitentiary Law of 1979 also expressly establishes resocialization as the overriding goal of prisons and security measures and extends it to all forms of detention, even at the pretrial stage. Resocialization is understood in the statement of intent of the law as "re-education and social reintegration." Rehabilitation efforts are "directed to prepare the re-entry of the offender into free social life in the best possible conditions in order to exercise freedom in society." Article 59,2 assigns to treatment the following goals: "to make from inmates persons with the intent and capacity to live respecting criminal law and provide to their own needs, and develop in them an attitude of self-esteem and of social and individual responsibility regarding their families and society in general.'' The sense of this provision, plus the law's insistent use of the word *reeducation*, amounts to giving rehabilitation an ethical content according to de la Cuesta.[75] Such an interpretation is reinforced by the Regulation of Prison Services of 1956, which allows personality-changing therapies. On the other hand, such integration is denied by a passage of the law's preamble pointing out that ''treatment should not aspire to impose a modification of the inmate's personality, but to provide him with the necessary elements to carry out a fruitful life in freedom.'' Apprehension about a rehabilitative concept based on value-oriented indoctrination is further diminished by other provisions of the new penitentiary law that make treatment voluntary (Articles 4, 2, and 61), as well as the constitutional proclamation of political pluralism as the basis of the Spanish system (Article 1,1) and the guarantee of religious and ideological freedom (Article 16,1). In this connection, the new penitentiary regulations of 1981 expressly acknowledge a right to refuse treatment, without any negative consequence for the inmate's legal status.

DO CRIMINAL OFFENDERS HAVE A CONSTITUTIONAL RIGHT TO REHABILITATION IN THE UNITED STATES?

Rehabilitation and Individual Rights

Although the concept of rehabilitation has profoundly shaped American sentencing and correctional policies, a constitutional right to rehabilitation remains unrecognized by U.S. federal courts. In sharp contrast, a number of European nations have included rehabilitation as a constitutional mandate.[76] Furthermore, customary international law has established a duty of rehabilitation as expressed, for example, in the 1955 U.N. Standard Minimum Rules for the Treatment of Prisoners, the later U.N. Covenant on Civil and Political Rights and the American Convention of Human Rights.

The extraordinary diffusion in the United States of indeterminate sentencing and its associated parole system reflects the wholesale acceptance of what Francis Allen called the rehabilitative ''ideal.''[77] Yet in this particular sentencing context rehabilitation is often seen by critics as working against individual rights. In fact, a pretense of rehabilitation has often been used to protract incarceration unduly or to mask overly intrusive treatment methods, such as the administration of constitutionally inadmissible drug therapies.[78] Although excessive penalties are not inherent in indeterminate sentencing and parole was originally conceived as a means of shortening the period of incarceration, a misuse of the rehabilitative concept helped to produce the opposite result.[79] Likewise, it was a travesty of rehabilitation that allowed the development of various intrusive behavior-modification techniques to obtain compliance from particularly unruly inmates.[80]

The association of rehabilitation with policies opposed to individual freedom is also evident in a series of judicial decisions that invoked a rehabilitative aim to justify the abridgement of the inmate's basic rights. At the same time, a diametrically opposed view of rehabilitation has been used in prisoners' rights litigation to bolster the very rights curtailed by repressive use of the concept. In several cases, for example, the two competing meanings of rehabilitation sustained divergent opinions within the same U.S. Supreme Court decision. In *Wolff v. McDonnell* the majority opinion held that application of due process safeguards to the deprivation of "good time" (for example by confrontation and cross-examination) would hinder rehabilitative goals.[81] Conversely, the dissenting opinion concludes that greater procedural fairness enhances rehabilitation. In *Procunier v. Martinez* the majority opinion justified a regulation authorizing prisoner mail censorship on the basis of the governmental interest in rehabilitation.[82] Justice Marshall's concurring opinion saw the regulation as thwarting a rehabilitative function—namely diminishing the crippling and "artificial increase of alienation"—by restricting communication with the outside world. On the one hand the idea of rehabilitation is used to justify disciplinary goals and paternalistic state intervention, while on the other, it serves to advance basic prisoners' rights, such as due process and free speech in the mentioned cases, as well as health or religion in other decisions.[83] This confusing ambivalence of the rehabilitative concept must be clarified before analyzing the plausibility of a right to rehabilitation in the United States.

Two contradicting models of rehabilitation—one authoritarian and paternalistic in nature and the other humanistic and liberty centered—underlie the contradictory statements of the Supreme Court regarding the functions and significance of the rehabilitative goal.[84] As explained in Chapter 1, the first model is in fact a subtler version of the outdated repressive model of corrections. In this view correctional treatment is essentially a technical device to manipulate offenders and ensure their compliance with an imposed pattern of behavior. Such "rehabilitation" easily becomes a mere instrument of institutional discipline and is bound to apply brainwashing methods incompatible with the individual's right to privacy.

The second model, which stems from an anthropocentric outlook, places no faith in individual transformation achieved through subtly imposed paradigms. It assumes instead that significant change can result only from the individual's own insight and moral choice, and uses dialogue as an essential tool to encourage self-discovery. This model does not rely on idealistic preaching to reintegrate offenders to a hostile society. Instead, humanistic rehabilitation offers inmates a sound and trustworthy opportunity to remake their lives. Thus this model seeks to awaken in inmates a deep awareness of their relationship with the rest of society, resulting in a genuine sense of social responsibility.

The humanistic model of rehabilitation affirms the conception of prison inmates as possessors of rights. This legal status generates feelings of self-worth and trust in the legal system, and favors the possibility of self-command and responsible action within society. This concept ultimately leads rehabilitative efforts toward the paradigm of the inmate as a full-fledged citizen.[85] The prisoners' legal status reinforces their eventual participation in the shaping and governing of society. Thus prisoners' rights can be qualified, using Ely's terminology, as representation reinforcing.[86] This continuum of rights culminates in the right to rehabilitation, which can be formulated as the right to an opportunity to return to society with an improved chance of being a useful citizen and of staying out of prison. This right requires not only education and therapy, but also a non-destructive prison environment and, when possible, less-restrictive alternatives to incarceration. The right to rehabilitation is consistent with the drive toward the full restoration of the civil and political rights of citizenship after release.[87]

The inclusion of rehabilitation in the sphere of individual rights does not necessarily exclude it as a goal of state penal policies. Such a right, however, constrains penal policy to maintain scrupulous respect for the dignity of prisoners and to provide for the genuine fulfillment of their basic human needs, which go beyond mere physical survival. But even in the absence of such initiative from the state, a right to rehabilitation makes the performance of rehabilitative services legally enforceable, allowing the courts to intervene in case of administrative reluctance.[88] According to Dworkin's distinction between rights and social goals, viewing rehabilitation as a right implies granting the rehabilitative claim a "certain threshold weight against collective goals in general."[89] Such a right becomes a "political trump," creating an area of exception against state punitive policies. It replaces purely vindictive justice with a constructive approach of social reintegration.

Consequences of the Recognition of a Right to Rehabilitation

In America, through a misapplication of the medical model to corrections, rehabilitation has strengthened the power of the state to act with oppressive paternalism, and it has increased the discretion of judicial and administrative sentencing authorities, and the power of correctional agencies. Without denying a legitimate governmental interest in rehabilitation, the emergent concept of rehabilitation as a right affirms a positive position for the individual in relation to the state.

The recognition of rehabilitation as a right of the prisoner not only grants rehabilitative undertakings a specific due process protection, but demands momentous changes in the sentencing and correctional systems. For example, it requires both new legal guidelines for the sentencing authorities or an improvement of the present ones to reduce prison overcrowding, which is incompatible with rehabilitation, and a considerable expansion of community-based alternatives to imprisonment.[90] It is possible that neither sentencing reforms nor community programs will totally alleviate overcrowding. Even so, a right to rehabilitation will mean that new prisons must meet stringent qualitative standards incompatible with a purely incapacitation-oriented approach to construction. On the whole, a strict implementation of the right to rehabilitation will reduce the present excessive reliance on imprisonment as a form of punishment in the United States.

Some may fear that recognizing rehabilitation as a constitutional right will mean less close surveillance of institutionalized offenders, with harmful results. True, rehabilitation introduces into the prison educational and treatment staff often unconcerned with the questions of custody, but the development of trust in incarcerated human beings within a rehabilitation-oriented institution warrants a relaxing of custodial standards. The liberty-centered notion of rehabilitation implied in the rights model is clearly detached from the disciplinary goals of the institution. Rehabilitative efforts can thus no longer be perverted by being used manipulatively. This clear distinction between rehabilitation and discipline does not deny the importance of order and security in correctional institutions. Furthermore, discipline problems would most likely diminish in a rehabilitation-centered institution where staff and inmates are devoted to a meaningful goal. Discipline is maintained even when the development of trust between inmates and custodians leads to the granting of different forms of furloughs and work release.

Recognizing a right to rehabilitation would impose some new costs on taxpayers. However, costs may be reduced by using nonprofessional personnel in rehabilitation-oriented activities. Moreover, cost savings will result from the reduction of recidivism. In any case, federal court rulings have held that monetary considerations are insufficient to override constitutional demands.[91]

While admitting the paramount importance of rehabilitation, the U.S. Supreme Court has consistently abstained from holding it to be included in the Bill of Rights. Even the most progressive federal judges, responsible for far-reaching transformations in state penal institutions, have hesitated to take this ultimate step, which could result in drastic innovations in the criminal justice system and transform the nature of imprisonment in the United States. Although hinting that the sociological theory of rehabilitation may eventually "ripen in constitutional law,"[92] they have denied the existence of a constitutional federal right to rehabilitation, at least in a positive form. The courts have, however, already attributed an essential role to rehabilitation in the overall prison environment. They have in effect acknowledged the right to rehabilitation in a negative form— the right to counteract the deteriorating effects of imprisonment. The courts have also granted the prisoner a limited right to psychiatric treatment. These openings in the present body of law, as well as the other avenues of interpretation that will be explored in this chapter, should provide ample basis for the right to rehabilitation "when [the courts] decide to recognize it."[93]

Lack of Rehabilitation as Cruel and Unusual Punishment

The federal courts have assigned the rehabilitative idea a significant role in the constitutional analysis of the conditions of confinement. The Eighth Amendment's prohibition against cruel and unusual punishment is the linchpin of such promising interpretative developments. The dynamic nature of the Eighth Amendment proscription was emphasized by a 1958 ruling that the proscription's meaning must be drawn "from the evolving standards of decency that mark the progress of a maturing society."[94] The flexibility of the clause precludes a specific definition that could thwart its broadening significance "as society tends to pay more regard to human decency and dignity and becomes, or likes to think that it becomes, more humane."[95]

In the 1970s, judicial decisions interpreted the Eighth Amendment clause as to require a purposive inquiry into prison conditions to measure them against permissible penal goals.[96] In *Gregg v. Georgia* the Supreme Court established that "the sanction imposed cannot be so totally without penological justification that it results in the gratuitous infliction of suffering."[97] The means-end test of prison conditions is premised on the belief that nontrivial deprivations or restraints additional to the fact of incarceration must be justified by their contribution to the achievement of legitimate penal objectives. If arbitrary, such deprivations or restraints constitute a violation of the cruel and unusual punishment clause.[98]

Since the 1970s, the application of the cruel and unusual punishment clause to penitentiaries was the basis of judicial challenges to state penal systems. The first of these cases, *Holt v. Sarver*, was brought by inmates of a correctional institution in Arkansas in 1970.[99] After an exhaustive evidentiary hearing, reflected in a detailed memorandum opinion, Chief Judge Henley concluded that conditions and practices in the Arkansas penitentiary system were such that confinement itself amounted to "cruel and unusual punishment," "even though a particular inmate may never personally be subjected to any disciplinary action."[100]

The absence of meaningful rehabilitation programs was an essential element in the *Holt* decision. The district judge was unwilling to hold that the Constitution required the institution "to run a school, or provide rehabilitative facilities and services which many institutions now offer."[101] However, the judge expressly stated that "the absence of an affirmative program of training and rehabilitation may have constitutional significance where in the absence of such a program conditions and practices exist which actually militate against reform and rehabilitation."[102] The absence of a meaningful rehabilitation program alone did not rise to constitutional relevance, rather it constituted "a factor in the overall constitutional equation" when this absence aggravated an already degrading and criminogenic prison environment.

After *Holt v. Sarver* prisoners' challenges to prison systems proliferated. This led to decisions introducing comprehensive institutional reforms, although their unsatisfactory implementation often resulted in embroiled litigation. Various decisions emphasized the rehabilitative element in assessing overall prison conditions against the Eighth Amendment's standard.[103] In some cases the courts even threatened to close the institutions as a means of overcoming administrative resistance.

In *Pugh v. Locke*, the district court determined that prison conditions were so debilitating that they necessarily deprived inmates "of any opportunity to rehabilitate themselves, or even to maintain skills already possessed." Without recognizing a positive right to rehabilitation, the decision nevertheless stated that "a penal system cannot be operated in such a manner that it impedes an inmate's ability to attempt rehabilitation, or simply to avoid physical, mental or social deterioration."[104]

Rehabilitation plays a dual role in the "totality of conditions" analysis of correctional institutions. On the one hand, the lack of rehabilitative programs is one of the elements making prison conditions unconstitutional; on the other hand, the inmates' opportunities to rehabilitate themselves or even to maintain skills already possessed serves as a yardstick against which to measure the constitutionality of the cumulative effect of prison conditions. The "totality of conditions" approach seemingly views rehabilitation as one element relevant only in the aggregate of prison conditions. The absence of rehabilitation often indicates unconstitutional conditions, but its presence is not required when other factors are satisfactory. In other words, rehabilitation seems to be reduced to a series of programs directed toward counteracting the harmful effects of the institution on the inmates. These programs become constitutionally mandatory when, without them, institutional flaws are serious enough as to make confinement cruel and unusual punishment.

The role of rehabilitation, however, does not stop there. According to the case law developing the "totality of conditions" concept, the cumulative effect of prison conditions is unconstitutional when they make it impossible to maintain acquired social skills or continue efforts toward self-rehabilitation.[105] Here the courts employ the concept of rehabilitation as a gauge of the totality of prison conditions. According to *Laaman v. Helgemoe*, the unconstitutionality lies in the unnecessary and wanton infliction of pain caused by recidivism and future incarceration made probable by the overall conditions of the prison.[106] Prison conditions are thus constitutional only when they make deterioration not inevitable and recidivism not likely, and then efforts toward self-rehabilitation are possible. A constitutional right to rehabilitation thus encompasses the right to a rehabilitative prison environment, which is one that does not make degeneration probable or self-rehabilitation impossible.

Laaman v. Helgemoe represents one of the most significant applications of the Eighth Amendment to the totality of prison conditions. The *Laaman* decision is significant both for its comprehensiveness and far-reaching constitutional analysis. It was based on an extensive in-depth study of the prison conditions and included seventy-five separate orders to correct them. It was established that the prison conditions were bound to result in "mental, physical and social degeneration" and were "counterproductive to the inmates' efforts to rehabilitate themselves." An institution "where degeneration is probable and self-improvement unlikely would cause unnecessary suffering in the form of probable future incarceration." "Punishment for one crime, under conditions which spawn future crime and more punishment, serves no valid legislative purpose and is so totally without penological justification that it results in the gratuitous infliction of suffering in violation of the Eighth Amendment.'' In short, the violation of the Eighth Amendment was found to result from the cumulative effect of various negative prison conditions threatening ''the physical, mental and emotional health and well-being of the inmates and/or creating a probability of recidivism and future incarceration.''[107]

In this manner, the *Laaman* decision established a negative indirect right to rehabilitation as a consequence of a right not to degenerate. In consonance with precedent, this right includes the freedom to attempt rehabilitation or the ''cultivation of new socially acceptable and useful skills and habits''[108] and the provision of adequate mental health care.[109] The corresponding obligation of the state to provide opportunities to stave off degeneration and to minimize impediments to reform is measured through the totality of the conditions of confinement. Remedial orders must be issued by the courts when these ''conditions create an environment in which it is impossible for inmates to rehabilitate themselves—or to preserve skills and constructive attitudes already possessed—even for those who are inclined to do so.''[110]

In this connection, following the existing precedents and the prisoner's right to work under New Hampshire statutes, the court ordered the prison administration to institute work opportunities and vocational training, ''in order to minimize degeneration and succor what rehabilitative attempts were being made by inmates.''[111]

The *Laaman* decision also held that unreasonable restrictions on visitations infringed the Eighth Amendment when ''failure to allow inmates to keep their community ties and family bonds promotes degeneration and decreases their chances of successful reintegration into society.''[112] The court also ordered the establishment of a classification system as ''absolutely necessary, if effective rehabilitation is to take place.''[113] Such a classification system was to be used for the application of specific educational, vocational, and rehabilitative programs. The provision of adequate mental health care was also a relevant rehabilitative element considered in the court's decree.[114]

As a means of advancing the rights of prisoners, the ''totality of conditions'' approach has encountered some setbacks in recent years. The Supreme Court decision in *Rhodes v. Chapman*[115] proved that this approach is a ''double-edged sword.''[116] In the concurring opinion of Justices Brennan, Blackmun, and Stevens, double celling was seen as just one condition among the many to be considered in determining the constitutionality of the cumulative effect. Following the reasoning of *Laaman*, the court stated that the ''touchstone'' of the Eighth Amendment inquiry is ''the effect upon the imprisoned.''[117] This rationale conceded that favorable conditions—adequate shelter, food, and protection plus opportunities for education, work, and rehabilitative assistance—compensated for, and ultimately offset, the harsher condition of double-celling. This interpretation could lead to the incorrect conclusion that some positive aspects of a prison can compensate for conditions that are clearly unconstitutional in and of themselves, such as horrendous overcrowding, racial discrimination, and the everyday occurrence of serious prison violence.[118] The fact that some violations of the Eighth Amendment result from an aggregate effect of several conditions does not mean that the observance of constitutional norms regarding a certain number of conditions can legitimate other conditions that alone are unconstitutional. The danger of such a mistaken inference demands a more precise definition of the role of rehabilitation in the "totality of conditions" approach.

True, lack of rehabilitative efforts is more visible when prison conditions descend to their lowest levels of squalor and degradation, but it would be totally discordant with a liberty-centered concept of rehabilitation to assert that the existence of a rehabilitation program could render intolerable deprivations constitutional. To consider, for example, that a vocational training program could legitimate the existence of cells infested with vermin demonstrates *ad absurdum* the vulnerability of such an argument. Within the "totality of conditions" approach, the role of rehabilitation is not to be traded off against flaws that have a specific remedy (e.g., cleaning the facilities), but to counteract the overall harmful effects of institutionalization, such as depersonalization or loss of self-determination. A rehabilitation-oriented institution depends less on particular programs than on improvements in overall prison conditions that reduce the level of desocialization or dehabilitation.

Rehabilitation is necessary even in well-functioning institutions as a consequence of incarceration itself. But between the filth and squalor described by John Howard in the eighteenth century[119] and the modern problem-solving communities within walls,[120] there is a continuum of harmfulness and deterioration. Where to draw the line that makes the absence of positive rehabilitative attempts unconstitutional depends on those "evolving standards of decency that mark the progress of a maturing society."[121] Besides, the *Rhodes v. Chapman* view that some favorable conditions could compensate for the constitutional violation of others overlooks the fact that a primary goal of rehabilitative endeavors is to fortify the legal status of prisoners. A genuine rehabilitative concept therefore can never be used as a pretext to justify the abridgement of prisoners' basic rights.

Another judicial trend adverse to the recognition of rehabilitation as a right departs from the "totality of conditions" approach. Some lower federal courts have recently denied that the cumulative effect of several conditions violates the Eighth Amendment in cases where no single condition is violatory.[122] This interpretation tends to undermine the significance attached by precedent to the lack of rehabilitation, insofar as the absence of rehabilitation alone was not considered unconstitutional. As a result, the failure of prisons to provide rehabilitative programs then loses its potential to contribute to the totality of conditions liable to violate the Eighth Amendment. This step back from the progressive interpretation of the Eighth Amendment jeopardizes the limited role recognized for rehabilitation since *Holt v. Sarver*.[123] Moreover, these decisions indicate a return to the hands-off policy that endangers the totality of prisoners' rights. This perilous judicial retreat coincides with the short-sighted complacency of the court in *Newman v. Alabama*, which held that stultifying and deteriorating prison life is constitutional so long as shelter, sanitation, medical care, and personal safety are provided. This ruling ignores the nature of human needs.[124]

A constitutionally permissible prison environment includes the rights of inmates not to degenerate or to be impaired in their own rehabilitative efforts. But in *Bresolin v. Morris* the Washington state supreme court held that such a negative right does not entitle a prisoner to claim for specific programs.[125] The majority decision rejected the notion that the Eighth Amendment gave prisoners a right to rehabilitative treatment for psychological dependence on drugs. The court based its ruling on the U.S. Supreme Court decision in *Procunier v. Martinez*, which considered rehabilitation a "governmental interest" and not an enforceable right.[126] The court also rested on a "realist" view of the prison situation, a skeptical appraisal of the results achieved by drug rehabilitation programs and an assumption that rehabilitation as a whole is ineffective.[127]

However, the dissenting opinion in this case warrants analysis as an important contribution to an alternative constitutional doctrine. In his dissent, Associate Justice Utter applied the idea of an indirect right to rehabilitation in the sense of a right to avoid deterioration. On this basis he affirmed the prisoner's constitutional right to a specific drug rehabilitation program, deeming its absence a violation of the Eighth Amendment. Justice Utter also relied on sociological data. Instead of accepting that imprisonment inevitably brings harmful consequences, Justice Utter affirmed a peremptory duty of the state to counteract these consequences. He underlined the responsibility contracted by the state by placing an inmate with an addictive personality in a closed setting where his addiction is exacerbated by an atmosphere of apparently uncontrollable dealing in and use of drugs. In *Estelle v. Gamble*, regarding the right of prisoners to medical treatment in general, the U.S. Supreme Court recognized that "it is but just that the public be required to care for the prisoner, who cannot, by reason of the deprivation of his liberty, care for himself." This duty of care for the prisoner, Justice Utter argued, is all the more pressing when an individual psychologically addicted to the use of narcotic drugs is placed in a situation of "continued explosive degeneration," inherent in state institutions, "creating thus a great likelihood that such individuals will do further injury to society when they are eventually released."[128]

The factual framework of the case presented a narrow, albeit important, issue concerning the constitutional right of inmates with addictive personalities to be protected from harm when they are unavoidably exposed to unlawful narcotics. In this case the lack of a drug treatment program implies the deprivation of needed medical care, which includes the healing of the mind. Such deprivation represents suffering beyond that of incarceration, thus constituting cruel and unusual punishment. The right to a specific treatment intended to avoid the intensification of an individual's psychological addiction is another instance of the right to counteract the degenerative effects of penal institutions. In the *Laaman* decision mentioned above, this right represents a negative type of the right to rehabilitation.

The Right to Psychological and Psychiatric Treatment as Part of the Right to Rehabilitation

The recognition of a limited right of prisoners to psychological and psychiatric treatment is represented at the federal level by the leading case *Bowring v. Godwin*.[129] This right stems from a progressive interpretation of the Eighth Amendment "and is also premised upon notions of rehabilitation and the desire to render inmates useful and productive citizens upon their release."[130] In *Bowring* the United States Court of Appeals for the Fourth Circuit formulated a test to determine when those needs should entitle a prisoner to psychological and psychiatric treatment. The court stated that if a physician or other health care provider, exercising ordinary care at the time of observation, concluded with reasonable medical certainty that the petitioner's symptoms evidenced a serious disease or injury, that such "disease or injury was curable or might be substantially alleviated, and that the potential for harm to the petitioner by reason of delay or denial of care would be substantial," then the prisoner had a right to treatment.

The *Bowring* decision recognized rehabilitation as a paramount goal of the corrections system even though it is not mandated by any particular constitutional provision.[131] The court also stated that this judicial recognition helped establish the right, based on the Eighth Amendment, to psychological treatment.[132] Psychotherapy is a principal ingredient of a modern rehabilitative concept, especially when applied to mentally disordered offenders. The concept of medical necessity on which the *Bowring* decision is based includes psychological disorder in its broader sense and thus confers the status of a right on this important aspect of rehabilitation.

Arguments similar to those of *Bowring* were used as a basis for a 1978 decision of the Supreme Court of Alaska.[133] The court affirmed that there is a public obligation to care for persons deprived of their liberties and cited the numerous precedents considering the lack of adequate food, clothing, shelter, medical care facilities, and staff as constitutional violations of the Eighth and Fourteenth amendments. The tests to determine when those needs should entitle a prisoner to treatment were derived from *Bowring v. Godwin*.

Besides the right to treatment derived from the Eighth Amendment and the common-law duty of care for the prisoner, "who cannot by reason of the deprivation of his liberty care for himself,"[134] the right to treatment for certain categories of offenders has also been premised on the Fourteenth Amendment. This approach originated in lower courts' decisions in the field of mental health.[135] Treatment in these cases needs to compensate for the restriction of procedural safeguards resulting from indeterminate confinement with alleged therapeutic purposes. The absence of the "quid pro quo" of treatment was seen as a violation of the due process clause of the Fourteenth Amendment. Courts recognized this right to treatment not only for involuntarily committed patients, but also for juvenile offenders and offenders with mental disorders. These include sexual psychopaths[136] and persons convicted under "guilty but mentally ill" statutes.[137] In extending a Fourteenth Amendment right to treatment to mentally disordered and juvenile offenders, the above-mentioned courts reasoned that "whenever the provision of care and treatment is part of the purpose of confinement, such must be accorded consistent with due process."[138] Some decisions have considered that a rehabilitative purpose for confinement must be inferred whenever the term of sentence is indefinite.[139] Although these decisions were made in the context of sexual psychopath statutes, the same rationale could be applied to the indeterminate sentencing of all prisoners.[140]

Arguments Based on the Equal Protection Clause

The affirmation of a constitutional right to rehabilitation based on equal protection assumes that the prisoner maintains all basic rights not incompatible with incarceration.[141] The leading case *Coffin v. Reichard* holds that prisoners retain all civil rights except those expressly taken by law or those whose removal is necessary to the attainment of legitimate penal goals.[142] The equal protection clause has been successfully invoked to remove inequalities within the prison system based on race,[143] sex,[144] or differential treatment, when not justified by valid circumstances.[145]

Morales v. Schmidt, although reversed on appeal,[146] opened an important line of argument to support a constitutional right to rehabilitation. The district court held that the equal protection clause applies not only among persons convicted of a crime, but also to governmental treatment that distinguishes this group from the general population. The governmental differentiation between those convicted of a crime and those not convicted of a crime "should not escape the judicial scrutiny borne by other governmental classifications for the purpose of differential treatment."[147] The court decided that if the distinction between the two classes bears on an individual interest considered to be "fundamental," then the burden will be on the government to show a compelling state interest in the differential treatment. In short, convicts and the general public were assimilated in their rights to the equal protection of law. Commenting on this decision, Dwyer and Botein asserted that "depriving prisoners of rehabilitation . . . would deny them equal protection if an almost identical right to rehabilitation applies to similarly situated non-prisoners."[148]

Dwyer and Botein's analysis presumes the existence of a disadvantaged sector of the general population in need of treatment services. This is, however, only a supplemental argument. The primary reference in the equal protection argument is the general public. This is important because it means that the right to rehabilitation does not depend on the existence of a right to treatment, a question left unsettled by the U.S. Supreme Court.[149] Rather, the right depends on the recognition that the offender is a citizen whose rights have been withdrawn or limited only to a degree strictly required by legitimate penal goals. This is consistent with the notion that convicted persons are "not sent to a penal institution to receive additional punishment: the fact of incarceration itself is the punishment."[150] Furthermore, the idea of equal protection is extended by Dwyer and Botein to require that prisons use the least-restrictive alternative, as in treatment cases within the general population. In their equal protection argument, Dwyer and Botein also demand a liberal construction of state constitutional and statutory provisions which establish rehabilitation as a right of prisoners.

Dwyer and Botein assimilate rehabilitation and treatment to a large extent, yet concede that the two concepts are not synonymous.[151] Psychotherapeutic treatment is only one component of the current concept of rehabilitation, which encompasses a variety of socialization offerings. The goal is to integrate a learning process that can overcome insufficiencies ranging from deep psychological conflict that prompts aggressive behavior to a lack of skills that prevents the individual from entering the labor market. Rehabilitation today encompasses meaningful work and education as well as treatment.[152] Furthermore, the recognition of the prisoner as a possessor of rights has a secondary rehabilitative effect. Many of the prisoners' basic rights allow them to maintain social relations with the world outside or increase their feelings of dignity and self-worth.

The application of the equal protection clause to a global rehabilitative concept should consider the various components of rehabilitation, involving therapy, education, or social learning. If prisoners should be entitled to the same rights as other citizens, except when public protection absolutely demands otherwise, the scope of the equal protection inquiry is enlarged considerably. An equal protection inquiry should first determine the extent to which education, work, vocational training, therapy, or any other rehabilitative component has become a legally enforceable right of the public. A second stage of the inquiry should establish if the exercise of such rights can be legitimately curtailed or abolished because one is imprisoned.

The question then arises whether the concept of legal punishment can be limited to deprivation of freedom. Rejecting this limitation is equivalent to accepting all the deteriorating effects caused by sterile warehousing in an atmosphere of idleness and potential violence. Denying the prisoner's right to counteractive measures amounts to a definition of punishment that includes a reversal of human development, the loss of capacity and of mental and social health. Such a concept of punishment could never claim to be civilized. If punishment is to conform to its overt legal objectives, the state must guarantee the equal protection of inmates' basic rights. Meaningful rehabilitative programs must be developed to counteract the degrading and socially detrimental situation of incarcerated prisoners. This legal obligation of the state implies that inmates have the same rights as other citizens to education, vocational instruction, and maintenance of acquired skills, mental health, and remunerated work.

Like the disabled, many criminal offenders suffer from social handicaps. This similarity suggests another application of the equal protection theory. Here comparative law offers an important precedent in the recognition of a constitutional right to rehabilitation via equal protection. The Constitutional Court of the Federal Republic of Germany, in the *Lehbach* case (1973),[153] declared the rehabilitation of criminal offenders to be an active duty of the state, based on its general constitutional duty to protect and care for the socially disadvantaged (*Sozialstaatsprinzip*).[154] The decision was premised on a view of criminal offenders as psychosocially handicapped and consequently in need of resocialization-oriented compensatory action. The assimilation of prisoners and former convicts to the vast group of those handicapped in personal and social development creates a new perspective for future applications of the equal-protection theory to the rehabilitation of criminal offenders. Such an interpretation should introduce into the constitutional equation the social welfare and rehabilitation programs to which the disabled are entitled.

Customary International Law

International law, applied as part of domestic U.S. law, is another source of constitutional interpretation supporting a right to rehabilitation. This principle, which includes the application of customary international law by American courts, was established by the Supreme Court in 1900 in *The Paquete Habana*.[155]

Customary international law is defined by the Statute of the International Court of Justice as a "general practice accepted by law" and binding on the world community.[156] Customary international law demands a "concordant practice by a number of states, and [their belief] that an action is required by, or consistent with, international law."[157]

In *Lareau v. Manson*, the court used customary international law as a basis for declaring the overcrowded conditions of the Hartford Community Correctional Center in violation of the Eighth Amendment.[158] The U.N. Standard Minimum Rules for the Treatment of Prisoners were cited as a significant "expression of the obligations to the international community of the member states of the United Nations . . . and as part of the body of international law (including customary international law) concerning human rights which has been built upon the foundation of the United Nations Charter."[159] In fact, the Standard Minimum Rules were adopted as a preamble to the Administrative Directives to the Connecticut Department of Corrections. Although the rules are not necessarily applicable in the United States, the court considered them "an authoritative international statement of basic norms of human dignity and of certain practices which are repugnant to the conscience of mankind."[160]

The Standard Minimum Rules were also invoked by the Supreme Court of Oregon in its decision that the search of male prisoners by female corrections officers violated Oregon's constitutional prohibition of cruel and degrading punishment.[161] The court held that the case involved the application of Oregon's bill of rights, stating that "laws for the punishment of crime shall be founded on the principles of reformation, and not of vindictive justice."[162] This interpretation is reinforced by both the Universal Declaration of Human Rights and the Standard Minimum Rules, which also establish rehabilitation as an essential aim of the penitentiary system.[163]

A variety of sources support the existence of a strong right to the rehabilitation of criminal offenders based on customary international law. The United Nations Standard Minimum Rules for the Treatment of Prisoners, adopted in 1955, provide in Article 58:

The purpose and justification of a sentence of imprisonment or a similar measure deprivative of liberty is ultimately to protect society against crime. This end can only be achieved if the period of imprisonment is used to ensure, so far as possible, that upon his return to society the offender is not only willing but able to lead a law-abiding and self-supporting life.[164]

In other articles this document prescribes detailed guidelines for an individualized and integral rehabilitative action. The U.N. International Covenant on Civil and Political Rights, in force since 1976, establishes in Article 10, ¶3: "The penitentiary system shall comprise treatment of prisoners the essential aim of which shall be their reformation and social rehabilitation."[165] The American Convention of Human Rights, entered into force in 1978, provides that "punishments consisting of deprivation of liberty shall have as an essential aim the reform and social readaptation of prisoners."[166]

State Constitutions

Several state constitutions provide significant sources for the constitutional status of a right to rehabilitation. During the 1960s, the U.S. Supreme Court relied on the federal Constitution to initiate more comprehensive protection of the rights of the people. But after the Court's retreat from political activism during the 1970s, the states' bills of rights gradually regained their prominent role. The principle of federalism is being used to expand rights, and state judges are scrutinizing state constitutions in order to create a body of civil liberties going beyond current interpretations by the U.S. Supreme Court.

The matter of rehabilitation is incorporated into the bill of rights of several state constitutions among their fundamental guarantees and safeguards. Article 18 of the constitution of New Hampshire, in effect since 1784, establishes: "All penalties ought to be proportioned to the nature of the offence . . . a multitude of sanguinary laws is both impolitic and unjust—the true design of all punishments being to reform, not to exterminate mankind." With this emphatic conclusion the provision links the sentencing goals with a concept of reform inspired in a philanthropic, religious, and humanitarian tradition. In the late eighteenth century, the idea of reform represented a barrier against the fearsome arbitrariness of the pre-Enlightenment exemplary punishment. Beccaria's humanistic and rational considerations on the legislative meting out of punishment were extended by the constitution of New Hampshire to the correctional field. But reform also had an evangelical content, going beyond utilitarian calculation.

In the nineteenth century the requirement of rehabilitation was included in the constitutions of Oregon, Indiana, Wyoming, and Montana. According to Elbert F. Allen these were simple embodiments of common law principle.[167] The Oregon Constitution goes far beyond the Eighth Amendment prohibitions, providing that punishment be based on "principles of reformation and not vindictive justice" (1859). The same language is used in §18 of the constitution of Indiana providing that "the penal code shall be founded on the principles of reformation, and not of vindictive justice" (1851). Likewise, the constitution of Wyoming (1889) commands that "the penal code shall be framed on the human principles of reformation and prevention."

Modern provisions can be found in the 1972 Montana Constitution and in the constitutions of Alaska and Illinois. Under the heading "Rights of the Convicted," the constitution of Montana provides that "laws for the punishment of crime shall be founded on the principles of prevention and reformation. Full rights are restored by termination of state supervision for any offense against the state."[168] The constitution of Alaska adds to the cruel and unusual punishment prohibition the following command: "Penal administration shall be based on the principle of reformation and upon the need to protect the public."[169] The Illinois Constitution establishes that "all penalties shall be determined both according to the seriousness of the offense and with the objective to restore the offender to useful citizenship."[170]

Especially when included as part of the bill of rights, such provisions are highly significant. They shape penal legislation and are a source of individual guarantees equivalent to the prohibition of cruel and unusual punishment. Occasionally, other clauses can be found prescribing humane or healthy conditions of imprisonment. Other rights granted by state constitutions impose a pattern or style on eventual rehabilitative undertakings. These are the right to privacy[171] and the right to conscience,[172] which exclude from treatment any form of brainwashing or ideological imposition. Such rights imply that rehabilitative action should respect the privacy of individuals and not curtail, but rather intensify, their capacity for self-determination.

Nonconstitutional Sources of a Right to Rehabilitation

The state's duty to try to rehabilitate convicted prisoners can emerge from a statute or a contract or from a situation that endangers the mental or social integrity of the prisoner through particularly grievous forms of imprisonment. The corresponding right of the inmate can be enforced through administrative litigation or tort claims against prison authorities.

In some states an enforceable right to rehabilitation could be derived from general statements of the purposes of the correctional system or general directives to the correctional system on how to treat the inmates (e.g., Massachusetts,[173] South Carolina,[174] Rhode Island, [175] New Jersey,[176] New York,[177] Washington,[178] and Montana[179]).[180] The Interstate Agreement on Detainers Act[181] establishes a right of prisoners to uninterrupted and unimpeded rehabilitation.[182]

Another possible source of a rehabilitative obligation on the part of the state is the parole contract, in which the inmate and the parole authority agree on a release date on the condition that the inmate complete certain obligations including rehabilitation programs. Cullen and Gilbert point out that the very existence of a contract system puts pressure on correctional officers to improve treatment services,[183] and they advocate mandatory contracts, obligating the state to rehabilitate.[184] "Mutual agreement programs" have proliferated in state prison and parole systems, and are also being applied in probation programs.[185] These comprise a variety of negotiations in which correctional authorities commit themselves to provide the rehabilitative resources that allow inmates to fulfill the conditions of their release.[186]

A third source of the duty to rehabilitate springs from the very fact that the state imprisons individuals. Imprisonment in America today is an intrinsically dangerous situation, requiring the state to take positive action to avert potential harm to prisoners' mental, social, and physical health. In some cases, imprisonment amounts to placing inmates in closed environments where they are exposed to "unlawful trade in and use of hard narcotics."[187] In others, the harm may be a permanent deterioration of the personality or a dramatic loss in social capacity and skills. Deprived of their liberty by state action, prisoners cannot handle these problems themselves. Forms of incarceration that threaten inmates' physical well-being and psychosocial maturation are not only unconstitutional but create, whenever an identifiable harm can be determined, the possibility of civil and even criminal liabilities.

NOTES

1. See p. 4.

2. See p. 33.

3. See p. 38.

4. David Garland, *Punishment and Welfare: A History of Penal Strategies* (London: Heinemann, 1985), 12.

5. John T. McNeill, *A History of the Cure of Souls* (New York: Harper & Brothers, 1951), vii.

6. See p. 28.

7. Mark H. Haller, *Eugenics: Hereditarian Attitudes in American Thought* (New Brunswick, N.J.: Rutgers University Press, 1984).

8. Ibid., 14.

9. Moral treatment according to Pinel was a therapy based on the creation of a therapeutic atmosphere. Although he occasionally assigned the ambiguous French word

moral an ethical significance, he most often used it as a synonym of *psychological*. See Walter Riese, *The Legacy of Philipe Pinel* (New York: Springer, 1969).

10. Günther Kaiser, "Krankheit, Behandlung und strafrechtliche Schuld heute," *Universitas* 4 (Apr. 1978): 407.

11. Michel Foucault, "About the Concept of the 'Dangerous Individual' in the Nineteenth-Century Legal Psychiatry," *International Journal of Law and Psychiatry* 1 (1978): 1–18.

12. Ibid., 5.

13. Ibid., 6.

14. On the medical myth, see Marc Ancel, "Examen de conscience de défense sociale: Le problème du traitement des délinquants," *Revue de science criminelle et de droit pénal comparé* (1978): 949 and R. S. Brody, *The Effectiveness of Sentencing—a Review of the Literature* (London: Her Majesty's Stationery Office, 1976), 55.

15. José Ingenieros, *Instituto de criminología* (Buenos Aires: Talleres Gráficos de la Penitenciaría Nacional, 1911).

16. See Lorenz Bollinger, *Psychoanalyse und die Behandlung von Delinquenten* (Heidelberg: C. F. Müller, 1979), 21–57.

17. Franz von Liszt, *Strafrechtliche Aufsätze und Vorträge* (Berlin: J. Guttentag, 1905), II: 435.

18. See Klaus Sessar, "Die Resozialisierung der strafenden Gesellschaft," *Zeitschrift für das gesamte Strafrechtswissenschaft* 81 (1969): 372 and Eduard Naegeli, "Die Gesellschaft und die Kriminellen," in *Verbrechen—Schuld oder Schicksal?* ed. Wilhelm Bitter (Stuttgart: E. Klett, 1969), 40–67.

19. George L. Engel, "The Need for a New Medical Model: A Challenge for Biomedicine," *Science* 196 (1977): 131.

20. Ibid., 132.

21. Earl A. Burch and Kay T. Burch, "The Congestive Heart Failure Model of Schizophrenia," *Journal of the American Medical Association* (1979): 1925.

22. The outstanding example is the Dr. van der Hoeven Clinic in Utrecht, Netherlands (see Appendix).

23. Erwin Goffman, *Asylums* (New York: Anchor Books, 1961).

24. Hans Toch, ed., *Therapeutics Communities in Corrections* (New York, Praeger, 1980), 18.

25. Ulrich Eisenberg, "Über sozialtherapeutische Behandlung von Gefangenen," *Zeitschrift für das gesamte Strafrechtswissenschaft* (1974): 1051.

26. John A. Clausen, "A Historical and Comparative Study of Socialization Theory and Research," in *Socialization and Society*, ed. J. A. Clausen (Boston: Little, Brown, 1968), 20–72.

27. Gerhard Wurzbacher, "Sozialisation—Enkulturation—Personalisation," in *Sozialisation und Personalisation*, ed. G. Wurzbacher (Stuttgart: Enke, 1974).

28. Orville G. Brim, "Adult Socialization," in *Socialization and Society*, ed. J. A. Clausen (Boston: Little, Brown, 1968), 183–226.

29. See Frieder Dünkel, "Statement," in *Actes du XIème Congrès International de Droit Pénal*, ed. H. -H. Jescheck (Baden-Baden: Nomos, 1980), 472.

30. The experiment took place at the Professor W.P.J. Pompe Clinic, in Nijmegen, Netherlands.

31. Werner Heinz and Salomon Korn, *Sozialtherapie als Alibi* (Frankfurt: Fisher, 1973), 203–31.

32. K. P. Rotthaus, "Die Sozialtherapeutische Anstalt," in *Strafvollzug in der Praxis*, ed. H. -D. Schwind and G. Blau (Berlin: De Gruyter, 1988), 95.

33. See Ralph Cormier, *The Watcher and the Watched* (Montreal: Tundra, 1975).

34. See Jacobus Reicher, "Psychoanalytically Oriented Treatment of Offenders Diagnosed as Developmental Psychopaths: The Mesdagkliniek Experience," *International Journal of Law and Psychiatry* 1 (1979): 87.

35. Günter Schmitt, introduction to "Sozialtherapie und Behandlungsforschung," special issue of *Zeitschrift für Strafvollzug und Straffälligenhilfe* (1980): 5.

36. Günther Kaiser, Frieder Dünkel, and Rüdiger Ortmann, "Die sozialtherapeutische Anstalt—das Ende einer Reform? *Zeitschrift für Rechtspolitik* (Aug. 1982): 198, 206.

37. See Rudolf Egg, *Straffälligkeit und Sozialtherapie* (Cologne: Karl Heymanns Verlag, 1984), 67–72.

38. Marc Ancel, *La défense sociale nouvelle* (Paris: Cujas, 1981), 288.

39. Ernest van den Haag, *Punishing Criminals: Concerning a Very Old and Painful Question* (New York: Basic Books, 1975), 259.

40. Charles Fried, *Right and Wrong* (Cambridge, Mass.: Harvard University Press, 1978), 108.

41. Besides the general depersonalizing impact of closed institutions described by Goffman (see note 23), some specific side effects of imprisonment demanding a counteracting action are the following: increased tendency to recidivism due to the creation of criminogenic inmates' social systems; victimization resulting from assaults or harassment by prisoners, various physical and psychological effects of prison stress, "gross deterioration and permanent scarring of . . . mental, emotional and behavioral integrity." See Ruthanne DeWolfe and Alan S. DeWolfe, "Impact of Prison Conditions on the Mental Health of Inmates," *Southern Illinois University Law Journal* (1979): 479, 507. See also Robert Johnson and Hans Toch, eds., *The Pains of Imprisonment* (Beverly Hills, Calif.: Sage, 1982). These effects are exacerbated with the current overcrowding of prisons. See Gerald Gaes, "The Effects of Overcrowding in Prison," *Crime and Justice* 6 (1985): 95–146; The Annals AAPSS, National Institute of Corrections, *Our Crowded Prisons* (Beverly Hills, Calif.: Sage, 1985), 478; and *Overcrowded Time* (New York: Edna McConnell Clark Foundation, 1982).

42. Edgardo Rotman, "La protection des droits de l'homme en matière pénale dans le droit Argentin et Latino-Américain," *Revue internationale de droit pénal* 47 (1976): 84.

43. Glauco Giostra, "Tre settore da differenziare nei rapporti tra giurisdizione ed esecuzione penale," *Rivista Italiana di diritto e procedura penale* (1981): 1375.

44. Emilio Dolcini, "La rieducazione del condannato tra mito e realtà," in *Diritti dei detenuti e trattamento penitenziario*, ed. Vittorio Grevi (Bologna: Nicola Zanichelli Editore, 1980), 57.

45. Ibid., 58.

46. Giostra, "Tre settore da differenziare," 1377.

47. Pietro Nuvolone, "Il problema della rieducazione del condannato," in *Sul problema della rieducazione del condannato*, ed. University of Padua (Padua: Cedam, 1964), 350.

48. Giuliano Vasalli, "Il dibatito sulla rieducazione" *Rassegna penitenziaria e criminologica* 1–2 (1982): 458.

49. Law of July 26, 1975, No. 354, in *Ordinamento penitenziario*, ed. Ministero di Grazia e Giustizia (Roma: Tipografia delle Mantellate, 1980).

50. Vasalli, "Il dibatito sulla rieducazione," 458.

51. Dolcini, "La rieducazione del condannato," 55.

52. Vasalli, "Il dibatito sulla rieducazione," 466.

53. Ibid., 471.

54. Decision of September 21–27, 1983, *Rivista Italiana di diritto e procedura penale* (1984): 801.

55. Vasalli, "Il dibatito sulla rieducazione," 462.

56. Dolcini, "La rieducazione del condannato," 63–67.

57. *Ordinamento penitenziario*, Art. 80, (4); Art. 20, (5), (6), (7), (8); Art. 19, and Art. 21, (2).

58. Thomas Würtenberger, "The Reform of the Execution of Penal Sentences in Germany and the Constitutional State," *Universitas* (1970): 75–86; Thomas Würtenberger, *Kriminalpolitik im sozialen Rechtsstaat* (Stuttgart: Enke, 1970), 222; and A. Müller-Emmert, "Resozialisierung als Verfassungsauftrag," *Deutsche Richterzeitung* 54 (1976): 65–68.

59. Heinz Müller-Dietz, *Strafzwecke und Vollzugsziel* (Tübingen: J. C. B. Mohr, 1973), 15–18.

60. *Decisions of the Federal Constitutional Court* 35: 202, 235; 36: 174, 188; 40: 276, 283.

61. *Decisions of the Federal Constitutional Court* 28: 264, 278; 32: 97, 109.

62. *Decisions of the Federal Constitutional Court* 33: 1.

63. See note 60.

64. Carsten Hoffmeyer, *Grundrechte im Strafvollzug* (Karlsruhe: C. F. Muller, 1979), 58, 59.

65. Müller-Emmert, "Resozialisierung als Verfassungsauftrag," 66.

66. *Decisions of the Federal Constitutional Court* 22: 181, 220.

67. *Decisions of the Federal Constitutional Court* 33: 1, 11.

68. Donald Clemmer, *The Prison Community* (New York: Reinhart, 1958).

69. *Decisions of the Federal Constitutional Court* 22: 181, 219, 220.

70. Bernhard Haffke, "Gibt es ein verfassungsrechtliches Besserungsverbot?" *Monatschrift für Kriminologie und Strafrechtsreform* (1975): 246–61.

71. Federal Prison Act, §3, ¶3 and other coincident provisions such as §6, ¶2; §8, ¶1; and §16, ¶3.

72. Federal Prison Act, §3, ¶1.

73. Federal Prison Act, §3, ¶2.

74. Jose Luis de la Cuesta Arzamendi, *El trabajo penitenciario resocializador* (Guipúzcoa: Caja de Ahorros Provincial, 1982), 255.

75. Ibid., 257.

76. See Italian Constitution, Article 27; Spanish Constitution, Article 25,2 ¶1 and decision of the Federal Constitutional Court of the Federal Republic of Germany in the *Lehbach* case (BVerGE 35,202). For the Argentine Constitution, see Edgardo Rotman, "Resozialisierungstendenzen im argentinischen Strafgesetzbuch," *Zeitschrift für das gesamte Strafrechtswissenschaft* 91 (1979): 475–98; Edgardo Rotman, "Dogmática y política criminal en la interpretación del Articulo 51 del codigo penal," *Revista la ley* (Buenos

Aires, 1981); and Eugenio R. Zaffaroni, *Tratado de derecho penal* (Buenos Aires, 1983), 1:63ff., 5:114ff.

77. Francis Allen, *The Decline of the Rehabilitative Ideal: Penal Policy and Social Purpose* (New Haven, Conn.: Yale University Press, 1981).

78. Nicolas N. Kittrie, *The Right to Be Different: Deviance and Enforced Therapy* (New York: Penguin Books, 1973) and Jessica Mitford, *Kind & Usual Punishment* (New York: Vintage Books, 1974).

79. Alan M. Dershowitz, "Indeterminate Confinement: Letting the Therapy Fit the Harm," *University of Pennsylvania Law Review* 123 (1974): 303.

80. See p. 102.

81. 418 U.S. 539, 591 (1974).

82. 416 U.S. 539, 562, 591 (1974).

83. In Nicolson v. Choctaw County, Alabama, 498 F.Supp. 295 (S.D. Ala. 1980), rehabilitation was considered to reinforce the First Amendment's arguments supporting the free exercise of religion. In Barnett v. Rogers, 410 F.2d 995, 1002 (D.C. Cir 1969), religion was considered as subserving the rehabilitative function by providing an area within which the inmate may reclaim his dignity and reassert his individuality. The right to health, protected in various decisions based on the totality of prison conditions, was specifically related to rehabilitation in Battle v. Anderson, 564 F.2d 388, 395 (10th Cir. 1977), and in Ramos v. Lamm, 639 F. 559 (10th Cir. 1980), *cert. denied*, 450 U.S. 1041 (1981), where a healthy rehabilitative environment was declared constitutionally mandated.

84. Edgardo Rotman, "Latest Trends in Crime Policy and Their Effect on Sentencing," in *Latest Trends in Crime Policy* (Syracuse Colloquium, 1982), ed. International Penal and Penitentiary Foundation (Bonn: I.P.P.F., 1984), 76. On the humanistic model of rehabilitation, see also Edgardo Rotman, "L'évolution de la pensée juridique sur le but de la sanction pénale," in *Aspects nouveaux de la pensée juridique (Melanges Ancel)* (Paris: Pedone, 1975), 2:163–76 and Edgardo Rotman, "Le sens de l'individualisation judiciaire," *Revue de science criminelle et de droit pénal compare* (1977): 437–44.

85. John Conrad, "Reintegration: Practice in Search of a Theory," in *Reintegration of the Offender in the Community* (Washington, D.C.: U.S. Department of Justice, June 1973), 21.

86. John Ely, "Toward a Representation-Reinforcing Mode of Judicial Review," *Maryland Law Review* 37 (1978): 451. In Ely's constitutional interpretation, the commitment to representative democracy, as opposed to a majoritarian republicanism, includes recognition of an exceptional class of positive rights. According to Frank Michelman ("Welfare Rights in a Constitutional Democracy," *Washington University Law Quarterly* [Summer 1979]: 659, 669–85), these include rights to the indispensable means of effective participation in the institutional system itself. Basic education, for example, does not amount to participation in the sense that acts of voting do, but it is a prerequisite to achieving the guaranteed democratic representation.

87. James B. Jacobs, *New Perspectives on Prisons and Imprisonment* (Ithaca, N.Y.: Cornell University Press, 1983).

88. Francis E. Cullen and Karen E. Gilbert, *Reaffirming Rehabilitation* (Cincinnati, Ohio: Anderson, 1982), 263. Cullen and Gilbert proposed a state obligation to rehabilitate through administrative accountability and parole contracts. They also advocated the exercise of political and moral pressure. The fact that judicial intervention has vastly improved the quality of prison life (see Comment, "Confronting the Conditions of Con-

finement: An Expanded Role for the Courts in Prison Reform,'' *Harvard Civil Rights– Civil Liberties Law Review* 12 [1977]: 367, 389), does not preclude other forms of action to further humanistic rehabilitative policies. ''Though courts and litigation will always remain vital [to the rights movement] David J. Rothman proposes to devote new attention to legislative and administrative concerns.'' David Rothman, ''Afterword'' in *Doing Good*, ed. W. Gaylin et al. (New York: Pantheon, 1981), 184.

89. Ronald Dworkin, *Taking Rights Seriously* (Cambridge, Mass.: Harvard University Press, 1977), 92.

90. Capps v. Atiyeh, 495 F.Supp. 802, 811 (D. Oreg. 1980).

91. Rozecki v. Gaughan, 459 F.2d 6, 8 (1st Cir. 1972); Jackson v. Bishop, 404 F.2d 571, 580 (8th Cir. 1968); Barnes v. Virgin Islands, 415 F.Supp. 1218, 1227 (D. V.I. 1976).

92. Holt v. Sarver, 309 F.Supp. 362 (E.D. Ark. 1970), *aff'd*, 442 F.2d 304 (8th Cir. 1971). See also John W. Palmer, *Constitutional Rights of Prisoners* (Cincinnati: Anderson Publishing Co., 1985), 179.

93. Peter Dwyer and Michael Botein, ''The Right to Rehabilitation for Prisoners— Judicial Reform of the Correctional Process'' *New York Law Forum* 20 (1974): 273, 274.

94. Trop v. Dulles, 356 U.S. 86, 101 (1958).

95. Holt v. Sarver, 309 F.Supp. 362, 380 (E.D. Ark. 1970), *aff'd*, 442 F.2d 304 (8th Cir. 1971).

96. Michael S. Feldberg, ''Confronting the Conditions of Confinement: An Expanded Role for the Courts in Prison Reform,'' *Harvard Civil Rights—Civil Liberties Law Review* 12 (1977): 393.

97. 428 U.S. 153, 182–83 (1976).

98. Feldberg, ''Confronting the Conditions of Confinement,'' 395.

99. Holt v. Sarver, 309 F.Supp. 362.

100. Ibid., 373.

101. Ibid., 379.

102. Ibid.

103. Rehabilitative considerations were included in Pugh v. Locke, 406 F.Supp. 318, 330 (M.D. Ala.), *cert. denied sub nom.* Newman v. Alabama, 438 U.S. 915 (1978); Barnes v. Virgin Islands, 415 F.Supp. 1218, 1227 (D. V.I. 1976); Miller v. Carson, 401 F.Supp. 835, 900 (M.D. Fla. 1975), *aff'd in part and modified in part*, 563 F.2d 741 (5th Cir. 1977); James v. Wallace, 382 F.Supp. 1177 (N.D. Ala. 1974); Taylor v. Sterret, 344 F.Supp. 411, 415 (N.D. Tex. 1972), *aff'd in part, vacated in part, and remanded*, 499 F.2d 387 (5th Cir. 1974), *cert. denied*, 420 U.S. 983 (1975).

104. 406 F.Supp. 318, 330 (M.D. Ala.), *cert. denied sub nom.* Newman v. Alabama, 438 U.S. 915 (1978). For an analysis of the process of institutional reform through litigation in Alabama, see Larry W. Yackle, *Reform and Regret: The Story of Federal Judicial Involvement in the Alabama Prison System* (New York: Oxford University Press, 1989).

105. See Dawson v. Kendrick, 527 F.Supp. 1252, 1315 (S.D. W.Va. 1981); Miller v. Carson, 401 F.Supp. 835, 900 (M.D. Fla. 1975), *aff'd in part and modified in part*, 563 F.2d 741 (5th Cir. 1977); James v. Wallace, 382 F.Supp. 1177 (N.D. Ala. 1974).

106. 437 F.Supp. 269 (D. N.H. 1977).

107. Ibid., 316, 323.

108. Ibid., 316.

109. Ibid., 319.

110. Ibid., 317.

111. Ibid., 318.

112. Ibid., 320.

113. Ibid., 319.

114. Ibid., 324.

115. 452 U.S. 337 (1981).

116. Comment, "Federal Intervention in State Prisons: The Modern Prison-Conditions Case," *Houston Law Review* 19 (1982): 931, 947.

117. Rhodes v. Chapman, 452 U.S. at 364.

118. Note, "Laaman v. Helgemoe: Degeneration, Recidivism and the Eighth Amendment," *Vermont Law Review* 3 (1978): 229, 243, 248.

119. John Howard, *The State of Prisons in England and Wales* (Warrington: William Eyres, 1777).

120. Hans Toch, ed., *Therapeutic Communities in Corrections* (New York: Praeger, 1980).

121. Trop v. Dulles, 356 U.S. 86, 101 (1958).

122. Hoptowit v. Ray, 682 F.2d 1237 (9th Cir. 1982), *cert. denied sub nom.* Franzen v. Duckworth, 107 S. Ct. 71 (1986) and Wright v. Rushen, 642 F.2d 1129, 1132 (9th Cir. 1981), *aff'd in part, rev'd in part, and vacated in part sub nom.* Toussaint v. McCarthy, 801 F.2d 1080 (9th Cir. 1986).

123. See note 104. 309 F.Supp. 362 (E.D. Ark. 1970), *aff'd*, 442 F.2d 304 (8th Cir. 1971).

124. 559 F.2d 283 (5th Cir. 1977), *cert. denied*, 460 U.S. 1083 (1983).

125. 80 Wash. 2d 167, 558 P.2d 1350 (1977).

126. 416 U.S. 396 (1974).

127. Spicer v. Williams, 191 N.C. 487, 490, 132 S.E. 291, 293 (1926) quoted by 429 U.S. 97, 104 (1978).

128. 80 Wash. 2d at 175, 558 P.2d at 1356 (Utter, J., dissenting).

129. 551 F.2d 44 (4th Cir. 1977).

130. Ibid., 48.

131. Ibid.

132. Ibid. See Note, "Prisoners' Rights—Bowring v. Godwin: The Limited Right of State Prisoners to Psychological and Psychiatric Treatment," *North Carolina Law Review* 56 (1978): 612, 614.

133. Rust v. State, 582 P.2d 134 (Alaska 1978).

134. Spicer v. Williams, 191 N.C. 487, 490, 132 S.E. 291, 293 (1926) quoted in Estelle v. Gamble, 429 U.S. at 104.

135. See Rouse v. Cameron, 373 F.2d 451 (D.C. Cir. 1966): Wyatt v. Stickney, 325 F.Supp. 781 (M.D. Ala. 1971), 334 F.Supp. 131 (M.D. Ala. 1971), 344 F.Supp. 373 (M.D. Ala. 1972), *aff'd in part, remanded in part, reversed in part sub nom.* Wyatt v. Aderholt, 503 F.2d 1305 (5th Cir. 1974). The Supreme Court, however, refused to affirm a constitutional right to treatment for mentally ill patients and expressly left the question unsettled. O'Connor v. Donaldson, 442 U.S. 563 (1975). The Supreme Court only recently recognized a right to a minimally adequate training and habilitation for the mentally retarded. Youngberg v. Romeo, 457 U.S. 307 (1982). See also Edgardo Rotman, "Rechtliche Voraussetzungen der Behandlung geistesgestörter Straftäter in den Vereinigten Staaten," in *Festschrift für Günter Blau*, ed. H.-D. Schwind (Berlin: De Gruyter, 1985), 555–72.

136. Humphrey v. Cady, 405 U.S. 504 (1972); Ohlinger v. Watson, 652 F.2d 775 (9th Cir. 1980).

137. See Comment, "Punishment versus Treatment of Guilty but Mentally Ill," *Journal of Criminal Law and Criminology* 74(2) (1983): 428–56. In Linda C. Fentiman, " 'Guilty but Mentally Ill': The Real Verdict Is Guilty," *Boston College Law Review* 26 (1985): 601, 652, the author pointed out that "in practice, the psychiatric treatment accorded [these] inmates tends to be either minimal or nonexistent." Denial of their constitutional right to treatment is one of the bases on which the author questioned the constitutionality of the "guilty but mentally ill" statutes.

138. Rone v. Fireman, 473 F.Supp. 92, 119 (N.D. Ohio 1979).

139. Ohlinger v. Watson, 652 F.2d 775 (9th Cir. 1980) and Slotkin v. Brookdale Hospital Center, 357 F.Supp. 705 (S.D. N.Y. 1972).

140. In a broad sense indeterminate sentencing refers to any sentence of confinement in which the actual term to be served is not known at the time of the judgment but will be subject, within a considerable range, to the later decision of a parole board or other sentencing authority. See M.E. Frankel, "Lawlessness in Sentencing," 41 *University of Cincinnati Law Review* (1972): 1, 28–39 at 28.

141. See Hudson v. Palmer 468 U.S. 517, 547–48 (1984) (Stevens, J., concurring in part and dissenting in part).

142. 143 F.2d. 443 (6th Cir. 1944).

143. Washington v. Lee, 263 F.Supp. 327, 331 (M.D. Ala. 1966), *aff'd mem.*, 390 U.S. 333 (1968).

144. See Note, "Women's Prisons: An Equal Protection Evaluation," *Yale Law Journal* 94 (1985): 1182–1206.

145. See Nason v. Superintendent of Bridgewater State Hospital, 353 Mass. 604, 233 N.E.2d 908 (1968) (upholding differences of treatment but recognizing the possibility of a violation of equal protection).

146. 340 F.Supp. 544 (W.D. Wis. 1972), rev'd, 489 F.2d 1335 (7th Cir. 1973). The district court decided that conviction was sufficient justification for differential treatment of prisoners without requiring a demonstration of "compelling state interest," id. at 1335, 1341–42.

147. Ibid., 550.

148. Dwyer and Botein, "The Right to Rehabilitation for Prisoners," 284.

149. See O'Connor v. Donaldson 422 U.S. 563, 573 (1975).

150. Barnes v. Virgin Islands, 415 F.Supp. at 1219.

151. Dwyer and Botein, "The Right to Rehabilitation of Prisoners," 284 n.60.

152. The importance of skill training as a rehabilitative option is underlined by Halleck and Witte, within the category of opportunity-changing programs. See Seymour L. Halleck and Ann D. Witte, "Is Rehabilitation Dead?" *Crime and Delinquency* 23 (Oct. 1977): 372–82.

153. Judgment of June 5, 1973, Bundesverfassungsgericht (Federal Constitutional Court) 35 BVerfGE 202.

154. Article 20, ¶1, of the West German Fundamental Law.

155. The Paquete Habana, 175 U.S. 677 (1900).

156. Comment, "Plyler v. Doe and the Right of Undocumented Alien Children to a Free Public Education," *Boston University International Law Journal* 2 (1984): 513, 523, citing Statute of the International Court of Justice, 59 Stat. 1055, T.S. No. 993, Article 338(1)(a).

157. Ibid.

158. Lareau v. Manson, 507 F.Supp. 1177 (D. Conn. 1980), *aff'd in part and modified in part*, 651 F.2d 96 (2d Cir. 1981).

159. 507 F.Supp. at 1188.

160. Ibid.

161. Sterling v. Cupp, 290 Or. 603, 625 P.2d 123 (1981).

162. 290 Or. at 616, 625 P.2d. at 128.

163. 290 Or. at 622, 625 P.2d at 131 n.21.

164. "The United Nations Standard Minimum Rules for the Treatment of Prisoners," in *Report on the First United Nations Congress on the Prevention of Crime and the Treatment of Offenders* (U.N. Pub., No.: 1956.iv.4).

165. U.N. International Covenant on Civil and Political Rights, Article 10, ¶ 3 G.A. Res. 2200 (xxi), 21 U.N. Doc. A/6316 (1967).

166. The American Convention of Human Rights, Article 5, ¶ 6 O.A.S. Treaty Series No. 36, at 1, O.A.S. Off. Rec. OEA/Ser. L/V/II.23 doc. 21 rev. 6 (1978).

167. Elbert F. Allen, "Sources of the Montana State Constitution," in *Montana Constitutional Convention 1971–1972* (Research Memorandum 4), (1972): 2.

168. Montana Constitution, Article III, ¶24.

169. Alaska Constitution, ¶12.

170. Illinois Constitution, Article I, ¶11.

171. E.g., Alaska Constitution, ¶22.

172. E.g., California Constitution, ¶4; Georgia Constitution, ¶XVIII; New Hampshire Constitution, Article 4.

173. Massachusetts Annotated Laws, ch. 24, 1(e)–(f) (Lawyers Co-op. 1981).

174. South Carolina Code Annotated, ¶24-1-20 (Lawyers Co-op. 1976).

175. Rhode Island General Laws, ¶42-56-31 (1984).

176. New Jersey Statutes Annotated, ¶30:1B-6, 30:4-91.1,-91.3,-91.6,-92 (West 1981).

177. New York Corrections Law, ch. 43, ¶136. (McKinney 1968).

178. Washington Revised Code, ¶¶72.08.101, 72.64.010, 72.01.150, 72.62.010 (1982).

179. Montana Code Annotated (1985), ¶53-1-201 (1985).

180. On the process through which rehabilitative services have gradually come to be seen as rights rather than privileges, see Richard E. Hardy and John G. Cull, *Introduction to Correctional Rehabilitation*, 2d ed. (Springfield, Ill.: Charles C. Thomas, 1973), 21.

181. 18 U.S.C., ¶2 (1982).

182. See Gray v. Benson, 458 F.Supp. 1209 (D. Kan. 1978).

183. Francis T. Cullen and Karen E. Gilbert, *Reaffirming Rehabilitation* (Cincinnati, Ohio: Anderson, 1982), 271.

184. Ibid., 273.

185. Daniel Glaser, "Protocol for Mutual Agreement Programs in Parole Release," in *Probation, Parole and Community Corrections*, ed. R. M. Carter, D. Glaser, and L. T. Wilkins (New York: Wiley, 1984), 269.

186. Research on the effectiveness of parole contracts has not yet provided conclusive results. See H. E. Allen, C. W. Eskridge, E. J. Latessa and G. F. Vito, *Probation and Parole in America* (New York: Free Press, 1985), 255.

187. Bresolin v. Morris, 88 Wash.2d 167, 175–76, 558 P.2d. 1350, 1354 (1977) (Utter, J., dissenting).

4

Against Rehabilitation

CRITICISM IN GENERAL

The recent crisis in rehabilitative policies makes it important to reexamine their conceptual basis. In fact, a theoretical clarification will help to correct the flaws pointed out by constructive criticism. The formulation of a revised rehabilitative concept, free from the errors of the past, can improve existing rehabilitative programs and inspire future ones.

A first step in this process of clarification is to set aside unfair criticism, which distorts the rehabilitative idea in order to dismiss it more easily. Often rehabilitation is blamed for the flaws of other concepts associated with it only contingently. It is, for example, unfair to hold rehabilitation responsible for the shortcomings of imprisonment. In fact, rehabilitation can no longer be identified with imprisonment, as the old penitentiary reform model did. Quite the contrary, rehabilitation today includes methods to counteract the noxiousness of incarceration as well as alternatives to avoid it altogether. Equally misleading is the criticism that confines rehabilitation to the old biomedical treatment model or identifies it with the negative aspects of indeterminate sentencing. Modern rehabilitation consists of learning processes and social opportunities that can also function within the framework of determinate sentencing systems.

Criticism of rehabilitation falls into four broad categories, based on (1) abuses perpetrated in the name of rehabilitation, arising either from overly intrusive therapies or excessively prolonged incarceration under discretionary sentencing based on rehabilitative considerations; (2) demand for increased punishment; (3) sociological theory and research; and (4) the alleged ineffectiveness of rehabilitative programs. The different types of criticism often interrelate and combine, even when their ideological origins are quite opposed. An ineffectiveness argument has been used, for example, to reinforce all the other forms of attack on rehabilitation.

CRITICISM BASED ON ABUSES

Use of Overly Intrusive Methods

In recent years rehabilitation has been held responsible for the abuse of intrusive therapies. The attacks applied primarily to the treatment of mentally disordered offenders, but also aimed at corrections as a whole. Overly intrusive programs in U.S. prisons have taken various forms. Small electric shocks were administered to child molesters while they were shown photographs of naked children,[1] and similar methods were used to treat shoplifters and bank robbers.[2] The most important therapeutic abuses perpetrated in the name of rehabilitation involved the use of biochemical means to control behavior and recondition the offender. Drugs were used to chemically castrate dangerous offenders, to tranquilize them, or to arouse pain and fear as a form of aversion therapy. The use of aversive conditioning as a therapeutic method in institutions became publicly known through court cases challenging its constitutionality.

One of the most frequently cited examples of therapeutic abuse was the use of intravenous succinylcholine (trade name Anectine), a neuromuscular blocking agent. The program consisted of associating violent acting-out behavior with the terrifying effects of the drug, which induced the cessation of respiration (apnea) for short periods, provoking sensations of suffocation and drowning.[3] During the suspension of breathing the inmate was admonished and exhorted to change his behavior. The drug was used at the Atascadero (California) State Hospital for persistent violent behavior, sexual deviation, and resistance to institutional treatment. The program was halted after the institution was criticized for not having obtained the inmates' informed consent. The California Medical Facility at Vacaville used the drug for prison transferees with mental disorders or mentally disordered offenders not judged to be insane, according to the decision of the California Department of Corrections. Unlike the Atascadero experiment, Vacaville used succinylcholine exclusively as a punishment or threat within a broader behavior-modification program, and complied with the requirement of informed consent.[4] However, this program too fell into discredit and was discontinued in 1970.

Another abuse was the use of Prolixin in prisons. This powerful tranquilizer, normally applied to schizophrenics, was indiscriminately used to pacify unruly prisoners, in massive doses capable of producing painful and harmful side effects.[5] More threatening still were the plans for psychosurgery to subdue violent inmates. In 1971 the California Department of Corrections drafted such a program for prisoners who volunteered as candidates for surgery. Strong opposition led to the abandonment of the project. An attempt to perform psychosurgery on a patient committed to the Kalamazoo State Hospital under the provisions of the

Michigan sexual psychopath statute gave rise to a leading case on the matter. The lawsuit was brought about by Gabe Kaimovitz, a Michigan legal services lawyer, on behalf of the candidate and twenty-three other patients who would also participate in a project sponsored by the Michigan state legislature.

The final decision of the Wayne County Circuit Court held that experimental surgery can never be used to eliminate antisocial behavior in institutionalized patients.[6] The suit argued that, because of their diminished capacity, involuntary mental patients were incompetent to make surgical decisions; thus their consent was meaningless. Another important argument concerned the lack of information about the possibly harmful consequences of psychosurgery, which belied the concept of informed consent. The court's decision was based on the fact that psychosurgery without valid consent amounted to battery, prohibited by tort law as well as by criminal law. As additional grounds for the decision, the violation of the constitutional rights to freedom of mental processes and to privacy was mentioned. No further cases of psychosurgery ever reached the courts. In that regard, Kaimovitz set a well-publicized precedent that significantly influenced future policies on performing psychosurgery on involuntarily institutionalized patients.

Liberals saw in behavior-modification programs the possible germ of new forms of political tyranny. Reminders of Aldous Huxley's *Brave New World* and George Orwell's *1984* nourished the fear of a highly technological state control using the sophisticated methodology offered by scientific progress.[7] Winick established, for didactic purposes, a useful "continuum of intrusiveness" along which the various rehabilitative techniques used on offenders may be roughly positioned.[8] He affirmed that the proposed therapy should not infringe a fundamental right unless there is a sufficiently compelling governmental interest and no less restrictive alternative available. Limits to therapy can be statutory, regulatory, or judicial or can arise from international law.[9]

Behavior-modification programs are always prone to abuses. Incentive programs, ingrained in correctional practices since the sixteenth century, enjoyed a new boom during the 1960s. Behavior-modification techniques based on token economies and operant conditioning were quickly adopted because they coincided with the interest of prison administrators in behavioral control. As Ross and McKay pointed out, "In many ways the new operant would be perceived by the administrators as just fancy, socially acceptable, professional, 'treatment appearing' versions of what generations of wardens had been providing for ages— incentive programs."[10] Scientifically fashionable and apparently simple, these behavior-modification programs appealed to correctional practitioners because they did not have to share their authority with the medical staff. They could accordingly deal with the most-difficult inmates in an administratively efficient, cheap, and quick way.[11]

A survey conducted in 1968 revealed that sixty-three correctional institutions in the United States and Canada had been involved since 1960 in some form of behavior-modification program.[12] Many of the so-called operant programs, however, "were operant in name only—they were a masquerade."[13] In effect these programs were disguised versions of highly punitive practices that had been used long before scientific research on operant conditioning was undertaken. After 1974 such programs fell into disrepute. The Federal Bureau of Prisons discontinued all behavior-modification programs under its jurisdiction, and the Law Enforcement Assistance Administration withdrew funding for those existing in corrections. They were also condemned by the General Accounting Office (the auditing agency for Congress) in three prisons: Leavenworth, El Reno, and Marion.[14]

One of the most renowned experiments on behavioral change was the Special Treatment and Rehabilitation Training Program, commonly known by the acronym START. Established by the Federal Bureau of Prisons at the federal hospital in Springfield, Missouri, in 1972, it aimed to produce institutional adjustment of maladaptive inmates of other federal prisons. The purpose of the program was "to promote behavioral and attitudinal change in that element of the prison institution that has chronically demonstrated inability to effectuate adherence to established regulations." Prisoners worked their way through a three-tier system, each tier subdivided into eight levels. Each successive level enlarged the scope of available privileges, thus creating incentives to progressive behavioral control. Conformity was rewarded with a "good day" report. The accumulation of such reports allowed the inmate to earn back the "good time" he had forfeited through unruly behavior and to gain other institutional privileges. The idea was that the inmate should work himself up in the system. To allow a considerable improvement as a prisoner moved up through successive tiers, the lowest level was one of extreme austerity.

START and similar behavior-modification programs were terminated as the result of lawsuits. The litigation was initiated by the American Civil Liberties Union National Prison Project on the basis of procedural due process violations. Placement at the bottom level, with its extreme deprivation, was tantamount to punishment without any procedural safeguards. Evidence was introduced to support the prisoners' claims of being shackled to their beds, not receiving sufficient food and even being forced to lie in their own excrement to create an initial atmosphere of deprivation that would increase the motivational force of rewards.[15] In *Clonce v. Richardson*,[16] the court found that the START prisoners were entitled to a due process hearing guaranteed by the Fifth Amendment. Petitioners in the START case claimed that the program violated the freedoms of speech and association and of religion, the rights connected with search and seizure, and the right to privacy.[17] The government replied that the contingency of those rights was the core of the treatment, as their uncertain exercise acted as a positive reinforcer to modify the behavior of the inmates. The point was declared moot by the court, because the program was discontinued by the Federal Bureau of Prisons before a decision was reached on inmates' right to refuse to participate.

It should be pointed out that the constitutional challenge to START did not involve the method itself, but the inclusion of punitive procedures in a particular institutional setting without the corresponding safeguards. The real flaw of the program, from the viewpoint of inmate rights, was that the scale of progress started below normal levels of liberty deprivation instead of extending upward. When behavioral therapy is applied on a nonresidential basis, there is some evidence that it is at least more effective than doing nothing, although causality has never been adequately demonstrated.[18] In correctional settings behavioral therapy has all the flaws inherent in the carrot-and-stick approach peculiar to post–Civil War penitentiary reform,[19] because it confuses genuine rehabilitation with institutional adjustment.

Because of strong liberal reaction, overly intrusive behavior-modification programs never went beyond limited and isolated experiments. However, these experiments increased the confusion among those who associated rehabilitation with brainwashing techniques. Their apprehension paved the way for others to propose increased punishment free of any of the feared "treatments."[20] The criticism of rehabilitation based on therapeutic abuse should not be allowed to paralyze humanistic initiatives of genuine and constructive help for the criminal offender. On the contrary, an awareness of the dangers of intrusive abuses should help inform a refined, liberty-oriented concept of rehabilitation, setting clear and insurmountable limits to state intervention.

Sentencing Abuses

Since the late 1960s the main argument against rehabilitating criminal offenders has been that the idea of rehabilitation has been used to justify indeterminate sentences. This particular form of sentencing became the target of liberal criticism because it gave both sentencing and correctional authorities discretionary power, which was thought to lead to disparity, arbitrariness, and inequality. Moreover, although indeterminate sentencing was originally intended to shorten the period of incarceration for trustworthy inmates, its practical application resulted in disproportionately high penalties.[21] This criticism was reinforced by the argument of rehabilitative ineffectiveness.[22] Thus rehabilitation was accused of being a mere rhetorical pretext to justify abusive indeterminate sentencing schemes.

Although modern rehabilitative policies are not associated with particular sentencing systems,[23] there is an historical link between certain configurations of the penitentiary and therapeutic models of rehabilitation and sentencing, which has varied considerably through time and space. An examination of this link will help in assessing the criticisms of rehabilitation based on sentencing abuses.

The modern idea of the indeterminate sentence has many historical precedents. In seventeenth-century Amsterdam houses of correction, indeterminateness served the goal of reformation through labor. Another precedent was the trailblazing Bavarian penal code of 1813, which included penalties of imprisonment for an indeterminate number of years, while the inmate was allowed to earn his freedom by showing evidence of genuine reform through work and good conduct.[24] The Continental trend, however, has followed a more determinate sentencing tradition, which began with the fixed penalties system of the French penal code of 1810 and was made gradually more flexible as subsequent legislation allowed for judicial individualization. The basic concern, however, was to contain the punitive power of the state within legal limits. Retributive punishment, strictly defined by a preexisting law, is preserved in civil law countries as a barrier against unrestrained state power over citizens.

In the modern Continental penal codes, and in many non-European countries that followed their system, the judge selects the particular sentence within a maximum and a minimum range fixed by the law for each offense. These milder forms of indetermination have prevented the most serious abuses. Within the statutory predetermined ranges, the sentencing judge has some latitude to consider rehabilitative needs. In fact, one of the most modern codes states that the sentence must take into account the future life of the offender in the community.[25] There are also flexible conditional release or parole regimes, creating what Donnedieu de Vabres called "concealed indeterminate sentences."[26] Furthermore, besides a basic system of relatively determined sentences, Continental penal legislation adopted indeterminate sentences for juvenile offenders and a system of nonpunitive security measures of indeterminate duration for dangerous abnormal and habitual offenders. As Dershowitz pointed out, the indeterminate sentence is not a unitary concept, "but a continuum of devices designed to tailor the punishment to the rehabilitative needs and special danger of a particular offender."[27]

The first modern legislation to provide nonpunitive security measures of indeterminate duration was the Norwegian penal code of 1902, which introduced the indeterminate detention of mentally abnormal offenders and of drunk and disorderly offenders judged to be a public danger. The Dutch penal code of 1881 had already prescribed indeterminate detention in mental hospitals for mentally disordered and defective offenders. The United Kingdom established the preventive detention of dangerous recidivists through the Prevention of Crime Act of 1908, while a 1927 Swedish law and the 1930 Belgian Social Defense Law provided for indeterminate measures of security for both dangerous abnormal offenders and recidivists. Nonpunitive security measures were also contained in the Argentine penal code of 1921, the Swiss penal code of 1937, and the Cuban Social Defense Code of 1936, among many other pieces of legislation.

Until the 1870s the sentencing system in the United States was similar to the European model. American statutes usually fixed only a maximum penalty, giving a wider range than the European codes, which provided a minimum and maximum term of imprisonment for each offense. In both systems, once the judge selected a particular sentence, it was immutable and the convict was bound to serve it to the end. The only exception was a governor's pardon, which as Dershowitz indicated was sometimes used to reduce partially served prison sentences.[28] The idea of the indeterminate sentence emerged in the United States during the 1870 National Penitentiary Congress at Cincinnati and gained ground through Zebulon Brockway's experiment at the Elmira reformatory.[29] The idea of reformation played a preeminent role at least in the theory of this first indeterminate sentencing scheme. It was supposed to provide incentive to the inmate, who worked his way toward release by participating in activities designed to be reformative. The potential for abuse was already present in Brockway's model, which was indicted in the 1970s for "exploiting the managerial potential of indeterminacy as a tool of institutional control" and "increasing the median length of time served by prisoners."[30]

The adoption of the medical "myth" in corrections, together with the hiring of experts in the behavioral sciences, justified the rapid expansion of indeterminate sentencing to most American statutory legislation. In practice, attempts at rehabilitation were only peripheral, but the spread of indeterminate sentencing led to disparities and arbitrariness that have been the object of modern criticism.

Parole became the indispensable complement of indeterminate sentencing in America. Its abuses and inadequacies during the progressive era are vividly reflected in the record of parole hearings, which led Rothman to conclude that despite certain elements of uniformity, "parole was at its core arbitrary and capricious" and that a parole board's predictions were no more than a game of chance.[31] Nor was postsentence supervision carried out with efficiency, due mainly to the lack of sufficient and competent parole officers. The function of parole was more disciplinary than rehabilitative. Contrary to public belief, it was not a form of leniency, but extended the state's period of control, supplementing imprisonment rather than substituting for it.[32]

The political abuses of indeterminate sentencing are illustrated by the case of George Jackson, author of the book *Soledad Brother*.[33] Convicted of a $70 gas station robbery, he became both a writer and a radical inmate leader. His alleged failure to achieve rehabilitation was used as an argument to delay his release for eleven years until his shooting in 1971 during an aborted escape attempt. In that same year the American Friends Service Committee published *Struggle for Justice*, which severely criticized the role of rehabilitation in the criminal justice system, aiming especially at what we have characterized as the penitentiary and therapeutic models.[34] The report did not confine itself to indicting the flaws of a carrot-and-stick methodology indissolubly linked to indetermination or to criticizing the medical myth that had led to abusive discretionary power. It pointed out "the concerns of the reformers to humanize criminal justice by reducing its severity and to carry fellowship, education and service directly to the prisoners in order to counteract some of the destructiveness of imprisonment."[35] These concerns also motivated the later efforts to dissociate rehabilitation from indetermination and from any other inadmissible threat to the prisoner's inalienable rights.

The current trend is to disengage as far as possible the idea of rehabilitation from any particular form of sentencing. The length of the prison term is still relevant because it affects the intensity of the efforts needed to counteract the noxious effects of incarceration, but imprisonment cannot be extended for the sake of rehabilitative considerations. In this context, Norval Morris's pioneering proposals should be mentioned. In *The End of Imprisonment* (1974) he attempted to separate treatment from indeterminacy and developed the idea of facilitated change as a substitute for coerced cure. He considered that it is "an abuse of power to extend the duration of an accused person's imprisonment on the basis of predictions of his future criminal behavior, while on parole or thereafter."[36] On these grounds he shifted the basis of parole decisions from prediction to testing. For that purpose he conceived a system of early fixation of the parole date, in which release was subject to the inmate's accomplishment of predetermined conditions. He tried thus "to minimize the corruptive link between time and treatment."[37] Morris also emphasized that when the date of release is made contingent on the accomplishment of a prison program, both staff and prisoners perceive the link between rehabilitation and time as fraudulent.[38]

Vulnerable to liberal attacks based on the protection of individual rights and safeguards, indetermination is also likely to work against a true rehabilitative concept. It can create tensions and uncertainties incompatible with a rehabilitative atmosphere. In this connection, Miriam Reich questioned the rehabilitative value of indeterminate sentencing and examined its actual impact on the individual prisoner.[39] She affirmed that the indeterminate sentence, "presumed to enhance the rehabilitative goals of the sentence, brings in its wake certain factors which undermine this objective."[40] Although she recognized its positive aspects, in giving the inmate some responsibility for the implementation of sanctions[41] or in using authority therapeutically,[42] she pointed out that

it can have a detrimental and aggravating effect on the whole process of imprisonment. The anxiety created by uncertainty can elicit stronger defensive attitudes than those experienced by the prisoner who has a definitive fixed sentence to serve and therefore makes some adjustment to this factor.[43]

Furthermore, she found a major obstacle in the "ambivalence which the therapist often feels concerning his role of authority and the vacillation between identification with the system, or a 'pure' therapeutic frame of reference."[44]

A determinate sentence, conmensurate with the offender's guilt, can also have a rehabilitative value per se. The determination of the penal sanction becomes an important element in a rehabilitative task conceived as a "pedagogy of responsibility," in which his culpability is explained to the offender in order to awaken a genuine feeling of responsibility.[45] In Germany, Arthur Kaufmann underlined the preventive function of the principle of culpability. He considered the experience of the guilt generated by the offense (*Schulderlebnis*) as a way to resocialization of the criminal offender.[46]

The rejection of indetermination is directly related to the idea of voluntary treatment. However, neither determination of sentences nor voluntariness should be transformed into an absolute dogma, and a new concept of rehabilitation should not be made contingent either. An uncompromising position could exclude from the field of modern social therapy those who need it the most.[47] Prospective candidates for social therapy are often reluctant to accept treatment and may not experience the anxiety that would normally impel them to seek professional help. In fact, some offenders who are ready to adjust to a social therapeutic program are also apt to find the rehabilitative resources in orthodox forms of imprisonment. Unfortunately, they sometimes apply for social therapy, seeking the benefits and privileges associated with such treatment-oriented institutions. The legal framework of determinate sentencing is not always suitable for the treatment of a certain type of persistent recidivists who lacks the will for autonomous decisions. Involuntary submission to rehabilitative treatment for strictly limited and short periods of time could, in certain cases, show the inmate the benefits to be derived from such therapy. This solution was recently proposed by the authors of the renowned Alternative Draft penal code of 1966, who cited the successful continuation of indeterminate treatment programs within indeterminate sentencing schemes in the Netherlands and Austria, emphasizing that the recent introduction of determinate sentencing in the United States has tended to increase the length of imprisonment.[48]

CRITICISM BASED ON THE DEMAND FOR INCREASED PUNISHMENT

Law and Order Policies and Rehabilitation

Advocates of a tougher reaction to crime also contributed to the crisis of rehabilitative policies, although differing from the liberal critics in both premises and goals. Both groups attacked the prevailing indeterminate sentencing system based on the rehabilitative medical model and the discretionary power of parole boards. But while liberals viewed this system as unjustly increasing punishment, conservatives complained of judicial and administrative leniency. Rehabilitative policies, they felt, weakened the punitive mechanisms of the state.

Discretionary measures entailing disparity in the treatment of a particular group of offenders can be interpreted in two ways. Some observers focus on the lenient treatment of those who benefit from discretion, while others emphasize its impact, equivalent to a penalty, on those excluded from such privileged treatment.[49] Moreover, the joint liberal-conservative indictment of rehabilitative policies reflects the existence of two opposed models of rehabilitation.[50] While liberals aimed at the authoritarian model, which is in fact a form of punishment, conservatives were attacking the liberty-enhancing effects of rehabilitative offerings.[51]

The conservative critiques unfairly blamed rehabilitation for the overall crisis in crime control, disregarding the many social, demographic, and economic factors that helped increase crime. Phenomena such as technological advance, industrialization, urban-rural migration and urban concentration, population explosion, unemployment, housing shortages, economic instability, ethnic and class conflicts, and changes in the family structure have transformed modern societies, eroding the old normative systems and reducing the effectiveness of social control. The consequent rise of violent crime, the emergence of new forms of criminality and the severe leaks in the criminal justice system have made obvious the need to reexamine the postulates of current crime policies. Although prevalent both in legislative proposals and in penal theory since the end of World War II, rehabilitation had not been consistently applied and could hardly be held responsible for the increase in crime.

The overhasty conclusion that rehabilitation had failed encouraged a revival of punitive models already proven inadequate. The harsh repressive model, worn out beyond repair, still offers a deceptive illusion of order and security, while the humanistic rehabilitative model,[52] which aims at improving the quality of society, has not yet had a fair chance to prove its worth. One is now at a bewildering impasse, forced to choose between retreating to former models and delving into the causes of failure and evolving creative modifications.[53]

The return to the harsh repressive model is linked to the feelings of fear and insecurity aroused by the upsurge of violent crime. Statistically, one's chances of becoming a victim of homicide, rape, burglary, assault, or robbery increased steadily in the 1960s.[54] The psychological impact on the public of violent and predatory crime was aggravated by other threats to the stability of the social values system: political assassinations, the Vietnam War, economic depression, prison revolts, unemployment and poverty, racial tensions, and turmoil in the ghettos and on the university campuses.

The gravity of the crime menace was magnified through mass media reports and exaggerated by politicians who favored more punitive solutions. So strong was the sense of powerlessness and insecurity that, according to Arzt, fifteen years of gradual education of the public in correctional matters were destroyed in scarcely three years.[55] In this field, as Sherman and Hawkins point out, "the dangers and inequities of a policy that follows too closely the shifts in vox populi are obvious enough to scare us all."[56] Such was the policy of cracking down on criminals by giving them longer prison terms to be served under the harshest possible conditions. Individual safeguards were regarded as cumbersome hindrances and rehabilitation as a costly and pointless appurtenance.

The issue of law and order was a leitmotiv over four presidential campaigns commencing in 1964.[57] The 1920s and 1930s, an era of gangsterism and prohibition, saw similar campaigns. The rising crime rates and a one-sided concern for the victims of crime were invoked in an attempt to revive past repressive models. During the Nixon era, the law and order movement projected "an image of incipient civil war."[58] A "war theory" of crime developed, whose ethic, as Allen incisively indicated, "conceives of the offender as an alien and in doing so induces a regression to primitive conceptions of penal justice."[59] In America, such attitudes influenced the unsuccessful penal policies of the last decade, which led to extreme overcrowding of prisons.

Law and order policies since the mid–1960s have demanded security for the citizen at home, at the workplace, and in the streets. Although this objective is obviously legitimate, such policies were flawed insofar as they held the expansion of rights and procedural safeguards responsible for the failure of the criminal justice system, ignoring the many social, demographic, and economic factors influencing the crime rates.[60] Another defect of these policies was the "legal superstition" that a harsh execution of prison sentences would prevent the inmate from relapsing into crime.[61] The fields of animal training and child rearing have long since discarded their belief in education through rigor and severity.[62] Besides, there is no evidence that milder forms of imprisonment increase criminality.[63] In fact it was precisely the ineffectiveness of the severe classic forms of imprisonment that inspired late nineteenth-century reform efforts to mitigate their harshness. Harsh punishment had not prevented an alarming increase of recidivism, but the general belief in its effectiveness barred all true rehabilitative possibilities.

The law and order movement tends to ignore the lessons of the past. Even in the eighteenth century, Blackstone and Montesquieu indicated that the certainty of punishment is more important to deterrence than its severity. Likewise, Beccaria's famous essay demonstrated the overriding importance of the promptness, certainty, and inexorability of punishment and its proportion to the crime committed.[64] His utilitarian arguments were so convincing as to render obsolete most of the earlier scholarly science based on a belief in exemplary cruel punishment. Today's champions of increased punishment have far too easily brushed aside the insights of the Enlightenment.

The Principle of Less Eligibility

Although considered "intellectually and morally bankrupt" by many, the principle of less eligibility has been invoked by critics of rehabilitation.[65] Earlier in the history of imprisonment, unnecessary pains and deprivations were deliberately added to the fact of incarceration. Such afflictive purpose permeated the various forms of *carcere duro* and *durissimo*, the irons and chains, hard labor, and the defamatory forms of penal servitude. The concern for specific deterrence—that is, the desire to make the experience of punishment dreadful—was even more important than the economic interest in exploiting the convicts' labor. The underlying assumption that prison was not enough punishment in itself was mirrored in the forms of unproductive and punitive work represented by the treadmill, the crank, and the shot drill.[66]

The limitation of imprisonment to the deprivations inherent in the loss of liberty is a hallmark of modern civilized punishment. But it is not enough simply to ban primitive forms of additional punishment. To avoid the harmful effects of incarceration on the mental and social health of the inmate, some positive action toward rehabilitation is essential.

Such action, which includes improvements in prison conditions and the economic opportunities of prisoners, encounters a serious obstacle in the principle of less eligibility. Formulated by Bentham in 1791, this principle holds that "saving the regard due to life, health and bodily ease, the ordinary conditions of a convict doomed to punishment" shall not be made "more eligible than that of the poorest class of citizens in a state of innocence and liberty."[67] To apply the principle of less eligibility strictly would mean maintaining prison conditions less favorable than those found in the worst slums or, in extreme situations, to push prisoners to the limits of starvation. This principle has been applied as a means to realize equity in social welfare policy. The implication is that the situation of the beneficiary of public relief should not "be made really or apparently so eligible as the situation of the independent laborer of the lowest class."[68] But there is a significant difference between maintaining the incentives to work in the free labor market and using the conditions of imprisonment as a supposed deterrence against crime.

In modern democratic societies, in which freedom is of the highest value, not even catastrophic social or economic conditions could make imprisonment attractive, however humane or civilized it might be, or neutralize its intrinsic deterrent potential. Although a few derelicts may commit minor offenses to obtain jail shelter during the winter, it is highly unlikely that the rehabilitative prospect of a correctional institution would diminish the deterrent effect of a long-term stay or motivate anyone to commit a felony. Even in times of crisis, the general population will derive its motivation for life from their margin of personal freedom, which is denied to prisoners. To prevent the wholesale deterioration of institutionalized inmates, it is indispensable to offer them a substitute for freedom.[69]

Conversely, under dictatorships, where the population at large has been already considerably deprived of its freedom, there is a tendency to make the prisoner "feel his position by other means."[70] It is therefore not surprising that during the eleventh International Penal and Penitentiary Congress, which met in Berlin in 1935, the delegation of a totalitarian Germany strongly adhered to the principle of less eligibility, demanding that the "prisoner's standard of life should not be superior to that of the poorest citizen."[71] In contrast, the English and Norwegian delegations stressed the abysmal differences between the life of the free population and those suffering the depressing effects of imprisonment, which made it "essential that a counterpoise should be found."[72] The English report emphasized that the privation of liberty is in itself the greatest of evils, to which Mannheim added, on the basis of expert opinion, that the length of imprisonment is more dreaded than its harshness.[73] There is, of course, a commonsense relationship between the state of a country's economy and its prison standards, but that does not condone an "artificially contrived" principle of less eligibility or, as he calls it, of "nonsuperiority."[74]

The Nature of Punitive Reactions

The punitive reaction toward crime is symmetrical in nature. Violence is opposed to violence, and fear, to fear. It is a mechanical response, governed and compelled by the behavior of the offender, incapable of breaking through the vicious circle of increased retaliatory violence. It makes impossible any creative solution, which could only spring from a free decision. Such freedom includes the freedom of not reacting, which does not necessarily mean offering the other cheek. Asymmetry is the outcome of inner freedom and the sole means to a creative response. It is essential to any significant change in human relationship.

The inability of symmetry to produce any significant change has been long known in natural science. Kant and Pasteur used the notion of asymmetry to explain the nature of sensibility,[75] and Pierre Curie held that it is the prerequisite for all physical phenomena. He further explained that "certain elements of symmetry may coexist with certain phenomena, but they are not necessary. What is essential is the non-presence of certain elements of symmetry. It is asymmetry that creates the phenomenon."[76] In interpersonal relations punishment is the typical symmetrical response, resulting from a primitive social-psychological conditioning. Its primacy is intellectually justified with the assumption that any reaction short of retaliation is equivalent to weakness or appeasement. This line of reasoning ignores the potential of the human mind for freedom and creativity, and its ability to go beyond automatic crystallized patterns of thought and behavior, such as the punitive reaction. Whatever social or psychological functions are served by punishment, it lacks the capacity to surmount the vicious circle of symmetrical reactions leading to mounting violence or the dead end of stubborn indifference. Only true rehabilitation offers the option of a nonmechanical reaction that might overcome the contradiction between the offender and society.

CRITICISMS BASED ON SOCIOLOGICAL THEORY AND RESEARCH

Sociological theory belies the one-sided model of rehabilitation based on a conception of crime as an exclusively individual pathology. Instead, it supports a social-learning model of rehabilitation in which the sociocultural context plays a preeminent role. Furthermore, constructive social criticism underscores the connection of rehabilitation with the restructuring of the community, while recognition of the criminogenic aspects of modern societies implies that individual change must go beyond mere readjustment into society. Sociological theories on crime also inspired new rehabilitative strategies, for example, the creation of anticriminal groups among the inmates of correctional institutions.[77] In addition, the theoretical recognition of the cultural element in crime has helped to dispel residues of biological determinism that undermined rehabilitative initiatives.

Rehabilitation is incompatible with rigid determinism, whether biological or social. An example of the latter is the affirmation of punishment as an absolute and exclusive element of social order. Durkheim believed, for example, the function of punishment as an inexorable response of the "conscience collective" makes rehabilitation irrelevant.[78] Equally antithetical to rehabilitation are the theories that explain the reaction to crime as totally determined by political or economic factors. But sociological theories that acknowledge the plasticity, dynamism, and unpredictability of human nature are not adverse to rehabilitation. On the contrary, the recognition of the possibility of individual change transforms social theory into a rich instrument to guide the renewal of rehabilitative undertakings.

Sociological theory made an important contribution to the revision of rehabilitative models by demonstrating the links of crime and the sanctioning system to basic traits of modern society. If society produces crime in various ways, blurring the limits between the criminal offender and the law-abiding citizen, the very notion of antisociality has to be redefined as a basis for conceptualizing rehabilitative goals. At the same time, the participation of society in the genesis of crime demands a broader social response to neutralize it. An overview of some major sociological contributions reveals the extent of their challenge to the traditional rehabilitative concepts built around an inadequate therapeutic model.

Since the 1920s and particularly after the 1950s, purely psychological theories of crime have had to compete in America with increasingly refined sociological explanations, which link crime with the sociocultural system. Dynamic models were constructed to represent the disintegration of preexisting normative systems, which began in the nineteenth century and gained momentum in the twentieth. Merton explained deviant behavior as the result of a process of anomie in which the exaltation of the objectives institutionalized by a given culture is followed by the deinstitutionalization of the means employed to attain them.[79] Sociological explanations of crime culminated in Cloward and Ohlin's analysis of the structural factors that block opportunities for legitimate access to valuable social goals.[80] This blockage produces organized delinquent subcultures, which provide illegitimate means to attain the denied social success. Disorganized slum neighborhoods generate instead violent types of crime or retreatist subculture.

Other theories have emphasized the role of society in the genesis of crime. The labeling approach and the interactionist perspective posed new challenges to the individual-centered crime theories that underlay the traditional notion of rehabilitation. As early as 1938 Frank Tannenbaum explained deviance as a process of labeling, definition, identification, and segregation.[81] In 1951 Lemert distinguished primary and undetected deviance from what he called secondary deviance. In the latter case, labeling created a psychosociological status that strongly conditioned future criminal careers.[82]

The discovery of the extent of hidden crime was a decisive blow against the individual-based therapeutic model of rehabilitation. Modern research on the relationship between official statistics and the real amount of crime, initiated by Guerry and Quetelet in the nineteenth century, reveals that a staggering amount of crime goes undetected. According to findings based on self-reported crime and victimization studies, offenders officially labeled as such are not representative of the crime problem. Most people have been involved in delinquent behavior at some point of their lives, and only a small fraction of overall criminal activities are touched by the criminal justice system.[83] And if few criminals are caught, fewer still are prosecuted and convicted. By 1970, criminological research had discovered an abyss between the official figures on crime and the underlying reality.[84]

These empirical findings, blended with psychoanalytical theory, led to the idea of the criminal offender as scapegoat for the emotional needs of the public.[85] The so-called psychoanalysis of the punitive society affirmed that criminal punishment helps nonoffenders to overcome their criminal drives through the surrogate experience of the punishment of others.[86] Its function is to allow the repression of the criminal impulse existing in the law-abiding citizen. The convicted criminal serves as a scapegoat for a large majority of undetected or unpunished offenders.

The difference between the offender and the nonoffender was further blurred as a consequence of criminological research on white collar crime, including political corruption, environmental crime, governmental violations of human rights, and various other abuses of political or economic power, as well as corporate and business crime. These sophisticated forms of criminality, originating in the "respectable" areas of society, demonstrated that antisociality was not confined to the "dangerous classes." Moreover, deep antisocial attitudes were discovered to extend beyond the limits of criminal law, although jeopardizing the very basic human values protected by the criminal codes.[87] Jaques Vérin proposed in 1970 that criminology should give the first priority to studying the criminal mechanisms that were pushing modern societies to the verge of a nuclear holocaust.[88] Leading criminologists have also associated the tendency to crime with basic features of modern society. Mannheim[89] and Jean Pinatel[90] analyzed the psychosocial mechanisms that generate criminal conduct under the expressive rubric "our criminogenic society," while Schur spoke of "our criminal society."[91]

Sociological findings, combined with social and institutional criticism, led to a questioning of the very foundations of the rehabilitative idea. As the distinction between the criminal and the law-abiding citizen blurred and the criminogenic dimension of society was revealed, rehabilitation seemed tainted with a basic contradiction. There was no sense in returning offenders to the very environment that had made them criminals.

The Radical Critique

Radicals resolved this dilemma by asserting that structural changes of society were needed before any effort could be made at the individual level. The possibility of individual improvement was either denied or condemned as propping up a society that ought to be overthrown. Radical criminologists negated the whole rehabilitative issue, considering it an excuse for avoiding social change. The maligned medical model, whose shortcomings had also been cited by other critics to dismiss all forms of rehabilitation, fueled the radical attack. For instance Taylor, Walton, and Young condemned all correctionalism as "irreducibly bound up with the identification of deviance with pathology." And "correctionalism," for these writers, meant anything less than normative action toward the "abolition of the inequalities of wealth and power." This condemnation of rehabilitative action also included social reform that did not conform to their radical standards.[92] Meanwhile, criminal offenders were expected to endure unchanged conditions, just as prescribed by the conservative opponents of human perfectibility. Thus the radical solution could lead to an inaction whose main victims are the imprisoned offenders. The willingness to sacrifice human beings in the name of an ideal is characteristic of antihumanist thinking.

It is also a serious misconception of radical theories to base social change on the powerless, especially those who are deprived of their liberty. Cullen and Gilbert exposed the fragility of strategies that use prisoners as pawns in political struggle, pointing out how easily such strategies are neutralized with disciplinary measures and transfers. The end result is to worsen prisoners' personal situations considerably.[93] Moreover, the radical accusation that rehabilitation amounts to brainwashing misses the point, for it focuses on ideological content rather than on the demeaning nature of the method itself. The real flaw of a brainwashing type of rehabilitation is not the indoctrination of middle-class or any other kind of values, but the fact of attempting to manipulate the offender. Radical criticism does not aspire to eliminate psychological conditioning altogether but to replace one ideology with another. In fact, the technique of brainwashing was actually developed in countries where the radical ideology has attained its fullest realizations.[94]

No political system avoids the deep links between the basic features of modern society and serious forms of antisociality. They are less pervasive, however, in democratic societies, where the rights of the individual provide protection against the antisociality of the powerful. The psychosocial mechanisms of antisociality function unbridled under dictatorships, where subjects are easily brainwashed or controlled through terror and propaganda, and penal and psychiatric institutions are used as an instrument for the rulers' goals. In fact, recognition of the antisociality of modern societies should bolster a liberty-centered model of rehabilitation that seeks to strengthen individual rights as a bulwark against state-produced alienation.

Radical attacks on rehabilitation were intertwined with arguments derived from the criticism of particular sentencing systems or of prisons in general.[95] Radicals joined with liberals in denouncing the potential for state intrusion through the medicalization of deviance and the misuse of discretionary sentencing authorities to reflect class or racial motivations. Claims about the ineffectiveness of correctional treatment were accepted at face value by radical critics to reinforce their arguments.[96] Anti-institutional criticism also provided grounds for attacking rehabilitation, which was seen as a means to cloak the mechanisms of social control through which prisons were perpetuating unjust structures of power. As Garland and Young pointed out, radical criminology "did not provide answers.''[97] Nor did it provide a "framework which took the penal realm, rather than some general concepts of control, as an object of knowledge." Thus radical proposals lead crime policy to a dead end.

Individual Transformation as a Response

Given the criminogenic aspects of modern society and the true breadth of anti-social behavior, adjustment is an insufficient aim for rehabilitation. Many dangerous criminals are quite well adapted to society. Furthermore, to return criminals to the same society that generated their criminality could undo any individual rehabilitative effort. Thus sociological findings demand a conceptual refinement of rehabilitation. Our initial inquiry led to a liberty-centered notion of rehabilitation, in which the goal was not to inculcate a particular moral content, but to develop a pedagogy of self-determination.[98] A criminogenic society requires a pedagogy that can transform its workings at the level of individual psychology.

This quest requires shifting the rehabilitative discourse to the basic issue of human transformation—that is, the dissolution of antisocial attitudes at a psychological level. Such attitudes arose from values that create patterns of conflict and aggression. The goal must be to dissolve conditioning influences and to dismantle the stereotypes imposed by a criminogenic society, first in the rehabilitative agents themselves and by themselves. Then the psychological energy caught in such stereotyped images and ideas can be restored to the individual, generating the possibility of a new action, deeply social and creative. In proposing that we reexamine the notion of psychological change, one is not suggesting to stop providing rehabilitative opportunity at the social level. One would simply observe that if the inner solution is neglected, purely external remedies will prove ineffective in the long run, and unresolved internal conflicts will annul external accomplishments.

Who should carry out this rehabilitative task at a deeper level? To help offenders unlock their consciences, rehabilitative agents themselves need to understand the psychological determinants leading to antisocial acts. Criminologists, judges, and the correctional officers need to acknowledge that they are human beings conditioned by the same society that generated the offender. They will draw their pedagogy of freedom from the experience of their own deconditioning. A true rehabilitative task cannot merely exchange one conditioning influence for another, but must dissolve the very process of psychological conditioning through insight.[99]

A new attitude toward offenders develops when their responsibility is seen as only a particular instance of social contribution to crime. The offender is no longer a different type of human being, as Garofalo used to proclaim,[100] or a stereotyped scapegoat at the service of the emotional needs of the public. By dissolving their own internal image of the criminal, rehabilitative agents and educators can help offenders overcome their own negative image of themselves, which is a major obstacle to rehabilitation. This is also the way to prevent or reverse the criminogenic effects of the criminal justice process and of prison sentences. Otherwise the offender is crushed by their demeaning psychological impact and false moral condemnation, which are sources of many iatrogenic illnesses.

A higher concept of rehabilitation does not necessarily deny that less ambitious efforts have value. Too simplistic an affirmation of the "antisocial" character of modern societies can lead to a rejection of many traditional rehabilitative approaches, creating the risk of falling back into the sterility of pure retribution. There are several levels of antisociality, which justify those modest but necessary efforts limited to helping the individual avoid breaking the law. The simple capacity to function in society without infringing its criminal law is a valid goal for rehabilitative endeavors, which is not necessarily equivalent to coerced compliance with society's value system. It does not destroy the capacity to criticize nor does it hinder the deeper form of rehabilitation that is the specific response to the challenge of the criminogenic society. On the other hand, the transformation of the criminogenic society at the individual psychological level implies perceptual and attitudinal change in the rehabilitative agents themselves, enhancing the quality of their human services.

In the social creation of crime, as the labeling theory points out, there is an important psychological component. Conversely, a change of attitude can decisively alter the response of the partner in the rehabilitative dialogue. It is well known that hatred tends to generate hatred, just as love tends to stir loving reactions. Likewise, human beings react according to the theory with which they are approached. "If one approaches another man with a fixed 'theory' about him as an 'enemy' against whom one must defend oneself, he will respond similarly and thus one's theory will apparently be confirmed by experience."[101]

When institutionalization is unavoidable, the labeling theory can provide significant insights to improve rehabilitative policies. Awareness of the labeling process can change attitudes among criminal justice professionals. Paternalistic supervision hindering the offender's future reintegration is replaced by efforts to create a relationship of trust and mutual respect based on the award of genuine opportunity. Thus the self-fulfilling prophecy inherent in the criminal label can be tackled at different levels, of which the psychological is not the least important. This psychological action should avoid the abuses of the medical model, which led to labeling. The recognition of a right to rehabilitation is the ultimate step to overcome the harmful labeling effects of the medicalization of deviance.[102] This new perspective should encourage the creation of opportunity-changing programs and active support for the offender reentering society, to minimize the stigma associated with processing through the criminal justice system.

Social Criticism and Collective Responsibility for the Rehabilitation of the Criminal Offender

If society helps to cause crime and if convicted criminals are the scapegoat for a larger proportion of actual lawbreakers, then it can be argued that society shares in the responsibility for individual offenses.[103] This idea provides the moral basis for viewing rehabilitative undertakings as a form of compensation, with many consequences at the level of action.[104]

The awareness of collective responsibility for a way of life that creates criminality, either through positive contribution or sheer indifference, gives the word *penalty* a totally new meaning. If criminal penalties are accompanied by a true rehabilitative aspiration, they are self-assumed—that is, voluntarily taken up not only by the convicted offender, but also to a certain extent by the rehabilitative agent conscious of the unfair distribution of guilt in society. Penalty in this context does not mean punishment based on moral condemnation, but a painful task, which corresponds to one of the meanings of the Latin word *poena*. This inner work was seen by Kierkegaard as a precondition to genuine human change. ''Ideas do not change men,'' he wrote, ''knowing the cause of a passion is not enough to overcome it; one must live it, . . . in short one must work oneself over.''[105] This self-assumed task consists primarily in dismantling in oneself the psychological structure that generates the criminogenic society.

Such a pedagogical attitude, which presupposes deep self-knowledge, is the way to pay (this time in good currency) the debt that the offense creates to both the offender and society. Insofar as the members of the criminal justice system are caught in the same psychological structure of society as the offender, they have to carry out their mission by a work of self-knowing and thus of dealienation.

The Transformation of the Community as Response

Constructive social criticism led to attempts to improve rehabilitative programs and expand them to reach the community. If society itself was the culprit, it was no good to revel in paralyzing condemnation of any reformative initiative. Instead, humanistic reformers undertook the realistic task of proposing creative models to transform the criminogenic community in nuclei of lasting support for rehabilitative undertakings.

Recognition of the harm done by institutionalization spawned new forms of community-based rehabilitative efforts. Going beyond the traditional institutional extensions in the community, such as halfway houses, reformers attempted to constitute real social subsystems with their own networks of relationships.[106] In youth corrections, the significance of the community led to the development of a new model of intervention, one that not only considers the individual offender, but ''directs action toward families, peers, schools and other youth-serving groups in the community.''[107] Pioneering attempts to reform the Massachusetts training schools and their ultimate closing were led by Jerome Miller between 1969 and 1973. This effort provided the Harvard Center for Criminal Justice, directed by Lloyd Ohlin, with first-rate material to establish a policy model for future correctional change. Successive studies identified a need that later became a leitmotiv in reform-oriented policy proposals: Outreach to the community is necessary for any long-run gain. ''To ignore the youths' family, peer group, school and work opportunities," the Harvard researchers affirmed "is to abdicate genuine responsibility."[108] To succeed in their goals they proposed to improve the quality of the linkages of programs with the community, systematic work with families, schools, and the world of work.[109]

In 1981, a panel of the National Research Council identified four "loci of intervention" besides the individual.[110] The family, the school, the workplace, and the community are all contexts for intervention. To reshape the interpersonal and learning environment of the offender it is essential to work with the family and the school. Intervention at the workplace improves legitimate opportunities for work and economic viability. The panel saw the further development of group- and community-focused intervention programs as a promising strategy for crime prevention and offender rehabilitation. Elliott Currie recently stressed the importance of wider community ties in crime prevention and the need to accompany rehabilitative programs with change in opportunities and intergroup relations. In his policy proposals he focused on "the broad conditions of community life into which offenders must return and on the conditions of early life that helped propel them into the justice system in the first place."[111]

CRITICISM BASED ON THE ALLEGED INEFFECTIVENESS OF REHABILITATIVE PROGRAMS

The Relevance of Rehabilitative Effectiveness

The claim that rehabilitative programs are ineffective has been used not only as an independent argument against rehabilitative policies, but also to reinforce criticisms of a different nature. New empirical findings have now changed the direction of the intellectual tide, however. More sophisticated research has revealed serious weaknesses in the data and methodology used by the detractors of rehabilitation, undercutting their conclusion that "nothing works." The result has been a considerable improvement in evaluative disciplines, with significant effects on the quality of the new rehabilitative programs. Although no longer seen as a universal panacea, rehabilitation has been proven effective under certain conditions for certain categories of offenders. Today rehabilitation implies a differential strategy with various levels of effectiveness.

The significance of rehabilitation, however, goes beyond empirical disputes on measurable outputs. Making support for rehabilitation contingent on its effectiveness has rendered it more vulnerable to the changing moods of policymakers, based on equally transient evaluative standards. If rehabilitation is recognized as a right, its value no longer hinges exclusively on its effectiveness.

A theoretical inquiry into the relevance of effectiveness should consider rehabilitation from two perspectives: as a right of the offender and as a governmental interest. The traditional one-sided view of rehabilitation as a governmental instrument to attain social goals led to an overemphasis on the question of its effectiveness. This view was associated with an authoritarian notion of rehabilitation, in which society is the only acting force and individuals, lacking any initiative, are mere passive recipients of such action. Like deterrence or incapacitation, rehabilitation was regarded as a social policy, without consideration of the offender's personal perspective.

The rights model, in contrast, views rehabilitation from the perspective of the offender, without losing sight of its societal impact. When rehabilitation is conceived as a right, effectiveness becomes a secondary consideration and no longer encroaches on other priorities related to offenders' needs for certain minimum assistance and opportunities to maintain or improve their sociopsychological status. According to the rights model, learning activities, dialogue, social interaction, and psychotherapy are provided without calculating their likelihood of ultimate success or guaranteeing their effectiveness.

A right to rehabilitation, however, includes the right to minimum standards of seriousness and quality in the performed services. In this respect a certain degree of efficacy is inherent in any serious rehabilitative undertaking. Such efforts should be likely to improve offenders' ability to live a crime-free life, enrich their skills, or improve their psychological condition according to the state of the art in psychotherapy. But the existence and force of the right is not dependent on the cost-effectiveness of its exercise or on any particular outcome.

A right to rehabilitation, and the corresponding duty of the state to render certain services, represents only an opportunity. Rehabilitation effectiveness is ultimately contingent on decisions made by offenders themselves, which cannot be observed or quantified. It is possible to make an abstract judgment of the rehabilitative potential of certain actions, but it is extremely difficult if not impossible to correlate them with changes in the mind of the offender. Nor is it feasible to evaluate rehabilitative agents accurately, for their quality depends to a great extent on imponderable human dispositions.[112]

The difficulties of measuring personality and attitude change were underlined by Lipton, Martinson, and Wilks, who concluded that few of the studies they surveyed have clearly interpretable results.[113] Especially meaningful are their observations on the significance of "improvement" and the criteria by which it is assessed. They questioned the value of examining test scores over time, because "improvements" may result from learning the appropriate response rather than from any change in attitude and personality traits. At the same time the criteria of improvement are ambiguous. Some changes that facilitate institutional adjustment may not have the same effect outside the institution. It is also probable that a self-image developed in the institution will change significantly under the pressure of the external world.

The rate of recidivism is by and large the most tangible outcome of rehabilitative treatment, and thus apparently the variable most suitable for measurement. The concept of recidivism, however, is fraught with confusion, and many attempts to agree on a definition have failed.[114] Besides, recidivism can be the result of a variety of factors and does not necessarily indicate the failure of rehabilitation any more than mere abstention from crime means rehabilitative success.[115] Identifying rehabilitation with the mere avoidance of recidivism reduces its true dimensions and ignores its unique traits. Enhancing the human potentialities of the offender is a specific feature of rehabilitative action, which is independent of its ultimate measurable outcome.

Viewed from the perspective of society, rehabilitation is part of governmental planning and social policy. At this level evaluation plays an undeniably important role. It is a legitimate governmental concern to report tangible results to the taxpayers. But the real value of accurate evaluation goes far beyond this rendering of accounts. Improved evaluation research will provide indispensable feedback to ongoing or future rehabilitative efforts. This guiding function is essential for critical policy decisions. Empirical research on sanctions, for example, may make it possible to adopt more humane and less intrusive penal policies, if they can be shown to be as effective as harsher ones.

When rehabilitation is seen as a right of the offender, its independence from its outcome becomes evident. Obsessive questioning of its effectiveness is understandable if rehabilitation is merely a governmental interest. The rights perspective encourages a shift in the focus of concern. One will still be interested in the effectiveness of rehabilitation, but the issue will not be assigned overriding importance. Instead, one will ask how much it matters and in what ways.

Evaluative Studies Undertaken before 1974

Although correctional treatment developed considerably after World War II, scientific knowledge about its effects long remained at a much more rudimentary stage. The few studies of correctional programs that were conducted seldom included statistical evaluations or used experimental or quasi-experimental design. In many projects the subjects were not selected on a random basis, nor were representative samples used.[116] Resistance to research at the correctional level is illustrated by John P. Conrad who recalled being advised never to use that threatening word *research* when he became director of the Special Parole Unit Project in California.[117]

Examining the state of knowledge in the field of delinquency and treatment in 1959, Barbara Wooton failed to arrive at a positive conclusion but did not despair. She called for a more careful consideration of treatment policy.[118] "Humanitarian treatment," she stated, "is justified on other grounds than a greater degree of effectiveness than other measures. One thing is certain, there is absolutely no shred of evidence that humanitarian measures are any less effective, and, what is more important, they are usually less costly."

Similar conclusions were reached in 1967 by Leslie Wilkins, in a systematic survey on the effectiveness of punishment reported to the Council of Europe.[119] Treatment can only be meaningful, he argued, if considered an interaction between the treatment and the treated; such consideration must refer to a typology. This subject has been consistently taken up by later studies and has become a basic principle of current evaluative research.

Doubts about the effectiveness of correctional treatment were reinforced by increasing skepticism of psychotherapy, mistakenly thought by many to be the backbone of modern rehabilitation. Since Eysenck's seminal study of 1952,[120] continued in 1960 and 1969, suspicion had grown that many positive outcomes of psychotherapy resulted from spontaneous remission or causes independent of the treatment. In this regard Rachman affirmed that "unlike faith healing, psychotherapy is recommended and practised by professionals who have undergone scientific and critical training. This is not, however, a guarantee that its use is justified on scientific grounds."[121] Pointing out the uncertainties of treatment, Wilkins quoted the discouraging conclusion of the American Psychoanalytic Association committee established in 1950 to evaluate psychoanalytic therapy: "In order to evaluate a subject, one must first know of what the subject consists and since apparently no two individuals, not only of the Committee but of society as a whole, would agree to a definition of psychoanalysis, the Committee was at a loss to know how they were to know what they were evaluating."[122]

A landmark in psychotherapeutic revisionism was the Cambridge-Somerville study on the prevention of delinquency.[123] Some 650 boys judged likely to become delinquent were studied over a period of eight years. A randomly allocated treatment group received guidance, counseling, and individual therapy based on psychoanalytic or nondirective techniques; the other boys served as a control group. Although therapists and patients reported success, the objective evidence showed a slight difference in favor of the control group. The study sponsors concluded that the data showed that the burden of the proof of effectiveness belonged to the therapists. Yet even without clear-cut evidence of its effectiveness, psychotherapy undoubtedly provides a measure of comfort and relief for many patients.

The first major survey questioning the effectiveness of correctional treatment was published by Walter Bailey in 1966.[124] Although positive results were apparent in roughly half of 100 studies of correctional outcomes between 1940 and 1960, he questioned the reliability of the evidence supporting the efficacy of correctional treatment. Bailey criticized the fact that positive outcomes were reported by the same people who instigated research studies. Gottfredson labeled this view a "treatment destruction technique." It is a mistake, he argued, to assume that meaningful findings can only be reported by someone other than the author of the research and that self-reports are inherently suspect."[125]

Hood and Sparks's assessment rejected the overall negative conclusion reached in Bailey's survey.[126] The deficiencies of earlier programs, they argued, merely underscored the need to examine a subject also emphasized by Wilkins: the interaction between the type of treatment and the type of offender. A treatment may have different effects on different types of offenders, and what is effective in reducing recidivism for some may actually increase the chances of recidivism for others. The most remarkable study to support this view was Stuart Adams's 1961 report on the Pilot Intensive Counselling Project (PICO Project).[127] The researchers concluded that the wrong kind of therapy for certain offenders can do more harm than good. Modern treatment research has shown definitively that there are no universally valid methods that can be applied successfully to every type.

Hood and Sparks's assessment of the effectiveness of punishment and treatment also sounded a cautionary note.[128] Although they did not consider the results of past research entirely negative, they stressed the limitations of existing knowledge on the subject. They warned against broad generalizations and, quoting Wilkins, observed that they were only at a stage where "the nature of our ignorance is beginning to be revealed."[129]

Well aware of the methodological shortcomings of earlier treatment research, Hood and Sparks, nevertheless, tried to draw out some meaningful inferences. For many offenders, they concluded, probation is likely to be at least as effective in preventing recidivism as an institutional sentence, while fines and discharges are more effective than probation for first offenders and recidivists of all age groups.[130] They also determined that the offenders most likely to improve after treatment are the "medium risks." Offenders with relatively good chances of avoiding recidivism are unlikely to benefit from an intensive treatment, and persistent offenders tend to be reconvicted despite any efforts made to help them.[131] Hood and Sparks also concluded from the existing studies that, contrary to the traditional belief, longer institutional sentences were no more effective in preventing recidivism than shorter ones. Robinson and Smith determined that the longer the offender is kept locked up, "the more will he deteriorate and the more likely is it that he will recidivate." Almost certainly, they added, "releasing men from prison earlier than it is now customary in California would not increase recidivism."[132]

In their more complete and detailed analysis of the related findings, Lipton, Martinson, and Wilks concluded that there is a curvilinear relationship between the length of sentences and recidivism: "Offenders serving very short sentences and those with very long sentences have lower rates of recidivism than those offenders serving sentences of an intermediate length."[133]

The Robinson and Smith survey proclaimed that the effects of different sentencing alternatives were basically equivalent, as had also been stated by Wilkins, and Hood and Sparks. In this determination, a central role was played by the influential conclusions of Lerman regarding the ineffectiveness of the Youth Authority's Community Treatment Project.[134] This project, started in 1961, involved community treatment of juvenile offenders who would otherwise have been sent to training schools. They were matched with a control group on the basis of random allocation. The wards treated in the community group were actively supervised. The project's findings seemed very promising, showing a much higher rate of parole violation in the control groups. Lerman, however, argued that the figures were misleading, because parole agents had shown more leniency toward members of the treated group who had committed offenses of low or moderate severity than toward those in the control group. Robinson and Smith agreed that "an ideological belief in the effectiveness of community treatment apparently altered the experimental results,'' but still supported community treatment on humanitarian and economic grounds.[135]

Other negative findings surveyed by Robinson and Smith concern the poor results of intensified supervision to ensure law-abiding conduct in parolees.[136] With considerably reduced caseloads, the agents were able to discover a greater number of minor technical violations, while the overall rate of prison return was even larger than under conventional supervision. These conclusions were supported by the results of the Special Intensive Parole Unit (SIPU) project, carried out from 1954 to 1964, and of the Work Unit Program in parole approved by the California legislature in 1964. The unpublished reports on these programs were adequately summarized by Lipton, Martinson, and Wilks.[137] The experiment was designed to test the possibility of reducing the time served in prison so as to avoid the need for new prison construction in California. Selected offenders were assigned to parole officers with reduced caseloads.[138] The independent variables were the date of release (significantly advanced for some inmates) and the size of the caseload, modified at various phases of the project. The dependent variable was always recidivism, defined as return to prison for a violation of the parole agreement or for the conviction of a new offense while under parole supervision.

According to Conrad,[139] this research was probably the first to use recidivism in an attempt to test hypotheses about correctional treatment, beginning with what Martinson called the California ''recidivism-only'' tradition.[140] Conrad pointed out, moreover, that caseload size was not really a homogeneous variable, because of the different qualifications and attitudes of the parole officers and the inconsistency of supervision methods within both the experimental and the control caseloads. There was really no methodology available to understand the meaning of the variations in recidivism from caseload to caseload, and Conrad doubted if parole or any ''therapeutical relationship can be satisfactorily studied by the 'classic' control group research design.''[141] A statistically significant difference in the number of serious offenses committed by parolees in the middle-expectancy range was achieved during one phase of the experiment by a combination of weekly group therapy and some financial assistance as needed. The really important discovery made by the SIPU research, Conrad pointed out, was that although the advance of parole dates substantially reduced time served, the rate of recidivism did not increase in either the experimental or the control caseload.

Group counseling is another important field in which rehabilitation has been criticized as ineffective. This contention was supported by the well-known study of Kassebaum, Ward, and Wilner.[142] The authors used a randomized assignment procedure and an adequate control group to test the effect of group counseling in prison on postrelease behavior. They found no significant difference in outcome for those in the various treatment programs or between the treatment groups and the control group. Robinson and Smith, however, considered that an improvement in the overall quality of group counseling could have an impact on recidivism.[143] The most serious objection to the Kassebaum, Ward, and Wilner study was raised by H. C. Quay in 1977, based on the lack of integrity of the program. [144] The study neither conceptualized the treatment adequately nor described it in operational terms. Two-thirds of the counselors did not believe that group counseling could have any effect on recidivism. Worse still, they were scarcely trained and hardly supervised. Inmate participation was involuntary, groups were extremely heterogeneous, and sessions were rated negatively by their members. Even Kassebaum, Ward, and Wilner indicated that the counseling groups were unstable and that counseling was poorly conducted. These and other deficiencies of the program led Quay to forcefully dismiss its pessimistic conclusions.[145]

The Publication of Martinson's "What Works?"

Although various studies cast doubts on the effectiveness of correctional treatment, sentencing policies were not substantially affected until the publication of Robert Martinson's epoch-making article "What Works?"[146] The article was based on an impressive survey of 231 studies published in the English language from 1945 to 1967. This survey, made with the collaboration of Douglas Lipton and Judith Wilks, was published only one year later. Despite the survey's many optimistic findings, Martinson's polemical essay emphasized only its negative aspects. Moreover, in the public discussion that followed, the content of the article was too often summed up as "nothing works." This distorted conclusion quickly spread among scholars and penal theorists and was frequently cited in academic and legislative debates on sentencing and correctional reform. It soon became an easy argument to reinforce the others that were then being raised against rehabilitation.

Martinson's essay dealt only with the effects of rehabilitative treatment on recidivism although the complete survey used several other criteria as well. He recognized that the studied groups were exceedingly disparate and that what works for one kind of offender may not work for others. Furthermore, he acknowledged uncertainty about the reliability and stability of the various studies. These reservations were ignored by the adversaries of rehabilitation. Critics quoted instead what Martinson called a "bald summary" of the survey results: "With a few and isolated exceptions, the rehabilitative efforts that have been reported so far have had no appreciable effect on recidivism."[147] In his analysis of the effects of different rehabilitative methods—such as education and vocational training, individual counseling, transformation of the institutional environment, graduation of the length of sentences, medical treatment, and noninstitutional alternatives—Martinson recognized instances of total or partial success. But because he did not find a single method endowed with general efficacy, he chose to seek ways to reduce recidivism "beyond the realm of rehabilitation."[148] Martinson's optimistic hope of finding more effective means of social control within the areas of retribution and deterrence helps to explain the general derogatory spirit of his approach to rehabilitative treatment.[149]

Shortly after the publication of Martinson's influential article, an important reply came from Ted Palmer, principal investigator of the California Youth Authority Community Treatment Project.[150] He challenged the pessimistic "nothing works" conclusion on the basis of "certain positive findings and relatively optimistic observations" included in Martinson's own presentation. Palmer quoted Martinson's expressed hope that treatment of properly selected amenable subjects would be effective, references to certain offenders' amenability to treatment, programs that seemed to work under specified conditions, successful reports of noninstitutional programs, and observations on an apparent relationship between type of offender and effectiveness of treatment when analyzing the impact of milieu therapy.[151] Martinson acknowledged that psychotherapy may work under specified conditions and that treatment may depend directly on the effectiveness and type of therapist, or at least on the therapist's motivation and skill.[152] Unlike Martinson, Palmer found significance in the instances of success and partial success, which he considers valuable in informing policy decisions. He accused Martinson of overlooking the clues provided by programs that achieved a certain degree of success, especially those related to the goal of matching appropriate treatment and offender types.[153] In Palmer's view, Martinson's skeptical summary conclusion is not only inconsistent with his own findings, such as his somewhat optimistic assessment of intensive supervision,[154] but reflects a one-sided search for methods that could be recommended across the board, a hope later diagnosed by Gendreau and Ross as "panaceaphilia."[155] Martinson's article asserted that positive evaluation results were confined to a "few and isolated exceptions." But when Palmer tabulated the results for the eighty-two individual studies (90 percent of all studies) that were mentioned in Martinson's article, he found that Martinson originally had referred to thirty-nine studies as having yielded positive or partly positive results.[156] In other words, Martinson used the phrase *a few and isolated exceptions* to refer to almost half the studies.

In his heated reply, Martinson began by denying that he had "demonstrated" that nothing works in corrections.[157] The apparent inconsistency or exaggeration picked up by Palmer in the expression "few and isolated exceptions" was due to a misunderstanding, Martinson maintained. Because *The Public Interest* wanted its articles to be free of jargon, Martinson had used the word "efforts" instead of "independent variable category." He had not meant to say that few studies reported positive results, but that few independent variables ("efforts") were associated with positive outcomes. Palmer had misinterpreted "efforts" to mean "studies."

Martinson also questioned Palmer's tabulation of the percentage of successful studies. Palmer counted the findings as "if the studies were peanuts in a sack," he charged, instead of weighing the evidence by comparing the findings of one study with those of another. Recognizing the falseness of the conclusion that "nothing works" in "intervention," Martinson attempted a more accurate statement: "The addition of isolated 'treatment' elements to a system (probation, imprisonment, parole) in which a given flow of offenders has generated a gross rate of recidivism has very little effect (and, in most cases, no effect) in making this rate of recidivism better or worse."[158] As Martinson's reply makes clear, he did not dogmatically deny the effectiveness of all correctional treatment. The studies that compose the survey were rigorously selected according to several methodological standards, but represented only the beginnings of a treatment effectiveness information base. Moreover, Lipton, Martinson, and Wilks expressly warned that "it is not suggested that any of the findings set forth in this survey should serve as the sole criterion for determining or for changing present correctional practices."[159] The authors expressed considerable uncertainty regarding the effects of treatment and awareness of the insufficiency of the findings. Nevertheless their survey succeeded in developing a cohesive body of knowledge out of heterogeneous and unconnected studies of different quality and scope. Its main flaw is its paucity of theory-grounded differentiations. Although it provided helpful guidance for future treatment and research projects, its prospects of finding cumulative knowledge "were limited from the outset by failure to organize its inquiry according to causal theory."[160]

Lipton, Martinson, and Wilks organized the results of evaluative studies by classifying them into categories defined by the intersection of independent and dependent variables. The seven dependent variables used to measure the effectiveness of the treatment outcome were recidivism, institutional adjustment, vocational adjustment, educational achievement, drug and alcohol readdiction, personality and attitude change, and community adjustment. The treatment methods (independent variables) were probation, imprisonment, parole, casework and individual counseling, skill development, individual psychotherapy, group methods, milieu therapy, partial physical custody (work release or halfway houses and residential centers), medical methods, and leisure time activities.

Dependent and independent variables were arrayed along the axes of a table, with cells defined by the intersection of any two variables. The authors filled each cell with the number of findings in the survey assessing that treatment method for its effect on that particular dependent variable.[161] This exercise showed that most findings had to do with recidivism and that no research was available for some of the other treatment/outcome combinations. The authors observed that available studies were often insufficient to prove some important point, for example, the impact of milieu therapy[162] or group methods[163] on institutional adjustment; or the effect of individual counseling,[164] probation, imprisonment, or parole[165] on community adjustment. This insufficiency was all the more troubling because these variables are major ingredients in a modern rehabilitative concept. The relationship of individual psychotherapy to community adjustment was represented by only one study of limited generalizability,[166] and studies of the effect of probation and other treatment measures on vocational adjustment were also wanting.[167]

Relationships between dependent variables also merit exploration, Lipton, Martinson, and Wilks pointed out. There may be significant interactions between vocational adjustment and recidivism,[168] for example, or community adjustment and recidivism.[169] The survey found some promise in the relationship between education or vocational training and recidivism:

There is evidence that vocationally oriented training for youthful offenders (over 16) both in institutions and in the community are associated with lower rates of recidivism than standard institutional care or standard parole. These programs appear to be most successful when they provide the offender with a readily marketable skill.[170]

Although there had been surprisingly little investigation of the effects of casework and individual counseling, the authors found evidence that community counseling, particularly if designed to meet the immediate needs of the offender, appears to reduce recidivism and increase community and vocational adjustment.[171] Many hints on successful rehabilitative possibilities were presented as incentives for further investigation of each particular method.

The Lipton, Martinson, and Wilks survey provided useful leads into the actual workings of various treatment measures. A good example is the analysis of the effects of imprisonment on offenders of different ages, although the conclusions can only be "viewed as highly tentative due to the equivocal nature of the research methods employed in the studies cited."[172] The survey found that institutionalized adult first offenders have lower recidivism rates when subjected to less stringent custodial care and that probation is more effective than imprisonment in directing the offender away from new criminal offenses. If juveniles are to be institutionalized, however, it is more productive to do so under fairly restrictive conditions for approximately two years.[173] This information is useful in suggesting a focus for future research that may eventually provide data for rational policy-making.

On the other hand, because of the vital interrelation between theory and research, empirical knowledge may lead to a more accurate conceptualization. For example, empirical studies on milieu therapy have led to a definition of community adjustment as "the individual offender's ability to meet environmental pressures in what are currently defined as socially acceptable ways—for example, meeting financial pressures by finding and keeping a job."[174] Similarly, the definition of counseling as a supportive aid in daily living within the community, rather than as something instrumental in personality change, is based on empirical evaluations.[175]

In 1977, the Panel on Research on Rehabilitative Techniques was organized by the National Research Council of the National Academy of Sciences to assess the state of knowledge about the effectiveness of rehabilitation.[176] After two years of work, the panel published its first volume, reviewing the influential work of Lipton, Martinson, and Wilks, as well as the literature published since 1968 not included in that survey. After careful examination, the panel upheld the Lipton, Martinson, and Wilks survey against its critics and accepted the substance of their work. However, the conclusions of the panel were less pessimistic, especially with respect to recent evaluations and rehabilitative research.[177]

The panel strongly opposed Martinson's famous derogatory conclusions, citing the many flaws in the tests of interventions on which those conclusions were based. Their weakness and lack of integrity would have undermined their credibility even if positive results had been found. The panel believed that some interventions not yet tested might prove effective in reducing recidivism rates and quoted recent reports on interventions involving work and financial support that might have a modest impact on postrelease criminal activity.[178] It also observed that even if the studies reviewed by Martinson did not report positive rehabilitative results, the results were typically no worse than with traditional punishments. The panel indicated the possibility of choosing the less expensive alternative, when treatments are equally humane.

The panel identified two principal kinds of obstacle preventing the assessment of rehabilitative effectiveness: problems of implementation and problems of evaluation. Problems of implementation arise from the difficulties of transforming scientific conclusions on human behavior into effective treatment programs. Programs are often poorly designed or poorly implemented.[179] The main flaw in the program designs is that they lack an adequate conceptual framework and a theoretical basis, leading to exaggerated expectations of results from partial or minimal interventions. Even when program design is exemplary, the treatment may not be delivered as intended.[180] As Quay asserted, the integrity of a program implies adequate conceptualization on the basis of previous empirical evidence, sufficient duration and intensity in its application in accordance to its description, qualification of the personnel, adequate supervision, and appropriateness of the subjects chosen to receive the treatment. These conditions are absent in many of the programs studied.

In regard to the problems of evaluation, the panel argued that an adequate scientific methodology must be used to demonstrate the effectiveness of rehabilitative programs. Such a demonstration would resemble the determination of the effectiveness of health services or other aspects of human welfare.[181] A stringent assessment of rehabilitation programs would consider the interests of taxpayers, relatives of offenders, members of the criminal justice system, and the offenders themselves.[182] The panel advocated the use of "true" experiments whenever possible. It also defended the powerful methodology of "true" randomized experiments and comparison groups against ethical objections. It is precisely the ethical imperative of offering the most effective treatment that demands an assessment of its effectiveness. The panel would require strict compliance with ethical guidelines for conducting research projects with prisoners, especially in the areas of informed consent and avoidance of harm.

The panel expressed hopeful expectations regarding ongoing rehabilitative programs and innovative possibilities. It mentioned a promising program involving economic subsidies to released offenders who committed crimes against property, enabling them to survive without having to turn to criminal activities while seeking legitimate employment.[183] These outcomes are still more favorable when subsidies are complemented with vocational counseling. Such is the case of a study designed to increase employment rates and community stability of released felons in Chicago.[184] The panel urged the exploration of innovative programs, combining methods and including early interventions.

Among such new alternatives it included the "quick dip" sanction, in which offenders apprehended for the first time are briefly exposed to a maximum-security penal environment. This experience is regarded as rehabilitative rather than as a specific deterrent to the extent that it provides information rather than punishment. In this connection the panel cited a report on a "shock parole" program in Ohio that gives adult felons early and unanticipated release from prison.[185] It also underlined the need to implement the concept of restitution, closely related to rehabilitation, and to carry out research on the subject. Prison furloughs were recommended as a reliable means of rehabilitation.

Alternative sentencing possibilities, such as the "in-and-out jail therapy" are also suggested. The in-and-out approach involves successive relatively brief periods of continuous confinement, interspersed with periods of release into the community. The release periods gradually expand, unless the wrong conduct of the offender causes a return to jail and a lengthening of the periods of confinement. The real rehabilitative ingredient is the possibility of maintaining family relationships and in some cases employment and education. The maintenance of links with the community was a common trait of many of the innovative possibilities mentioned by the panel. It strongly recommended noninstitutional forms of intervention, which would probably be cost-effective even if major investments were required in their testing phases.[186]

In 1981, the Panel on Research on Rehabilitative Techniques issued a second report based on the 1979 assessment of the effectiveness of rehabilitation efforts.[187] In the second phase of its work, the panel used this knowledge to prescribe possible directions for developing new rehabilitative programs and evaluating them scientifically. It encouraged the exploration of promising extrainstitutional programs, including not only community-based corrections, but also programs designed to reach individuals not yet delinquent but at a high risk of becoming so.[188] It did not ignore the difficulties and dangers of such programs, which include their potential for expanding surveillance and control.[189]

The panel's second report insisted on the importance of a conceptual framework "making explicit the assumptions that underlie intervention efforts and making the process as rational, systematic, and incremental as possible."[190] Theory should also guide action toward rehabilitation. Social scientists should be involved in the planning of experimental programs and should acquaint administrators and practitioners with the existing bodies of relevant theory. And theory should guide the measurement of the outcomes, not only in terms of recidivism but also with respect to a program's ability to affect "relevant" intervening variables. For this purpose the panel included a comprehensive review of the most important theories of crime. It also expressed the hope that future theories would be fewer, more comprehensive, and interdisciplinary, but recognized the need for multiple theories to deal with different types of criminal and criminal behavior as well as theories specifically focusing on behavioral-change processes.[191]

In this context, Glaser established the importance of theory in correctional research evaluation practice. Such evaluation focuses only on samples relevant for a given kind of program. It concentrates on the consequences of abstract potentially policy-guiding ideas "that could be expected from a particular kind of program for a specific kind of subject."[192] Glaser warned that research that neglects theory has little long-run impact. Vice versa, theory research sampling allows one to predict with greater certainty what programs applications can be made from the results of the research, to identify from the outset concurrent research, and to make tests more rigorous.[193] The Lipton, Martinson, and Wilks survey could not contribute "to cumulative knowledge on the validity or invalidity of any correctional principle" because neither the survey nor the original studies were grounded in behavioral or social science theory.[194]

The panel also discussed the "conditioning variables" that should be considered in the design of effective rehabilitative programs.[195] Here the questions were "when," "for whom," "how much," and "under what conditions." Effective planning should take into account target populations and offender types; the strength of the treatment; the integrity with which the intervention is implemented and measured; the timing of interventions in terms of offenders' age and stage in the development of their criminal careers; and the social, environmental, legal, and ethical limits.[196]

The panel proposed a "template-matching technique" to direct rehabilitative and evaluative resources to the people most likely to benefit from treatment. The templates are sets of descriptors of the kind of people who would be expected to do best according to the theory underlying a particular rehabilitative technique. A different template could be created for each intervention. For example, the report described a template that might be used for the initial selection of candidates for a rehabilitative job-training program.[197] The people likely to gain the most from such programs would be those who do not possess marketable skills but are capable of learning the job skills to be taught, who have the motivation to learn and to seek out employment, and who are in a position to use those job skills relatively soon after acquiring them.

Some of the panel's most significant innovations were simultaneous evaluations of programs currently under way. Knowledge gained early through such evaluation could enrich the program itself. The panel suggested a model for field experimentation in which "the intervention and its evaluation are jointly developed as a single, coordinated activity designed to test one set of explicitly detailed theoretical propositions."[198] The working model, inspired by Empey, consists of five interlocking elements: definition of the project goals, with emphasis on the intermediate goals; selection of the target population; theoretical statement of the program's assumptions on why and how the goals should be attained; development of intervention and research strategies; and assessment of the implications for theory, policymakers and practitioners, and future research.[199]

To bridge the gap between rehabilitative programs and knowledge acquired through evaluative research, the panel also outlined a "strategy for incremental development and evaluation of programs that maximizes the interplay between research results and program features and their design."[200] Multiple research approaches and methodologies should be used in program development. The panel recommended the "succession evaluation" model described by Tharp and Gallimore.[201] In this approach the results of the first intervention are taken back to the planning stage to determine what might be done to improve the program. The program is then redesigned, implemented, and retested until it achieves its intended goals or proves to be unworkable.

The panel also explored new avenues of rehabilitative intervention and research beyond the institution. A better understanding of offenders' interpersonal environment should make it possible to design programs to alter their behavior by reshaping that environment. Several promising areas for intervention were analyzed in the report, each affecting a wide spectrum of individuals and groups and providing a leverage point for altering behavior.[202] These loci are the family, school, workplace, and community. In these areas, rehabilitative action conceived as a true social-learning process tends to strengthen the links of individual offenders with their socialization nuclei. These socialization strategies, not devoid of legal and ethical problems, coincide with modern trends in crime policy to act in a nonpunitive way on groups that shape the interpersonal environment of the offender.

Rehabilitation Works: New Responses to the "Nothing Works" Conclusion

Rehabilitation received new support in the late 1970s and in the 1980s. Indisputable evidence refuted the claim that "nothing works."[203] The new studies demonstrated that the quality of both treatment and research has greatly improved in recent years,[204] largely invalidating the long, heated debate based primarily on treatment-evaluation studies published before 1967.[205] With proof that some programs had worked, Ross and Gendreau concluded that "some treatment programs, when they are applied with integrity by competent practitioners to appropriate target populations, can be effective in preventing crime or reducing recidivism."[206] The assertion that no treatment can be effective is inconsistent with the basic uncertainty inherent in social sciences. To exclude offenders from the benefit of rehabilitative offerings on the basis of such dubious conclusions can hardly be regarded as scientific. In 1987 Gendreau and Ross made a comprehensive review of the abundant literature on rehabilitation since 1980, including more than 300 titles that testify eloquently to the revival of rehabilitation in both theoretical and empirical research.[207]

Farrington, Ohlin, and Wilson affirmed that randomized experiments do not show that "nothing works," but that "the effects of general help, counseling, guided group interaction, and other 'talking therapies' are not notably successful with all types of offenders, but equally these methods may be successful with some types of offenders."[208] They indicated various positive results obtained in well-designed experimental research and recommended building on those results. They also urged combining those findings with longitudinal-experimental research projects in a way that has not been attempted before.[209] One aim "involves studying the impact of interventions on specific features of criminal careers in the context of long-term information about development."[210] It is hoped that a number of these longitudinal-experimental projects will increase our knowledge about the causes, prevention, and treatment of crime.[211]

In addition to describing successful programs, better conceived or more accurately evaluated than those of the pre–1967 era, the advocates of rehabilitation identified some fundamental flaws in the underpinnings of the "nothing works" arguments. Gottfredson, for example, explored the fallacies of "treatment destruction techniques," exposing the strategies used to discredit the rehabilitative idea and to ignore many valuable results of past programs.[212] In the same spirit, Martinson acknowledged the shortcomings of his own survey. The *enfant terrible* of rehabilitation research noted in 1978 that he and his coauthors had needlessly rejected significant pieces of their mammoth work because of methodological imperfections; in effect they "threw out the baby but clung rigorously to the bath water."[213]

Gottfredson identified several pseudoscientific methods used to "prove" the ineffectiveness of any and all treatment modalities in the criminal justice system. The first is the "contamination of treatment." Because it is difficult to establish the causality between rehabilitative efforts and the desired outcome, critics can always invoke other causes to explain the successful result and thus reject any rehabilitative claims. This treatment destruction technique ignores the possibility of cumulative research capable of detecting and excluding the competing factors.

Any study is vulnerable to this sort of treatment. Because there are no universally reliable criteria, a study that has, for example, taken convictions as an indicator of illegal behavior may be attacked on the grounds that arrests would be a better indicator or vice versa. Even recent major improvements in measurement can be countered with new ambiguities. For example, any criterion of criminality may measure the behavior of social control agents as much as that of the treated. Thus it can be argued that apparently successful efforts at rehabilitation merely altered the behavior of the agents of social control. Lerman, for example, claimed that the California Community Treatment Program only influenced the labeling and social control process.[214] Gottfredson also showed that opponents of rehabilitation relied on studies that concealed the scarcity of scientifically acceptable evaluation studies on rehabilitative effectiveness—only one a year, on average, between 1940 and 1965. The effect was to exaggerate the extent of demonstrated failures in rehabilitation. Thus opponents unfairly discounted the legitimate protest of treatment advocates that rehabilitation had never been systematically tried.[215]

Despite its excesses, criticism of rehabilitation served some useful purposes. It dispelled the falsely idealistic optimism that worked against the quality of programs, and it forced evaluation research to adopt higher methodological standards. Criticism of rehabilitative programs brought the existing studies into the spotlight, revealing the difficulties of attaining accurate evaluations as well as the dangers of the prevailing inaccuracy. The result was an extraordinary development of evaluation methodology. Instead of simply determining whether a program works in an overall sense, new evaluation methods provide valuable feedback for improving ongoing programs.[216]

NOTES

1. See Jonas Robitscher, *The Powers of Psychiatry* (Boston: Houghton Mifflin, 1980), 299.

2. Ibid., 300.

3. Jessica Mitford, *Kind & Usual Punishment: The Prison Business* (New York: Vintage Books, 1974), 140.

4. Michael T. Nietzel, *Crime and Its Modification* (New York: Pergamon Press, 1979), 144.

5. The use of tranquilizers for disciplinary purposes was vividly described by Jack Abbot in an account of his own prison experiences. See Jacques Henry Abbot, *In the Belly of the Beast* (New York: Vintage Books, 1982), 42.

6. This decision, although not officially reported, is known in law books as *Kaimovitz v. Michigan Department of Public Health*. See John Monahan and Henry Steadman, *Mentally Disordered Offenders* (New York: Plenum Press, 1983), 181.

7. On the characteristics and problems posed by the new technologies of surveillance, see Gary T. Marx, *Undercover: Police Surveillance in America* (Berkeley: University of California Press, 1988), 206–33.

8. Bruce J. Winick, "Legal Limitations on Correctional Therapy and Research," *Minnesota Law Review* 65 (1981): 331–442.

9. Bruce J. Winick, "A Preliminary Analysis of Legal Limitations on Rehabilitative Alternatives to Corrections and on Correctional Research," in *New Directions in the Rehabilitation of Criminal Offenders*, ed. S. E. Martin, Lee B. Sechrest, and R. Redner (Washington, D.C.: National Academy Press, 1981), 330–38.

10. Robert R. Ross and Bryan McKay, "Behavioral Approaches to Treatment in Corrections: Requiem for a Panacea," in *Effective Correctional Treatment*, ed. R. R. Ross and P. Gendreau (Toronto: Butterworths, 1980), 40.

11. Ibid., 43.

12. Ibid., 39.

13. Ibid., 45.

14. Ibid.

15. Robitscher, *The Powers of Psychiatry*, 300.

16. Clonce v. Richardson 379 F.Supp. 338 (1974).

17. Nietzel, *Crime and Its Modification*, 238.

18. Ibid., 181.

19. See pp. 38–41.

20. On the exaggeration of such abuses, see Francis T. Cullen and Karen E. Gilbert, *Reaffirming Rehabilitation* (Cincinnati, Ohio: Anderson, 1982), 162.

21. Alan M. Dershowitz, "Indeterminate Confinement: Letting the Therapy Fit the Harm," *University of Pennsylvania Law Review* 123 (1974): 303.

22. See pp. 120–35.

23. See pp. 14–16.

24. See Gernot Schubert, *Feuerbachs Entwurf zu einem Strafgesetzuch für das Königreich Bayern aus dem Jahre 1824* (Berlin: Duncker & Humblot, 1978), 63, 240.

25. See p. 51.

26. Marc Ancel, *The Indeterminate Sentence* (New York: United Nations, Department of Social Affairs, 1954).

27. Dershowitz, "Indeterminate Confinement," 298.

28. Ibid., 306.

29. See pp. 40–41.

30. *Struggle for Justice: A Report on Crime and Punishment Prepared for the American Friends Service Committee* (New York: Hill & Wang, 1971), 28.

31. David Rothman, *Conscience and Convenience: The Asylum and Its Alternatives in Progressive America* (Boston: Little, Brown, 1980), 173.

32. Ibid., 194.

33. George Jackson, *Soledad Brother, The Prison Letters of George Jackson* (New York: Coward-McCann, 1970).

34. See *Struggle for Justice*.

35. Ibid., 27.

36. Norval Morris, *The End of Imprisonment* (Chicago: University of Chicago Press, 1974), 33.

37. Ibid., 43.

38. Ibid., 50.

39. Miriam Reich, "Therapeutic Implications of the Indeterminate Sentence," *Issues in Criminology* 2(1) (1966): 8.

40. Ibid., 7.

41. Ibid., 24.

42. Ibid., 26.

43. Ibid., 24.

44. Ibid., 26.

45. Marc Ancel, *La défense sociale nouvelle* (Paris: Cujas, 1981), 249–56.

46. Arthur Kaufmann, "Dogmatische und kriminalpolitische Aspekte des Schuldgedankes im Strafrecht," *Juristenzeitung* (1967): 556.

47. See p. 68.

48. Heinz Schöch et al., "Rettet die sozialtherapeutische Anstalt als Massregel der Besserung und Sicherung!" *Zeitschrift für Rechtspolitik* 8 (1982): 207–12.

49. James Vorenberg, "Narrowing the Discretion of Criminal Justice Officials," *Duke Law Journal* (Sept. 1976): 651, 663.

50. See p. 8.

51. On the blurring in practice of the distinction between an authoritarian therapeutic

concept and punishment, see Herbert Packer, *The Limits of the Criminal Sanction* (Stanford, Calif.: Stanford University Press, 1968), 29.

52. See pp. 8–9.

53. Edgardo Rotman, "Latest Trends in Crime Policy and Their Effect on Sentencing," in *New Trends on Criminal Policy* (Proceedings of the Fifth International Colloquium), ed. International Penal and Penitentiary Foundation (Bonn: International Penal and Penitentiary Foundation, 1984), 75.

54. See reports on criminal victimization in Günther Arzt, *Der Ruf nach Recht und Ordnung* (Tübingen: J.C.B. Mohr, 1976), 30–33.

55. Arzt, *Der Ruf nach Recht und Ordnung*, 68.

56. Michael Sherman and Gordon Hawkins, *Imprisonment in America* (Chicago: University of Chicago Press, 1981), 18.

57. James O. Finckenauer, "Crime as a National Political Issue: 1964–76" *Crime and Delinquency* 24 (Jan. 1978): 13–27.

58. Francis A. Allen, *The Decline of the Rehabilitative Ideal: Penal Policy and Social Purpose* (New Haven, Conn.: Yale University Press, 1981), 38.

59. Ibid., 26.

60. Edgardo Rotman, "Latest Trends in Crime Policy," 75.

61. Arzt, *Der Ruf nach Recht und Ordnung*, 64.

62. Ibid., 65.

63. Ibid. See also Kevin N. Wright, *The Great American Crime Myth* (Westport, Conn.: Greenwood Press, 1985), who examined how the media distort and overdramatize crime information. He questioned the assertion that crime is becoming quantitatively and qualitatively worse.

64. Cesare Beccaria, *Dei delitti e delle penne* (Florence: Le Monnier, 1945), 231–38.

65. Andrew Rutheford, *Prisons and the Process of Justice* (London: Heinemann, 1984), 94.

66. George Ives, *A History of Penal Methods* (Montclair, N.J.: Patterson Smith, 1970), 188–94.

67. Jeremy Bentham, *Panopticon or the Inspection House: Postcript*, Part II (London, 1791), 7.

68. English Poor Law Commissioners' 1834 statement, quoted by Neil Gilbert and Harry Specht, *Dimensions of Social Welfare Policy* (Englewood Cliffs, N.J.: Prentice-Hall, 1974), 41.

69. Hermann Mannheim, *The Dilemma of Penal Reform* (London: George Allen and Unwin, 1939), 70.

70. Ibid., 71.

71. *Proceedings of the Eleventh International Penal and Penitentiary Congress* (English ed.) (n.p., 1937), 135.

72. Mannheim, *The Dilemma of Penal Reform*, 68.

73. Ibid., 71.

74. Ibid., 70.

75. Albert Lautman, *Essai sur l'unité des sciences mathématiques dans leur développement actuel* (Paris: Union Generale des Éditions, 1977), 239, 240.

76. Pierre Curie, quoted in ibid., 240.

77. In this regard, Cressey tried to adapt Sutherland's differential association theory

to treatment. See Donald R. Cressey, *Delinquency, Crime and Differential Association* (The Hague: Martin Nijhoff, 1964).

78. See David Garland and Peter Young, "Durkheim's Theory of Punishment: A Critique," in *The Power to Punish: Contemporary Penalty and Social Analysis*, ed. D. Garland and P. Young (London: Heinemann Educational Books, 1983), 56. For a different interpretation of the link between determinism and rehabilitation, see Michael R. Gottfredson, "The Social Scientist and Rehabilitative Crime Policy," *Criminology* 20 (May 1982): 29, 31.

79. Robert K. Merton, *Social Theory and Social Structure* (London: Free Press, 1964), 131.

80. R. A. Cloward and L. Ohlin, *Delinquency and Opportunity: A Theory of Delinquent Gangs* (New York: Free Press, 1960).

81. Frank Tannebaum, *Crime and the Community* (New York: Columbia University Press, 1938), 19.

82. Edwin M. Lemert, *Social Pathology: A Systematic Approach to the Theory of Sociopathic Behavior* (New York: McGraw-Hill, 1951).

83. See Edwin Sutherland, *White Collar Crime* (New York: Holt, Rinehart and Winston, 1967), 3–10.

84. Manuel Lopez Rey, *Crime, An Analytical Appraisal* (London, 1970), 99 and Chaps. 1, 2.

85. See Klaus Luderssen, *Strafrecht und "Dunkelziffer"* (Tübingen: J.C.B. Mohr, 1972) and Dennis Chapman, *Sociology and the Stereotype of the Criminal* (London: Tavistock, 1968).

86. See Arno Plack, *Pladoyer für die Abschaffung des Strafrechts* (Munich: Paul List, 1974).

87. Edgardo Rotman, "Le sens de l'individualisation judiciaire," *Revue de science criminelle et de droit pénal compare* (1977): 437–44.

88. Jacques Vérin, "Les critères de priorité en matière de recherche criminologique," *Revue de science criminelle et de droit pénal compare* (1970): 909.

89. Hermann Mannheim, *Comparative Criminology* (London: Routlege and Kegan Paul, 1970), II:419.

90. Jean Pinatel, *La société criminogène* (Paris: Calmann-Levy, 1971).

91. Edwin M. Schur, *Our Criminal Society: The Social and Legal Sources of Crime in America* (Englewood Cliffs, N.J.: Prentice-Hall, 1969).

92. Ian Taylor, Paul Walton, and Jock Young, *The New Criminology: For a Social Theory of Deviance* (New York: Harper, 1974), 281–82.

93. Cullen and Gilbert, *Reaffirming Rehabilitation*, 288–92.

94. Ibid., 289.

95. See Erik Olin Wright, *The Politics of Punishment* (New York: Harper & Row, 1973).

96. Günther Kaiser, "Strafrechtssoziologie—Dimension oder Partitur der Kriminologie," *MschrKrim* (1979): 58.

97. David Garland and Peter Young, "Towards a Social Analysis of Penalty" in *The Power to Punish*, ed. D. Garland and P. Young (London: Heinemann Educational Books, 1983), 7.

98. See p. 7.

99. Edgardo Rotman, "Las técnicas de individualización judicial frente a un moderno concepto de resocialización," *Revista de derecho penal y criminología* (1972): 115.

100. Ricardo Garofalo, *Criminología* (Madrid: La Espana Moderna), 342.

101. David Bohm, *Wholeness and the Implicate Order* (London: Ark Paperbacks, 1980), 6.

102. See p. 69.

103. On the origin of this idea see Peter Noll, *Die Etische Begründung der Strafe* (Tübingen: J.C.B. Mohr, 1962), 14.

104. Edgardo Rotman, "L'évolution de la pensée juridique sur le but de la sanction pénale," *Aspects nouveaux de la pensée juridique (Hommage à Marc Ancel)* (Paris: Pedone, 1975), 175.

105. Soren Kierkegaard, quoted in Jean-Paul Sartre, *The Search for a Method* (New York: Alfred A. Knopf, 1963), 12.

106. R. B. Coates, A. D. Miller, and L. Ohlin, *Diversity in a Youth Correctional System: Handling Delinquents in Massachusetts* (Cambridge, Mass.: Ballinger, 1978), 6.

107. Ibid., 10.

108. Ibid., 178.

109. Ibid., 182–86.

110. Susan E. Martin, Lee B. Sechrest, and Robin Redner, eds., *New Directions in the Rehabilitation of Criminal Offenders* (Washington, D.C.: National Research Council, National Academy of Sciences, 1981), 135.

111. Elliot Currie, *Confronting Crime: An American Challenge* (New York: Pantheon, 1985), 244.

112. Peter W. Greenwood and Franklin E. Zimring, *One More Chance: The Pursuit of Promising Intervention Strategies for Chronic Juvenile Offenders* (Santa Monica, Calif.: Rand Corporation, 1985), R–3214–OJJDP and Edgardo Rotman, "Le sens de l'individualisation judiciaire," 440.

113. Douglas Lipton, Robert Martinson, and Judith Wilks, *The Effectiveness of Correctional Treatment: A Survey of Treatment Evaluation Studies* (New York: Praeger, 1975), 621.

114. *Summary of the Proceedings of the Third International Congress on Criminology* (London: The Organizing Committee, 1957), 11.

115. Ancel, *La défense sociale nouvelle*, 325.

116. Paul Gendreau and Robert R. Ross, "Effective Correctional Treatment: Bibliotherapy for Cynics," in *Effective Correctional Treatment*, ed. Robert R. Ross and Paul Gendreau (Toronto: Butterworths, 1980), 6.

117. John P. Conrad, "A Lost Ideal, a New Hope: The Way Toward Effective Correctional Treatment," *The Journal of Criminal Law & Criminology* 72(4) (1981): 1711.

118. Barbara Wooton, *Social Science and Social Pathology* (London: Allen & Unwin, 1959).

119. Leslie T. Wilkins, "A Survey of the Field from the Standpoint of Facts and Figures," in *The Effectiveness of Punishment and Other Measures of Treatment* (Council of Europe: Strasbourg, 1967), 81.

120. H. J. Eisenck, "The Effects of Psychotherapy: An Evaluation," *Journal of Consulting Psychology* 16 (1952): 319.

121. S. Rachman, *The Effects of Psychotherapy* (Oxford: Pergamon Press, 1971), 1.

122. Wilkins, "A Survey of the Field," 25.

123. Edwin Powers and Helen Witmer, *An Experiment in the Prevention of Delinquency: The Cambridge-Somerville Youth Study* (New York: Columbia University Press, 1951).

124. Walter C. Bailey, "An Evaluation of 100 Studies of Correctional Outcome," *Journal of Criminal Law, Criminology and Police Science*, 57 (June 1966): 153–60.

125. Michael R. Gottfredson, "Treatment Destruction Techniques," in *Effective Correctional Treatment*, ed. Robert R. Ross and Paul Gendreau, (Toronto: Butterworths, 1980), 69.

126. Roger Hood and Richard Sparks, *Key Issues in Criminology* (London: Weidenfeld and Nicolson, 1970), 192.

127. Stuart Adams, "Interaction Between Individual Interview Therapy and Treatment Amenability in Older Youth Authority Wards," in *Inquiries Concerning Kinds of Treatment for Kinds of Delinquents*, ed. California Board of Corrections (Sacramento, Calif., 1961).

128. Hood and Sparks, *Key Issues*, 171.

129. Ibid., 25.

130. Ibid., 186, 88.

131. Ibid., 191.

132. James Robison and Gerald Smith, "The Effectiveness of Correctional Programs," *Crime and Delinquency* 17 (Jan. 1971): 72.

133. Lipton, Martinson, and Wilks, *The Effectiveness of Correctional Treatment*, 81.

134. P. Lerman, "Evaluating the Outcome of Institutions for Delinquents," *Social Work* (July 1968).

135. Robison and Smith, "The Effectiveness of Correctional Programs," 69, 70.

136. Ibid., 76.

137. Lipton, Martinson, and Wilks, *The Effectiveness of Correctional Treatment*, 116–64.

138. Conrad, "A Lost Ideal, a New Hope," 1711.

139. Ibid., 1712.

140. Robert Martinson, "California Research at the Crossroads," *Crime and Delinquency* 22 (Apr. 1976): 180–91.

141. Conrad, "A Lost Ideal, a New Hope," 1712.

142. G. Kassebaum, D. Ward, and D. Wilner, *Prison Treatment and Parole Survival* (New York: Wiley, 1971).

143. Robison and Smith, "The Effectiveness of Correctional Programs," 74.

144. H. C. Quay, "The Three Faces of Evaluation: What Can Be Expected to Work," *Criminal Justice and Behavior* 4 (1977): 341–54.

145. See Gendreau and Ross, "Effective Correctional Treatment," 7 and Martin, Sechrest, and Redner, *New Directions*, 40, 41.

146. Robert Martinson: "What Works? Questions and Answers about Prison Reform," *Public Interest* 35 (Spring 1974): 22–56.

147. Ibid., 25.

148. Ibid., 49.

149. Ibid., 50.

150. Ted Palmer, "Martinson Revisited," *Journal of Research in Crime and Delinquency* 22 (July 1976): 133–52.

151. Ibid., 133, 134.

152. Ibid., 136. The quality of rehabilitative agents and their degree of commitment

are hardly quantifiable elements, demonstrating the difficulties of measuring rehabilitative effectiveness. See note 112.

153. Ibid., 137.

154. Ibid., 136, 138.

155. Paul Gendreau and Robert Ross, "Offender Rehabilitation: The Appeal of Success," *Federal Probation* 45 (Dec. 1981): 45, 46.

156. Palmer, "Martinson Revisited," 142.

157. Robert Martinson, "California Research" 180–91.

158. Ibid., 190.

159. Lipton, Martinson, and Wilks, *The Effectiveness of Correctional Treatment*, 4.

160. Daniel Glaser, "Concern with Theory in Correctional Evaluation Research," *Crime and Delinquency* 23 (Apr. 1977): 177.

161. Lipton, Martinson, and Wilks, *The Effectiveness of Correctional Treatment*, 7.

162. Ibid., 320.

163. Ibid., 311.

164. Ibid., 488.

165. Ibid., 490.

166. Ibid., 499.

167. Ibid., 334.

168. Ibid., 337.

169. Ibid., 507.

170. Ibid., 194.

171. Ibid., 574.

172. Ibid., 519.

173. Ibid.

174. Ibid., 506.

175. Ibid., 178.

176. Lee Sechrest, Susan O. White, and Elizabeth D. Brown, "Introduction," in *The Rehabilitation of Criminal Offenders: Problems and Prospects*, ed. L. Sechrest, S. O. White, and E. Brown (Washington, D.C.: National Academy of Sciences, 1979).

177. D. P. Farrington, L. E. Ohlin, and J. Q. Wilson, *Understanding and Controlling Crime: Toward a New Research Strategy* (New York: Springer, 1986), 123.

178. Sechrest, White, and Brown, *The Rehabilitation of Criminal Offenders*, 32.

179. Ibid., 35, 37.

180. Ibid., 40.

181. Ibid., 54.

182. Ibid., 55.

183. Ibid., 88.

184. Ibid., 89.

185. Ibid., 92.

186. Ibid., 94, 95, 96.

187. Martin, Sechrest, and Redner, *New Directions*.

188. Ibid., 12.

189. D. F. Greenberg, "Problems in Community Corrections," *Issues in Criminology* 10 (Spring 1975): 1–33.

190. Martin, Sechrest, and Redner, *New Directions*, 30.

191. Ibid., 35, 36, 79.

192. Daniel Glaser, "Concern with Theory," 175.

193. Ibid., 176.

194. Ibid., 177.

195. Martin, Sechrest, and Redner, *New Directions*, 80.

196. Ibid.

197. Ibid., 81.

198. Ibid., 103.

199. L. T. Empey, "Field Experimentation in Criminal Justice: Rationale and Design," in *Handbook of Criminal Justice Evaluation*, ed. M. W. Klein and D. S. Teilmann (Beverly Hills, Calif.: Sage, 1980).

200. Martin, Sechrest, and Redner, *New Directions*, 103, 112, 113.

201. R. G. Tharp and R. Gallimore, "The Ecology of Program Research and Evaluation: A Model of Succession Evaluation," in *Evaluation Studies Review Annual*, Vol. 4, ed. L. Sechrest, M. Philips, R. Redner, S. West, and W. Yeaton (Beverly Hills, Calif.: Sage, 1979).

202. Martin, Sechrest, and Redner, *New Directions*, 135.

203. Gendreau and Ross described some of the most effective programs conducted between 1973 and 1978, citing ninety-five studies reporting success in treatment of antisocial behavior, based predominantly on a social-learning approach, in "Effective Correctional Treatment," 13.

204. Robert R. Ross and Paul Gendreau, eds., *Effective Correctional Treatment* (Toronto: Butterworths, 1980), xiv.

205. Gendreau and Ross, "Effective Correctional Treatment," 4.

206. Ross and Gendreau, *Effective Correctional Treatment*, xiii.

207. Paul Gendreau and Robert R. Ross, "Revivification of Rehabilitation: Evidence from the 1980s," *Justice Quarterly* 4, no. 3 (Sept. 1987): 349–407.

208. Farrington, Ohlin, and Wilson, *Understanding and Controlling Crime*, 93.

209. Ibid., 94.

210. Ibid., 152.

211. Ibid., 176.

212. Michael R. Gottfredson, "Treatment Destruction Techniques," 55.

213. "Martinson Attacks His Own Earlier Work," *Criminal Justice Newsletter*, Dec. 4, 1978, 4.

214. Paul Lerman, quoted by Gottfredson, "Treatment Destruction Techniques," 60.

215. Ibid., 61.

216. Ronald Roesch and Raymond P. Corrado, "Evaluation and Criminal Justice Policy," in *Evaluation and Criminal Justice Policy*, ed. R. Roesch and R. P. Corrado (Beverly Hills, Calif.: Sage, 1981), 9.

5
Rehabilitation: How It Works

REHABILITATION AND IMPRISONMENT

Rehabilitation and the Crisis of Imprisonment

Prisons were originally designed as multifunctional devices serving the various preventive and retributive goals sought by penal sanctions. In practice these aspirations have largely failed, and the effectiveness of prisons has been challenged at every level. Moreover, imprisonment has been increasingly denounced for its harmful and counterproductive effects. Today, one hears little idealistic rhetoric about prisons, and there is a growing interest in investigating what they actually are. It is important for this purpose to determine the meaning of freedom deprivation and concomitant deprivation phenomena.

Prison means first and foremost deprivation of time through the imposition of an alien time, often mutilating a substantial part of the inmate's life span. Dostoyevski made this point eloquently by titling his account of his own life as a convict *Memoirs from the House of the Dead*.[1] In fact, the value of time in freedom has increased in modern democratic societies because of improvements in the standard of living, making the penalty of imprisonment more grievous than in the past. The value of time as a commodity in the industrial world is reflected in the concern for its precise measurement. (Rothman finds the stopwatch emblematic of this unprecedented emphasis on time.[2]) In fact, deprivation of freedom became the normal form of criminal sanction only when individual freedom rose significantly in the market of social values.[3]

Imprisonment uproots inmates from their network of social relationships, including family, friends, and workmates, depriving them of the choice of companionship. Deprivation of space is another important aspect of incarceration, particularly given the modern overcrowding of prisons. Gerhard Mueller asserted that imprisonment is always cruel and unusual, because it entails "caging" human beings, whose natural instincts for ranging and roaming require satisfaction as much as the hunger drive or the sexual urge.[4] Furthermore, the sociological study of total institutions revealed new forms of deprivation. Prisons have been exposed as places of psychological deformation, loss of self-esteem and initiative, and depersonalization. In this atmosphere of constant coercion and intimidation, inmates not only lose their self-determination but are socialized into antagonistic subcultures based on values markedly more violent and authoritarian than those of the external society.

The realization that prisons as such do not rehabilitate precipitated a crisis of confidence in rehabilitation, especially in those countries where the myth of prison rehabilitation had the strongest influence on sentencing practices.[5] The utter demise of the old monastic belief in the reformative value of incarceration per se prepared a rebirth of rehabilitation, however. A renewed concept of rehabilitation, according to the humanistic model, no longer relies on imprisonment to attain its goals.[6] It is rather a counteractive force to imprisonment, creating duties on the part of the state to neutralize the unwarranted negative effects of freedom deprivation. The provision of appropriate human services and the opportunity for social reintegration after release not only heals excessive and illegal wounds of imprisonment, but protects both offenders and society from prison-related recidivism. Furthermore, rehabilitation becomes a prisoner's right reinforcing all the others, preventing human deterioration, and keeping punishment within its legal and constitutional limits. On the other hand, rehabilitative effort to prepare the inmate for release is recognized as crucial. It is at this stage, modern research suggests, that the key to rehabilitative effectiveness is to be found.[7]

Not even the staunchest critics of imprisonment deny that it is necessary for at least a small circle of extremely dangerous offenders.[8] It is, therefore, important not only to neutralize the desocializing effects of imprisonment, but also to develop some kind of positive action to help inmates to lead a crime-free life in the community. Experiments with mentally disordered offenders offer an important contribution to this enterprise. Although abuses have been committed in the past under the pretext of therapy, certain recent undertakings in social learning should inspire corrections as a whole.[9] The transformation of the institutional environment and the structure of interpersonal relations inside the prison are legitimate rehabilitative goals. It is also valid to help prisoners to become aware of their inner states and to deal with them in other ways than antisocial acting out. Moreover, there is no false pretense in educating the inmate for a future life in freedom without further lawbreaking. The social-therapeutic attempts to overcome the abyss of distrust, hate, and fear that separates the staff and inmates, transforming each side's images and stereotypes of the other, should be encouraged. A social-learning environment also helps to counteract the depersonalizing effect of the institution, to fortify the social links of the inmates, and to create within the institution's walls a society of mutual cooperation, resembling life outside the prison as much as possible.

Deprivation of liberty through coercive state actions seems in principle foreign to the complex and highly delicate human task of facilitating the change of the offender for the better. In this sense the expression *prison rehabilitation* compounds two antithetical concepts. Paradoxically, however, the very fact of imprisonment creates the need to rehabilitate the inmate from its own desocializing influence. Basic human deprivation and the ravages of imprisonment demand a strong compensatory rehabilitative action. Moreover, as sociologists have shown, modern prison environments are extremely complex. Besides having shattering effects on the personality of inmates, some modern American megaprisons have become an amplified version of social conflict and anomie, influenced by gang cultures developed outside the walls of the penitentiaries. New sociopedagogical actions and strategies will have to be developed beyond rehabilitative efforts to neutralize the wave of organized violence from inside and outside the prison. This systemic action must eventually come to grips with the extreme antisociality wildly growing today in modern urban centers. The new language and socializing action must counteract the jungle-law criteria that now influence an important segment of the population of correctional institutions.

Rehabilitation and the Aims of the Correctional System

Today most prisons do not rehabilitate; when they occasionally do, this is not their specific purpose. The purposes of imprisonment are to punish criminal offenders, to incapacitate them, or both. Still, rehabilitation is the overriding aim of a progressive correctional system. The distinction between the purpose of imprisonment and the aims of a correctional system can be understood by examining the housing and sustenance of the inmates. One cannot seriously maintain that the purpose of a prison sentence is to provide offenders with housing or food services. But such services are an unavoidable and costly issue for the correctional system. Likewise, people are not sentenced to be rehabilitated. But the correctional system cannot ignore the fact of their future reentry into society. From the viewpoint of both society and offenders, there is an overriding interest to avoid the prisoners' deterioration and to make it possible for them to lead law-abiding lives in the future. In fact, the most-advanced rehabilitative model regards such an opportunity as an offender's right, worthy of constitutional standing.[10]

The specific function of corrections is to process and carry out prison sentences. For a modern and democratic correctional system, however, the way this function is performed is crucial. Beyond administering the punishment prescribed by the sentencing authorities, corrections must assume responsibility for protecting inmates' bodily and psychological integrity and providing for basic educational and developmental needs inherent in their human condition. The aim of a progressive correctional system is to build on its basic penal function to preserve human life in every respect consistent with the required deprivation of freedom. This means in the first place the creation of a rehabilitative atmosphere, which presupposes a series of positive duties that have their correlate in the rights of prisoners. A minimally decent environment, security, medical assistance, recreation, and fair treatment are not only prerequisites for whatever programs a correctional institution may offer, but are part of the rehabilitative offering itself. Thus the rehabilitative potential of a prison is indissolubly linked to the maintenance of certain standards in the rest of the prison system. The chance of a successful future return into the free society requires not only specific programs, but also an environment that can counteract the deteriorating effects of freedom deprivation.

However problematic rehabilitation may appear in many penal systems, the difficulties of the task do not diminish its urgency or justify hopeless surrender to the sterility of merely repressive social control. To dismiss all possibility of improving the rehabilitative potential of present-day prisons is as unreasonable as yesterday's affirmation of the rehabilitative value of incarceration per se.

Rehabilitation and Discipline

The creation of a rehabilitative prison atmosphere serves the interests of both the state and the offender. The state is interested in maintaining discipline and order and avoiding riots and violence. All these perils considerably diminish when the institution is oriented toward the rehabilitation of its inmates. Rehabilitation-centered institutions tend to create a problem-solving atmosphere that helps to tackle other critical aspects of prison life. At the same time, the inmate benefits not only from the programs themselves but also from the prison standards that make them possible. For example, a skill-enhancing program can hardly be offered in a climate of continuous conflict and violence. Thus a clean and secure atmosphere, free from the danger of personal assault, helps both inmates and staff.

The concurrent interest of state and prisoners in rehabilitation creates the risk of slipping from a liberty-centered model of rehabilitation into an authoritarian one. Discipline may be confused with rehabilitation, or rehabilitation may be imposed in order to achieve discipline. A liberty-centered model of rehabilitation does not exclude a common area of interest shared by the inmates and the staff, and certainly benefits from institutional peace. But although rehabilitation facilitates order and security, it should by no means be confused with such order and security. A liberty-centered concept of rehabilitation is not made of the same stuff as is imprisonment. The former is life enhancing, whereas freedom deprivation is a reduction of a central ingredient of human life. Rehabilitation is perverted when it is invoked to curtail rights and to coerce. The authoritarian model can be identified by its potential for increasing serfdom. A liberty-centered model, in contrast, tends to relax the strictures of prison deprivation through furloughs, anticipated release, and other forms of trusting the inmates and making them self-responsible. The epitome of liberty-centered forms of institutional rehabilitation is the open prison. Furthermore, the heart of modern rehabilitation lies in the community, quite independent from institutionalization. In fact, rehabilitative opportunity flowers much better outside of than within the prison walls.

Although rehabilitation should not be used as a pretext to maintain prison discipline, it is true that demoralized prison staff, unless performing a humanly worthwhile mission, will have to rely on violent coercion for the accomplishment of their custodial task. This attitude inevitably aggravates deep institutional conflicts. As long as the aim of a rehabilitative venture remains focused on enhancing the future life prospects of the individual offender, its tangential use to improve intrainstitutional human relations does not infringe the aspiration of a liberty-centered model. The relationship between rehabilitation and discipline varies according to the size and characteristics of the institution. In a social-therapeutic establishment discipline flows from the very structure of the establishment, with a minimum need for coercion and state control.[11] In the mammoth violence-ridden penitentiaries, on the other hand, an increase of state control is inevitable and, paradoxical as it may sound, should be welcomed in certain cases on purely humanitarian grounds. If staff involvement reduces the number of murders and rapes in inmate-run establishments, the strict disciplinarian approach may be more humane than the anarchical reign of aggression and self-administered justice. If human beings have to be incarcerated at all, they should be prevented at all costs from killing each other. But the real answer is a rehabilitation-oriented correctional activity that would exclude the sources of prison violence.

Rehabilitation and the Length of Prison Sentences

The conflict between prison and rehabilitation was first addressed in the struggle against short-term prison sentences that raged at the end of last century and recurred during the 1960s, leading to important legislative reforms. As the result of the prevailing retributive considerations, penal codes of the last century (such as the French code of 1810, the Bavarian penal code of 1813, the Prussian penal code of 1851, and the German penal code of 1871) provided for extremely short terms of imprisonment, some of only a few days. The German official statistics for 1884 show that 68.5 percent of all convicted recidivists had previously served sentences not longer than three months.[12] In 1886, prison sentences amounted to 66.87 percent of all effectively applied sanctions. Of these, 80 percent were under three months long, 20 percent of three or more months' duration, and 96 percent of less than one year.[13]

Rehabilitation was used as an important argument in the fight against short-term prison sentences. Although these sanctions were deemed to have no chance of exerting an educational or reformative influence or a significant deterrent effect, they damaged offenders irreparably, cutting them loose from their social context, breaking their work and family relationships, and exposing them to the criminogenic influence of other inmates. Von Liszt was a champion of the crusade against short-term prison sentences. In effect, because this type of sanction was so predominant, his criticism became an indictment of the entire prison system. Von Liszt wrote in 1889, ''Our whole system of criminal law today is based almost exclusively on short prison sentences. From that we can further conclude that if the short-term prison sentences are not effective, our whole criminal law system today is worthless.''[14] His rejection of imprisonment was not total, because he believed in its reformative efficacy when it lasted long enough to influence the criminal.

The fight against short-term prison sentences generated valuable alternatives to imprisonment, namely fines and suspended sentences. True success of this policy came only in 1969, when the first law of reform of the penal code of the Federal Republic of Germany (FRG), inspired by the still more advanced Alternative Draft, substantially altered the lower limit of prison terms.[15] The minimum term of imprisonment was raised to one month, and prison sentences of less than six months were reserved exclusively for cases in which ''special circumstances concerning the offense or the personality of the offender render confinement indispensable to influence the offender or protect the legal order.''[16] This reform, which considerably diminished the rate of imprisonment in the FRG, came at a time when the rehabilitative concept that inspired it was on the wane, especially in Sweden and the United States. The penal philosophy of ''just deserts,'' a new bottle for the old retributive wine, led to a rebirth of short-term prison sentences. The new just deserts theories were right to consider that long-term imprisonment per se was not more rehabilitative than the maligned short-term sentences. In fact, the length of exposure increases the risks of deterioration and criminal contagion.

In the 1950s, the idea emerged of an exceptional use of short-term prison sentences as a psychological shock, which was presumed to have rehabilitative consequences. This amounted to a limited return to the idea of the *poena medicinalis*. The idea was embodied in what English penologists called the ''sharp short shock.'' In fact, the effects of this type of sanction are primarily deterrent, rather than rehabilitative. Modern policymakers have proposed such penalties for white-collar crime offenses, whose perpetrators were presumed to be more sensitive to the shame and social discredit inherent in a prison sentence.[17] This strategy not only uses the short stay in prison as a specific deterrent, but also uses the abstract threat of imprisonment as a form of general prevention. In Scandinavia, current policy rejected the ''treatment ideology'' and related indeterminate sentencing. There, short-term prison sentences are now incorporated in a penal system believed to be more progressive and humane.[18] In the Netherlands, the belief that longer sentences mean less chance of rehabilitation led to a preference for short custodial sentences, to make clear that certain kinds of conduct are unacceptable.[19]

The rehabilitative aim also inspired new policies against excessively long prison sentences. Roxin observed that "after criminological experiences, it is an unquestionable fact that with the exception of some rare and atypical cases, convicted offenders should not remain incarcerated more than ten years or fifteen at the most. Whoever remains incarcerated for a longer period loses all possibility of social reorientation and falls into ruinous psychological atrophy."[20] Accordingly, the 1966 Alternative Draft Penal Code established a maximum of fifteen years for penal sanctions entailing temporary deprivation of freedom and considerably liberalized the conditions for parole.[21] Even life imprisonment—still a sentencing option—could be suspended with probation. Roxin saw these rules as arising from the conviction that the state's mission is not to destroy a human being and that many of the more serious crimes are perpetrated in a conflictive situation that is very unlikely to repeat itself.[22]

The rehabilitative aim has also improved the legal structure of imprisonment by gradually eliminating earlier forms of penal servitude, hard labor, and defamatory forms of freedom deprivation. As Feuerbach noted, forced labor in public sites deprived the prisoner of all feelings of dignity, eroding the impulse toward reform and return to an orderly and productive life.[23]

Liberty-Centered Corrections

Realistic rehabilitative efforts within the prison environment should begin with a clear perception of their concrete field of action. Each particular prison system offers its own obstacles and footholds to such efforts, and many sociological, legal, architectural, technical, and economical factors must be considered in each case. At the same time, prisons have some common traits that should shape broad rehabilitative policies. Participation in rehabilitative activities can be an antidote against the loss of self-determination and the depersonalization inherent in total institutions. Combating social isolation and affective annihilation should also be a top priority. The breach of social bonds makes it more difficult for the offender to attain a law-abiding lifestyle in the future. In this regard, the structure of the prison can be modified so as to create propitious rehabilitative channels. The opening of the prison, both inwardly and outwardly, is a cornerstone of recent penal reform.[24] This effort ranges from the encouragement of visitation to the actual open prison, in which all the elements are oriented toward freedom. The inmate should also be supported at the educational, work, and social assistance levels.

A basic principle of modern corrections, directly linked with rehabilitation, is to replicate in prison, as far as possible, the conditions of life outside the prison. Some modern prisons house both men and women, and inmates may be directly responsible for their cooking and shopping, as in the modern Danish establishment of Ringe.[25] All inmates' activities can be tailored so as to prepare them for their life after prison and to counteract the loss of self-respect and initiative and other factors that tend to stultify prisoners and deal with them as objects.

The entire rehabilitative aim is at stake in prison work. The belief that making men work would render them honest goes back as far as Voltaire and Howard and underlays the reformative goals of the early houses of corrections.[26] The abyss between this alluring aspiration and prison realities has proven very difficult to bridge. In practice the idea of work as punishment, inherent in many forms of forced labor and penal servitude of the past, tended to prevail over the more generous reformative ends. The very idea of imprisonment is explained by Thorsten Sellin, developing an idea of Radbruch, as a form of exploitation of cheap labor.[27]

In modern correctional policies, work has a predominantly rehabilitative content. As de la Cuesta Arzamendi pointed out in his thorough study of the subject, work is a decisive element in building a penitentiary regime consonant with the rehabilitative aim.[28] Labor is an indispensable element in restructuring the prison so as to minimize its evils and bolster rehabilitative undertakings. Work relates the closed universe of the prison to the demands and economic realities of the society outside. Thus it is a useful instrument for bringing prison life closer to the open environment.

The rehabilitative potential of prison work depends to a high degree on its integration with free labor in its broad economic function.[29] Prison work should be meaningful, useful, productive, realistic, and should meet the requirements of the market.[30] Moreover, it should improve the economic prospects of inmates after their release.[31] Educational and formative in nature, rehabilitative prison work is a way to learn how to work.

As in the era when labor was devised as a purely afflictive component of imprisonment, most prison regulations require inmates to work. However, insofar as work is considered a rehabilitative instrument and not a means of punishment, it should not be obligatory. As de la Cuesta Arzamendi rightly held, incentives may be offered to perform rehabilitative prison work, just as occurs in the free labor market; as far as possible the external market's structure of rights and duties should be maintained.[32] The Spanish Constitution of 1978 not only expressly forbids forced labor for prisoners, but also introduced a right to remunerated work and social security benefits for convicted offenders.[33] However, the General Organic Penitentiary Law of 1979 maintained a prisoner's duty to work. The right to work is especially difficult to implement in times of unemployment, because public opinion generally adheres to the Benthamite principle of "less eligibility," believing that prison conditions should not be more favorable than those of life in freedom.[34]

MODEL PRISONS

Ringe

Ringe prison in Denmark is the foremost current experiment in prison rehabilitation. The meaning of rehabilitation has changed since the days when the ideology of treatment prevailed. The new concept emerged from a sobering and fruitful process of rejecting old abuses and recognizing the undesirable nature of imprisonment. Punishment is acknowledged as the only justification for such detrimental measures as prison sentences. The Danish legislation enacted in 1973 states explicitly that punishment is the goal of sanctions entailing the deprivation of liberty. Such reforms are a reaction against the indeterminate sentence and the underlying abusive therapeutic model prevailing in the past. At the same time, the rejection of the medical myth and its dangerous corollaries makes it possible to face the grim realities of imprisonment directly and counteract them. Thus a new form of rehabilitation emerges, whose goal is to reduce the noxiousness of imprisonment and to prepare inmates to live as normal members of society after their release.

Ringe prison is a good example of what Dünkel called opening the prison inwardly.[35] Inside the prison, inmates have a high degree of locomotive freedom and such typical ingredients of prison security as bars and armored glass are absent. This is nevertheless a closed maximum-security prison, thanks to an inconspicuous surrounding wall and a sophisticated video system. The prison is built on a plateau, in such a way that the surrounding walls are sunk in a depression of the terrain, permitting pleasant views of the scenery from many parts of the building. The walls are also camouflaged from the outside with buildings and vegetation. The workshops and a gymnasium intended also for the neighboring population stand outside the walled perimeter and are reached through a passage from the main building.

The main prison building is divided into six wings connected to an ample common corridor, which on the opposite side communicates with a large auditorium. Five of the wings each contain sixteen rooms, whereas the sixth has ten rooms and an infirmary. The total capacity of the prison is ninety inmates. During my visit in September 1983 there were close to seventy inmates, of whom approximately twenty were women. The prison was originally planned for juvenile offenders, but the 1973 law reform repealed all special measures for juveniles. The present population is made up of young adult offenders between twenty and twenty-five years old and women who do not qualify for open prisons.

The general principle in Denmark is that all sentences should be served in open prisons.[36] Assignment to a closed prison depends on the nature and importance of the crime and the length of the sentence. It is also mandated for cases of drug addiction or distribution of drugs and for offenders who have violated the obligations of open prisons. The abandonment of the therapeutic model is mirrored in the fact that the main criterion of selection for men is age, not abnormality or personality disturbances. Another selection criterion, implicitly reflecting dangerousness, is nonqualification for open prisons. This rule applies to both sexes.

The counteractive model of rehabilitation is embodied in the idea of approximating the conditions of the outer world as far as possible. Each week an employee of a local bank gives inmates cash, including the wages earned in the workshops and a basic allowance for subsistence. There is no central kitchen in the establishment; inmates must purchase their own food in a branch of a local supermarket functioning inside the prison and cook it in their own housing units. (Food for the ill and for those being punished in an isolation section is brought from a neighboring prison.) The prisoners must prepare their own budgets. If they run out of cash, no advance loans are made and they must depend on the solidarity of their fellow prisoners. All these strategies are intended to develop a sense of responsibility in the inmates. Whenever possible, they are expected to carry out by themselves all the necessary steps and procedures before administrative, labor, and employment agencies. No social workers are permanently employed by the institution, and they are only occasionally assigned for situations that cannot be handled by the inmates themselves. This policy aims to avoid a social welfare mentality and to encourage self-reliance.

Another consequence of the rejection of the therapeutic model is the deprofessionalization of the staff. The "standard officers" concentrate on the functions of prison guards, work instructors, and counselors. This counseling is not performed psychotherapeutically, but at the level of the reasonable man or woman. It includes helping the inmates with problems arising from their social life and in preparing for their release. The standard officers can be assigned to any function, from group leader in the living units to carpentry instructor in the furniture factory.[37] Specialization is deliberately avoided to prevent the usual conflicts between custodial and therapeutic staff or with work instructors. With only a few exceptions, the people hired as standard officers have no previous work experience in prisons. The ratio of staff to inmates is about 0.7 to 1, as in open prisons, whereas in other closed Danish prisons the ratio is 1.4 to 1.

A striking feature of Ringe for foreign observers is the experiment of mixing the male and female populations. However, as Rotthaus pointed out, this practice should be considered as merely an extension of conjugal visits, which are a matter of course in Danish corrections.[38] Women inmates occupy two of the wings in approximately the same proportion as men. Social and sexual intercourse between the inmates occurs on a regular basis. Staff members intervene only to prevent forced relationships or any kind of exploitation between the sexes. Contraceptives are sold in the prison supermarket. From the viewpoint of discipline, the system has worked smoothly, and participants seem to be less aggressive and more polite than in other institutions.

As its director Erik Andersen observed, there is a flow of new ideas at Ringe, especially concerning work.[39] This keeps the pioneering spirit alive. Inmates constructed a solar-receiving system, for example. Andersen did not believe in treatment, which, combined with indeterminate sentencing, results in a form of manipulation,[40] but believed that "inmates leave Ringe less bitter toward society, and that may, indirectly, have some effect on rehabilitation."[41] The rehabilitative significance of Ringe is underlined by Hans Toch in his discussion with Andersen.

You described some strong relationships between your guards and your inmates and the feelings of loyalty that the guards have. You described a staff culture that supports the

inmates. You described the strong commitment to building responsibility and normalization. And you noted that these inmates become so heavily involved in their work that
they continue to work beyond what is required. You even described giving the inmates
a sense of completion in meaningful tasks. Why is it that you refuse to concede the
possibility that what you're doing may have an impact that surpasses the experience of
prisonization? Is it a matter of semantics?[42]

"You provide more treatment than Butner does, but they call what you do
treatment," he continued.[43] In the same discussion, John Conrad, after questioning the applicability of the Ringe experiment to the United States, conceded,
"I agree with you; we have to start trying. I think one of the evils of our present
situation in this country is that, because of misadventures, because of disillu-
sionment, because of explosive ideas, we stopped trying."[44]

Ringe prison is the most tangible expression of the recent transformation of
the rehabilitative concept. The new concept is not considered applicable to
offenders with diminished responsibility, such as those arising from immaturity
or mental disturbance, thus excluding the traditional idea of treatment inherent
in the biomedical model. Inmates are deemed to be fully responsible, and the
goal of their imprisonment is punishment. However, rehabilitation plays an
important role insofar as staff members are supposed to keep in close contact
with the inmates, become aware of their problems, and help them overcome
their difficulties in coping with life in freedom.[45] This counseling is not carried
out by high-level, specialized therapists, however, but by average staff members.
In this way inmates are prompted to work out by themselves the practical solutions
to their problems. Rotthaus emphasized the living groups as the key to the Ringe
success and more generally as a major asset in modern social therapy.[46]

The Federal Correctional Institution at Butner, North Carolina

The Federal Correctional Institution at Butner, North Carolina, is an excellent
example of a noncoercive concept of rehabilitation. Inspired by Norval Morris's
idea of facilitated change, this model institution made voluntary rehabilitation
possible.[47] Butner's population consists of three groups: a research population
of chronic and violent offenders, a mental health population of inmates in need
of psychiatric diagnosis and treatment, and a general population of inmates to
be released in the Carolinas and surrounding states. Program participation is
independent from the inmate's release date, and inmates in the research population maintain their privilege of opting out. When they choose to stay in the
institution they participate in planning their own programs and can rely on a
supportive atmosphere that makes rehabilitative efforts meaningful.

Butner offers a wide range of educational, recreational, and training programs.
But, as Ingram stated, "the uniqueness of Butner revolves around the institutional
atmosphere rather than any single program."[48] The institution maintains a rehabilitative atmosphere that reduces coercion, grants responsibility to the in-

mates, increases communication with the staff, respects privacy, and, at the same time, offers realistic opportunities. Allowing a human ventilation of conflicts also makes the environment safer—an important prerequisite for the success of any rehabilitative attempts. With Butner, the Federal Bureau of Prisons actually sought "to create a safe and humane environment which was conducive to change and to finding new and more effective ways of providing correctional programs for offenders."[49]

Although located in the countryside, the institution is fairly close to urban areas and university centers. A visitor receives an extremely positive first impression. A barbed wire perimeter is the only outward sign that this is a prison. Inside, Butner feels like an open prison. A pleasing architectural design complements the natural environment, with a view of the surrounding woods. Inmates are allowed to move freely during the day and to wear civilian clothes. The atmosphere is cheerful, reminiscent of both college campuses and modern industrial parks. Reflecting the bureau's functional unit concept, the institution is composed of two clusters of housing: three mental health housing units, and four correctional program units. Although overcrowding is a potential threat to Butner's high standards—its current population of about 700 is 50 percent above design capacity—the institution's special characteristics seem to make the problem less taxing than in other prisons.[50]

Imprisonment at Butner proceeds through three phases: orientation; a continuation phase, in which the inmate chooses, within certain limitations, his work or self-improvement activities; and a graduated-release program, with increased levels of independent functioning. The emphasis is put on the inmates' taking responsibility for themselves. The prisoner, "aware of release date and of a graduated release plan can focus his attention on acquiring self-knowledge and self-control."[51] Individualized contracts between staff and inmates establish their duties and rights, anticipating furloughs and community programs. Craig T. Love, Jane G. Allgood, and F. P. Sam Samples, in their evaluation of Butner's optional programming aspect, wrote, "It has been clearly demonstrated that a group of sophisticated and dangerous offenders can be successfully housed in an environment predicated on the concept of humane incarceration which includes emphasis on individual rights and freedom as part of the confinement."[52] The evaluation also reported more program participation and fewer disciplinary problems than are typical of similar inmates in other institutions.

REHABILITATION IN THE COMMUNITY

The idea of rehabilitation encompasses not only efforts to improve the institutionalized offender's sociopsychological situation, but also the search for noninstitutional alternatives. Such arrangements avoid the desocializing effects of imprisonment and allow the use of the existing community resources to make the offender better able to lead a law-abiding life. Community corrections can be defined negatively, as encompassing all the varieties of state reaction against crime *other than* institutional confinement. In addition to the traditional exits from the criminal justice system—probation, parole, and suspended sentences—this would include more recent innovations such as diversion in the narrow sense or community service.

The free community offers a better terrain than institutional settings for rehabilitative initiatives. An uncoerced environment largely avoids flaws such as stigmatization, depersonalization, isolation, and many forms of alienation inherent in institutions. Assistance, therapy, and education may achieve remarkably favorable results when supported by the community in a free environment. The community possesses a variety of rehabilitative resources that can never be matched by the limited opportunities that are offered by even the best institutions. Furthermore, a well-designed community corrections program helps to reduce prison overcrowding and to free financial resources to improve the overall rehabilitative potential of the correctional system. It also helps to develop the social responsibility of community members, involving them in vital aspects of crime prevention. Rehabilitation in the community is at the heart of humanistic and liberty-centered crime policies, offering the rehabilitative agent the possibility of dialogue without the constraints of freedom deprivation. In fact, it was a constructive spirit of forgiveness and reconciliation that motivated the first modern experiments in dealing with the offender in the community, represented by the institution of probation.

In many countries there is an unfortunate tendency to expand state intervention through sanctions originally conceived as alternatives to imprisonment into areas of human conduct otherwise considered private. A liberty-centered concept of rehabilitation can never support such a ''net-widening'' or ''net-straying'' effect, particularly if rehabilitation is recognized as a right.[53] Within a liberty-centered crime policy, imprisonment is the last resort of state reaction against crime. Accordingly, genuine community corrections replaces imprisonment and is never taken as a pretext to extend the sphere of state intervention beyond the indispensable minimum.

If rehabilitation is seen as a right, it cannot be used as a pretext to impose restrictions greater than are essential to further legitimate governmental interests. Rather, the recognition of a right to rehabilitation implies the use of the least restrictive setting, minimal intrusion, and the least drastic methods by which legislative aims can be achieved. This principle is tantamount to a right to rehabilitation in the community. It is also consistent with a sentencing system in which alternative sanctions are substituted for imprisonment whenever objective legal conditions are met, according to procedural safeguards of fair treatment and equality. Thus parallel to a right to rehabilitation in the least restrictive setting, there is also, at the sentencing level, an implicit right to the least restrictive sanction legally available (i.e., a right to probation, to community service, or to a fine).

Humanistic rehabilitation coexists with imprisonment and institutional discipline, while countering its harmful effects. In the same way community alternatives to imprisonment coexist with a certain degree of surveillance and control. To the extent that these nonincarcerative sanctions substitute for institutional confinement, they are a mitigated continuation of its security and disciplinary functions. They thus generate duties for offenders, restrictions to their freedom, and coercive requirements, whose fulfillment is supervised or controlled by the state. But the supervision and control in community alternatives should never be confused with the genuine rehabilitative opportunity that is concurrently offered nor should they be justified as forms of forced ''rehabilitation.'' Their true rationale is to maintain the general preventive function of criminal punishment or to protect the public against potentially dangerous offenders. Punishment or control, whether retributive, incapacitative, or deterrent, has to be justified in its own right and carefully distinguished from the offer of voluntary rehabilitative opportunities.

Rehabilitation plays a preeminent role in the design and enactment of nonincarcerative criminal sanctions. At the legislative level, concern for rehabilitation favors the enactment of sanctions that do as little damage as possible to the offender's personality while accomplishing their punitive goals. Fines, community service, and restitution impose economic or time deprivations that do not necessarily affect the process of socialization as imprisonment does. Quite the contrary, they offer the opportunity to raise the social awareness of convicted offenders and allow them to come to terms with society.

In many European countries, the fine has become the most important alternative to short-term and even to medium-term imprisonment.[54] A particularly successful form is the day-fine system, which takes into account both the seriousness of the offense and the financial capacity of the offender. The judge sentences the offender to a certain number of units proportionate to the gravity of the offense and calculates the value of the fine unit according to the financial means of the particular offender. The Vera Institute of New York has been carrying out comparative research since 1980 to adapt the day-fine system to American courts. In 1986 a day-fine system was designed for the Richmond County Criminal Court (Staten Island, New York), to be applied after mid–1988 by the Richmond County judges and the district attorney's office, to replace fixed fines and other sanctions.[55]

At the policy-making and legislative levels, rehabilitative considerations will support the expansion as far as possible of the legal conditions for eligibility for community-based programs. At the sentencing level, rehabilitative considerations may also lead the sentencing authority to choose a less desocializing sanction, when such choice is made possible by a given sentencing system. However, the notion of rehabilitation as a right will curtail such discretionary powers of the sentencing authority, instead making the community alternatives mandatory when predetermined objective conditions are met.

Advocates of community-based rehabilitation should guard against viewing the community as a panacea. Just as earlier reformers were mesmerized by the idea of the asylum, some advocates are lost in an idyllic dream of the virtues

of the community. With the anti-institutional ideology that developed in the mid–
1960s, the community was seen as "the opposite of alienation, estrangement,
rootlessness, loss of attachment, disintegration of the social bond."[56] This image
of the community can lead to the naive assumption that deviance can be overcome
by the mere elimination of institutions, with their labeling and stigmatization.
Indeed, the community by itself does not necessarily become an effective instrument of human transformation. It can also be oppressive, authoritarian, or
even deadly as in the Guyana mass suicides of 1978. Similarly, chain gangs put
inmates to work outside the prison walls, but did not produce the kind of relationships with the community that are the goal of community-based corrections.[57]

To provide an operative concept of community for correctional efforts, it is
essential to focus on the quality of community relationships. Coates, Miller, and
Ohlin defined community as "the smallest local territory that incorporates a
network of relationships providing most of the goods and services required by
persons living within the boundaries of the territory." This implies a network
of relationships that would surpass neighborhood boundaries without necessarily
reaching the size of a metropolitan area. The essence of a community-based
program lies in its linkages with the network of relationships that make up a
community.[58] The first step toward using an actual community as a correctional
means is to scrutinize it carefully to determine its degree of cohesion, educational
and moral resources, and criminogenic potential. A rehabilitation-oriented community requires not only specific forms of interaction and participation, but also
certain positive attitudes of trust and cooperation on the part of individual members. In other words, the rehabilitative attempt should be supported by a true
community, understood as a body of interrelational and reciprocal assistance.
No rehabilitative program can hope to achieve long-term effects without opening
itself to community interactions and engaging in problems and relationships that
await the offender after release into unsupervised life in the community.[59]

Probation

Probation was the first device to open the community to rehabilitative efforts.
The specific rehabilitative function of probation consists in avoiding the harms
of prisons while actively guiding and training the offender. Probation orders
usually require the probationer to participate in activities of high rehabilitative
value. Thus probation introduced a range of constructive possibilities, from
apprenticeship to a trade to outpatient psychotherapy. All in all, probation is
today an essential element of a rehabilitation-centered criminal justice system.

The first modern, systematic probation experiment began in Boston in 1841.
After its early philanthropic stage, probation was taken over by the state and
professionalized officers typically replaced unsalaried volunteers. Today, however, volunteers are increasingly supplementing probation programs. Probation
became widely practiced in the United States during the progressive era. Statutory
legislation on probation began in Massachusetts in 1878 and later spread to other

states, mainly between 1900 and 1920. Most statutes determined the criteria for granting probation, defined the duties and responsibilities of the probation officer, organized the presentence investigation, and defined the conditions of probation and of its revocation. The role of the probation officer was initially one of constructive friendship, which included gaining the trust of the offender, encouraging his progress and initiative, and securing his employment. After World War I the emphasis on psychological treatment led to an alternate model of the probation officer as social worker.[60] Today the probation officer is seen primarily as a broker for social services or a community resources manager.

Statistics show very positive results in the early years of probation. In Boston among 2,803 persons sentenced to probation between 1879 and 1883, there were only forty-four cases of recidivism.[61] After the widespread judicial application of probation during the progressive era, results were less encouraging. Probation staff lacked adequate qualifications and training; too few in number, probation officers had to carry an unreasonably heavy caseload. Probation in practice has been criticized on several grounds. It was alleged that offenders who are relatively well adjusted socially are more likely to qualify for probation, while its benefits are denied to those suffering from extreme economic and cultural deprivation. In addition, some see probation as extending state supervision to persons who would otherwise have remained in the community without surveillance. However, the most frequent criticism of probation has to do with the inaction of overworked probation officers.

None of these flaws is beyond correction with proper criminal justice planning, legal regulations, and administrative and judicial controls. The rehabilitative significance of probation justifies all efforts toward improvement. Probation is premised on the idea of maintaining or reintegrating offenders into the community, strengthening their social contacts, helping them improve their social and working skills, and allowing the support of significant social institutions such as the family, school, and employers. Today, when institutional resources are strained by prison overcrowding, probation is all the more essential. Moreover, probation is a fruitful field for creative innovation. Two examples are "shock probation," which combines a short-term incarceration with increased use of probation, and probation subsidies, by which probation activities are funded with the costs saved by reducing incarceration.[62]

The most recent development is intensive probation supervision, which considerably increases the supervision of the probationer in the community and is often combined with community service orders. Although this form of probation is only at an initial stage, ongoing evaluations in Georgia, New Jersey, and Massachusetts yielded some promising results.[63] The heightened concern for community protection does not preclude a parallel rehabilitative function.[64] If the probation officer is totally involved in surveillance, of course, he or she may have little time left to serve as an advocate or counsel for the probationer. But the two functions are not inherently incompatible and could be accomplished by separate agencies or through distribution of functions within one organization.

One must remember, however, that supervision, controls, restrictions to freedom, and coercive requirements are not rehabilitation. To identify the two functions with each other would be much the same mistake as confusing imprisonment with rehabilitation. Rehabilitation in community-based alternatives coexists with supervision just as it coexists with prison discipline and deprivation of liberty in institutional sanctions. Supervisory effectiveness is essential for the survival and expansion of community-based programs that genuinely replace imprisonment. In this regard, by guaranteeing the avoidance of imprisonment the very intensity of supervision contributes indirectly to the achievement of the primary goals of humanistic rehabilitative policies.

Suspended Sentence

The suspended sentence is another early alternative to modern imprisonment. It interrupts the punitive reaction, giving the individual offender a chance to abide by the law without the execution of retributive punishment. Initially, the warning and reprimand implicit in a suspended sentence were deemed to have enough preventive force to make further punishment unnecessary. Unlike probation, this sanction did not originally provide for active rehabilitative measures. Suspended sentences emerged as a humanitarian means of avoiding pointless sufferings and preventing the desocialization of the socially adjusted offender. In Europe, they became a central feature of the crime-policy movement of the late nineteenth century. They functioned as a powerful instrument to individualize penal sanctions: indeed, Saleilles declared that they entailed the highest degree of individualization.

A major breakthrough in European penal legislation, the suspended sentence was the Continental equivalent to probation, modifying the retributive principle and introducing some flexibility into the crime-punishment equation. Originally drafted in France by Berenguer in 1881, the suspended sentence was first introduced into positive law in Belgium in 1888, as the result of the initiative of Lejeune. It was seen as a major instrument in the fight against short-term prison sentences, which were considered not only harmful to offenders and their relatives, but also lacking in preventive value for occasional offenders, who would probably not recidivate in any case. Berenguer considered that for such offenders, whose crime was due to exceptional circumstances, a sense of honor and a healthy fear of prison were enough and the threat of punishment could be as effective as its actual execution. The value of the warning or admonition, advocated by Bonneville de Marsaigny, had already been recognized in nineteenth-century legislation.[65]

In general, sentences may be suspended when the offender has no previous convictions and the rehabilitative prognosis is favorable. Such prognosis is really a disguised judgment on the dangerousness of the candidate. From a liberty-centered perspective, the decision to suspend a sentence should be based on predetermined objective requirements, not left to judicial discretion. The various legal forms of suspended sentence usually encompass a series of conditions with which the defendant must comply during a certain period of time; suspension is revoked in the case of noncompliance. The most common conditions are that the offender maintain a fixed place of residence; avoid bars, pubs, and gambling establishments; and pursue professional instruction or work.

Suspended sentences can become instruments of increased punishment, and a tool conceived as a brake can easily turn out to be an accelerator.[66] This aggravating effect results from employing a suspended sentence rather than a fine, thus making imprisonment mandatory after a second conviction. In addition, judges, who know they are expected to suspend relatively short sentences, have sometimes imposed longer sentences to ensure that the offenders were imprisoned.

New functions were added to suspended sentences, especially after World War I, under the influence of Anglo-American probation. The introduction of orders and instructions implied a more active rehabilitative role, which also meant a greater degree of supervision. In this way, with the addition of probation, suspended sentences came to serve multiple functions, although the basic structure was different from that of Anglo-American probation. In 1967 through a process of reciprocal influence, England adopted the Continental institution of suspended sentences, while maintaining its practice of probation. Both devices coexist in the progressive Swedish penal code of 1962. Belgium, the first country to enact a law on suspended sentences, today practices four sentencing variations, according to a 1964 law. The sentencing decision may be simply suspended (with or without probation); alternatively, the sentence may be pronounced but its execution suspended (with or without probation). Marc Ancel indicates three stages in the relationship between suspended sentence and probation: total divorce, increasing influence of probation on suspended sentence, and differentiated coexistence.[67]

On the basis of rehabilitative considerations, the 1975 reform of the Penal Code of the FRG expanded the scope of the conditional suspended sentence with probation. This measure was introduced in 1953. Following the French-Belgian model, it called for pronouncement of the sentence and suspension only of its execution. Provisions for probationary orders and the appointment of a probation officer were inspired by the Anglo-American model. The suspended sentence in the FRG was originally limited to offenders who had been sentenced only once in the previous five years and to a prison term not exceeding six months. After the 1975 reform, the mere existence of a prior sentence was no longer considered an obstacle in itself, and the upper limit for sentences that could be suspended was raised to two years. However, the "protection of the legal order" can be invoked as an obstacle to suspending sentences between six and twelve months. Thus in certain cases the upholding of legal values and the general preventive component are given priority over the rehabilitative aim. Rehabilitative considerations seem less important in the legal regulations concerning the criminal records. A conviction and sentence remain recorded even when, after five years of probation, the sentence is canceled. In the more progressive Alternative Draft, the cancellation is retrospective and the conviction is expunged from the records in order to favor rehabilitation.

The institutions of suspended sentence and probation embody two distinct concepts of rehabilitation. The suspended sentence basically relies on the responsibility and conscience of the offender. It is a reformulation of the legal threat to a particular individual, who is assumed to be capable of acting according to the values that inform criminal law norms and also apt to be deterred by the possibility of imprisonment. A suspended sentence has rehabilitative value in the negative sense, by preventing the desocializing influence of short-term incarceration. In addition, as Jescheck underlined, it has a sociopedagogical effect, impelling the convicted offender to assume the task of integrating into the order of the community.[68] Probation, in contrast, involves active support of the offender's social reintegration, through assistance and guidance during the difficult probationary period.

Community Service and Restitution

Besides the traditional alternatives to imprisonment, community service sentences and restitution have achieved remarkable rehabilitative success. In community service orders, noninstitutional punishment is combined with positive interaction with the community.

European countries' recent introduction of community service orders is an innovation of particular significance for the reform of the American criminal justice system. The spectacular success of community service in the last few years is particularly surprising in view of the high rates of unemployment in Europe.[69] There is, however, a strong pragmatic motivation for favoring community service and noncustodial sanctions in general: the increasing overcrowding of prisons. Although overcrowding has not reached the alarming proportions we see in the United States, it has exhausted the capacity of available institutions. Even in countries such as the Netherlands, with a traditionally low prison population, the increase of crime rates, especially in drug trafficking, has created an urgent problem of diminished prison capacity. In short, there is a growing awareness in Europe of the financial impossibility of addressing the challenge of increasing criminality by increasing prison capacity.

Another reason for the widespread acceptance of community service is the need to create a more favorable basis for rehabilitation. In 1976 the Committee of Ministers of the Council of Europe adopted a resolution asking its member states to study various new alternatives to prison sentences with a view to their possible incorporation into national legislation. In particular, states were asked to look into the advantages of community work, which allows offenders to make amends by doing community service and allows the community to contribute to rehabilitation by accepting their cooperation in voluntary work.

England led the way with the Criminal Justice Act of 1972, introducing community service sentences among other innovations. In time, this legislation became a model for English-speaking countries and for a number of European countries. Community service is a penal sanction, requiring the performance of unsalaried work under the supervision of a specialized officer or other appointed person. As with day training centers, also established by the 1972 act, the punitive ingredient resides in the restriction of free time. Not only are the harmful effects of imprisonment avoided, but the sanction has strong rehabilitative potential derived from the creation of contacts and interaction with the community. Its effectiveness depends on the presence of actively committed persons in the community and a positive social attitude and disposition toward this type of service.[70] Unlike the traditional social casework approach of probation, community service is an ability-oriented mode of rehabilitation, performed in the full view of the community, with a fixed and limited content and clearly defined objectives.[71]

Community service has rapidly expanded in England and Wales. In 1980 it was used in 4 percent of cases involving adult indictable offenders, and 8 percent of cases involving young adults aged seventeen to twenty-one.[72] In the Criminal Justice Bill of 1981–1982 it was extended to juvenile offenders aged sixteen. From England, where it was first used as an independent penal measure, it was exported to several Canadian provinces, Australia, New Zealand, and the United States, where it is used in some states as a form of nonstatutory pretrial and presentence diversion.[73] There has been no national survey of community service programs in the United States, although a 1977 study of the U.S. Law Enforcement Assistance Administration (LEAA) contains important information.[74]

Community service orders are an exceptionally successful combination of punishment (the loss of free time) and rehabilitation (the encouragement of a constructive occupation of leisure, the creation of regular working habits, and the development of social responsibility). Through meaningful social participation, this sanction reduces the estrangement of the individual from society.[75] It is cost efficient and offers a direct benefit to society, through charitable and constructive services. Community service should be designed strictly as an alternative to imprisonment and used only in cases where coercive state intervention is required. In practice, community service has not always achieved these goals, which should be related to a general policy of decarceration.[76]

In the Netherlands, community service was started under experimental conditions in 1981.[77] Its explicit goal was to replace short prison sentences (up to six months). The modalities most frequently used during this experimental phase were the postponement of judgment (with specification of penalty) and community service in the context of pardon. At the beginning, no more than 150 hours could be imposed, to be completed within six months. The limit was later raised to 240 hours. Research carried out during the experiment showed that community service was successful in replacing prison sentences of six months or less. It was used for offenses more serious than those for which fines were imposed, but less serious than those for which short-term prison sentences were imposed. Half of the community service offenses were property offenses, 25 percent were traffic offenses, and only about 10 percent were acts of aggression or personal violence. The community service experiments were carried out under adequate supervision, and research provided persuasive evidence that the program could work, winning support among members of the judiciary and the criminal justice system who had initially opposed the idea.

A draft bill written in 1985 gives legal basis to community service in the Netherlands. Its main aim remains the same as that of the experiments: reduction of the number of short-term prison sentences. The community service order is to be a penalty in its own right, consisting of an agreement to carry out work within a period of six months for the benefit of a private or public agency, institution, or service such as neighborhood centers, hospitals, homes for the, elderly, sporting clubs, forestry, environmental protection institutions, schools, and churches. The maximum number of hours is 240, with the number of hours a day to be negotiated between the offender and the institution where the unpaid work will be done. When suspension of a sentence of imprisonment of less than six months is revoked, the judge may impose a community service order instead of requiring that the sentence be served. A third form of community service, within the framework of a conditional pardon, was foreseen in a separate draft bill of pardon. In no case can the judge impose a community service order without the express consent of the accused, because §4 of the European Convention on Human Rights prohibits the imposition of forced labor as a penalty. To some extent, community service is seen as a right of the offender, because the judge cannot arbitrarily reject an offer of community service by the accused and must state his motives for a refusal.

In France, work in the interest of the community (*travaux d'interet general*) was introduced by a bill enacted in 1983 as an alternative to prison sentences.[78] It can also be applied as a condition for a suspended imprisonment (that is, as a form of probation). It was not intended to be applied to serious crimes. As in England, such orders have not entirely replaced short-term prison sentences, but tend to substitute for fines. In comparison with British practice, France applies community service orders relatively rarely (to about 2,231 adult offenders from an adult prison population of 85,018). In the United Kingdom, approximately 30,000 community service orders are pronounced each year, and the number is increasing. In France, nonfulfillment of a community service order made as the principal sentence is a punishable offense in itself, for which the accused may be given a prison sentence of two months to two years, although this may be suspended.

In Portugal, the 1983 Penal Code foresees community service orders as an alternative to prison sentences of up to three months.[79] Denmark and Norway have also been experimenting with community service since 1982 and 1984, respectively. Community service was proposed in Finland in 1985 and is still at an initial phase of experimentation. Community service is used in Switzerland, Italy, and the FRG as an alternative to imprisonment following default on a fine.

In the FRG, it is also used as a condition for a suspended sentence and can be applied within the framework of a conditional waiver (Article 153a of the Code of Criminal Procedure), a conditional release (§57 of the Penal Code), and a warning with deferment of sentence (§59 of the Penal Code). In Luxembourg, community service can substitute for prison sentences of up to one year by means of a pardon. This modality has also been provided in the recent Dutch draft bill on pardon. In short, most European countries have introduced community service orders in their legal systems. In some countries, such as Spain or Belgium, the idea has been well received but not implemented, because adequate infrastructure is lacking. Sweden has been critical of the measure, because of the difficulty of employing generally unskilled people in a highly professionalized society and a reluctance to use work as a sanction.

Restitution is another alternative to incarceration with high rehabilitative potential. This sanction requires offenders to make payment of money or service to victims or to their representatives. With precedents in ancient civilizations, it has long been employed as a sentencing alternative by American judges.[80] It has considerably developed since the 1970s as the result of interest in protecting the rights of crime victims and in finding alternatives to incarceration and probation casework. Restitution is simultaneously a form of victim compensation and a rehabilitative measure. The restoration of equity in the relations between the victim and the offender is deemed to have significant psychological effects. Besides reducing guilt feelings, its rehabilitative value lies in requiring "the offender to give of himself or herself to benefit another," providing a "clear task that relates to the harm caused," and producing "visible rewards for the other."[81] Behavioral changes in offenders are derived, according to Martin, from a change of attitude toward themselves, the victim, and the community, offering offenders the opportunity to take steps toward their own reformation.[82]

Diversion

Community-based corrections are part of a wider system of decentralization, which includes placement of offenders under supervision either at home, at an educational facility, in a halfway house, in a foster family, or in group living arrangements. These residential facilities and community support are also being used as an alternative to prosecution (e.g., Project Crossroads in Washington, D.C., offers deferred prosecution supplemented by a structured program of pretrial services). Other community programs focus on alternatives to arrest and pretrial detention as a way to avoid one of the most desocializing aspects of the criminal process. The first objective of a systemic rehabilitative policy is to avoid incarceration at the initial stages of the criminal process.

The basic form of pretrial action within the community is the "release on supervision," for cases in which defendants do not meet the requirements for a release on bail or on their own recognizance. Release on supervision involves the surveillance by and assistance of a professional or volunteer officer appointed by the court. In addition, there are various programs of pretrial diversion. An example is the Manhattan Court Employment Project, which diverts criminal defendants, after their arraignment on felony or misdemeanor charges, into a program of group therapy and employment counseling. If the offender gets a job, criminal charges are dropped.

Mediation and arbitration of minor criminal cases by community representatives have become fruitful alternatives to adjudication in the courts. Dealing with such disputes in a more thoughtful, thoroughgoing and humane manner than is possible through adjudication has significant rehabilitative value. The experience of peaceful and rational conflict resolution represents an important form of social learning and a powerful factor for attitude change. Pilot programs, mainly directed to cases involving individuals linked by a personal relationship, have been implemented in Boston; Philadelphia; Rochester, New York; Columbus, Ohio; New York City; and Washington, D.C.[83]

Conflicts between family members, friends, neighbors, landlords and tenants, merchants and customers, and coworkers resulting from behavior offensive to criminal law are solved more effectively by lay members of the community or criminal justice paraprofessionals. Snyder analyzed the Dorchester Urban Court Program in Boston. He reported that mediation during the first two years achieved "some impressive results as a process for the settlement of certain kind of minor criminal and potentially criminal disputes involving parties engaged in an ongoing personal relationship."[84] Mediation provides neglected urban populations "with a forum for meaningful ventilation of social problems" and a means to reduce urban tensions. Results of the Dorchester program strongly suggest that the process works remarkably well.[85] A recent study found community dispute resolution programs using conciliation, mediation, or arbitration are faster and of higher quality than a court's intervention and also make justice more accessible for citizens.[86]

Electronic Surveillance

At a time of unprecedented prison overcrowding and prohibitive construction costs, electronic monitoring technology facilitates various sentencing options used to avoid incarceration. This technology can be applied to monitor alternatives such as pretrial diversion, weekend sentences, work release, or intensive supervision. It can also make house arrest a more feasible sentencing option.[87] One of the most common applications is an electronic device that is attached to the offender's wrist, neck, or ankle and that transmits radio signals. Any violations are signaled through a receiver annexed to the offender's phone, which communicates with a central computer. This makes monitoring relatively simple and accurate, although some technical and economic problems remain unsolved.[88]

The rehabilitative value of electronic surveillance is purely negative: avoidance of the harm of incarceration. It cannot be considered a rehabilitative means except that it makes possible a sanction less restrictive than imprisonment. It can be certainly justified as a means to protect society that is less harmful than imprisonment, but it should not be used "to instill a sense of discipline which can be rehabilitative for the probationer."[89] That rationale reflects an outdated and oppressive concept of rehabilitation. No one should be supervised electronically "in order to be rehabilitated" in the same way that no one should be imprisoned for that purpose.

Electronic surveillance is designed for nonviolent offenders with records that would otherwise have led them to incarceration. The replacement of incarceration is a risk calculation reflecting the need to ease prison overcrowding, that has to be made in criminal statutes or sentencing decisions. This type of surveillance is primarily designed to prevent dangerous behavior, while allowing the offender to leave the monitored area at specific times to go to work, perform community service, or receive medical or psychological treatment. Electronically monitored house arrest can also be a punishment in itself, accomplishing purely retributive and deterrent goals. Besides its still-questioned potential to reduce prison populations, electronic surveillance has been advocated as a way of reducing the traditional supervisory function of probation officers.[90] The mechanical monitoring of the central computer would allow probation officers to use their time for rehabilitation-oriented activities.[91] The counterargument is that electronic monitoring deprives probationers of the chance to demonstrate trustworthiness, thus frustrating one purpose of probation.

Community Corrections for the Juvenile

Experimental research shows that communities are "the most effective center of action on delinquency problems" and that "the most strenuous and dedicated efforts to reform delinquent youth in institutional settings removed from the community will avail little unless the problems of community support for reintegration are solved as well."[92] Rehabilitation in the community will increase the likelihood of an offender's ability to get jobs, reduce the attraction of gangs, and avoid stigmatization, because it reflects a social definition of the offending youth as one needing services, rather than a dangerous threat.[93]

The need to rehabilitate juvenile offenders seems more pressing and at the same time more promising than in the case of adult offenders. It was this idea that originally inspired and shaped a special subsystem of criminal justice for the juvenile. But as with adults, lip service to rehabilitation was used to justify abuses in intervention and institutionalization. Institutions for juveniles became mere warehouses of custody and incapacitation, overcrowded and harshly punitive. The juvenile justice system not only failed to rehabilitate, but generated criminality through stigmatization and contact with other inmates, creating or consolidating delinquent subcultures. The situation was made worse by the lack of procedural safeguards against the power of the state to intervene under the *parens patriae* theory.

A reaction against abuses was initiated in the 1960s by a series of Supreme Court decisions, which considerably increased the procedural safeguards for youths in the juvenile courts.[94] The treatment of juveniles became more like criminal punishment of adults. A salutary development insofar as it prevented abuses against the individual rights of the juvenile, this shift also allowed an increase in punishment and a neglect of youth's special needs for care and support. A right to rehabilitation in the form of education and socialization is diametrically opposed to the type of intervention practiced by the juvenile institutions, which desocialized offenders in the name of an oppressive notion of rehabilitation. But a right to rehabilitation is equally violated by state inaction and indifference to the needs of wayward youths. Genuine rehabilitative programs, in which intervention is limited to the indispensable and the youths are provided with true opportunity, are at once a fulfillment of the juveniles' rights and a legitimate state strategy against crime. Such programs presuppose a high degree of deinstitutionalization and reliance on community resources. It is only abusive institutionalization or brainwashing intervention that contradicts a liberty-centered notion of rehabilitation.

Parallel to the transformations in the legal structure of the juvenile justice system, criminological findings posed a new challenge for the policymaker. The discovery that a small group of chronic offenders are accountable for a high percentage of serious crime led to a resurgence of the idea of dangerousness and a series of studies advocating incapacitation as the panacea for crime control.[95] In 1982, Greenwood proposed selective incapacitation strategies as a means to reduce crime significantly without increasing the total number of offenders incarcerated.[96] The author recognized the limitations of selective incapacitation and the practical difficulties of implementing it. Despite efforts to establish reliable predictor variables, chronic offenders can be identified with only about 50 percent accuracy. A 50 percent rate of false positives is enough to discourage any direct legal measure based on such predictions. In 1985, Greenwood and Zimring offered a breakthrough for crime control strategies with the idea of an early rehabilitative intervention. Their study pointed out that "the seeds of chronic delinquency are often sown at a very young age,"[97] and claimed that if school performance and home situation are included in the available information, chronic delinquents may be identified as early as their thirteenth birthday.

Greenwood and Zimring's proposal for an early preventive intervention recognized the obvious risk of targeting a special group of potential delinquents. They accepted that prevention programs should address wider social problems such as drug abuse, school dropouts, and unemployment.[98] For this purpose they indicated four types of program: early education, parent training, effective schools, and voluntary youth programs. The public school, they recognized, is the only alternative to juvenile court for prevention programs that are other than voluntary. But such programs would have to "evolve as school-wide adjuncts to the general educational experience rather than specially labeled and targeted attempts to identify high-risk groups."[99] A mandatory program aimed at a special population within the public school would be constitutionally inadmissible. Their study offered abundant examples of promising rehabilitation programs for adjudicated delinquents that could advantageously replace the traditional training schools. Such programs included outdoor education (survival training and wilderness experience), small secure treatment units, group homes, and tracking programs.[100] Their promise argues for expanding the rehabilitation of juveniles in the community and continuing to dismantle institutions for delinquent juveniles as far as possible.

Ross and Gendreau provided new evidence of successful experiments in their highly informative review of community-based programs for juvenile offenders. Some examples will suggest the creativity of such correctional experiments. In the ''Buddy System'' used in Hawaii, nonprofessional adults served as behavior-change agents for juveniles in their own community.[101] Youngsters were referred by the schools, courts, police, social welfare agencies, and community residents. An important warning derived from this experience is that ''intervention may have salutary effects with some clients but deleterious (iatrogenic) effects with others.'' Some of those who had not previously committed offenses started to do so following the treatment. But the program benefited those who had a recent history of offenses.

Project CREST (Clinical Regional Support Teams) was carried out in Florida with young hard-core probationers by teams of university students, who used a nonauthoritarian counseling approach instead of the usual threat of sanctions to obtain conformity.[102] Research findings revealed genuine effectiveness.[103] The Michigan Behavioral-Employment Intervention Program implemented a successful job employment program by ensuring motivation and a positive disposition from offenders and employers.[104] Its methods included praising job employment and job-appropriate behaviors, as well as contingency contracting.

A follow-up study of a program developed by Shore and Massimo in 1961 and 1962 revealed that ''comprehensive vocationally oriented psychotherapy continues to show promise as a technique for reaching the so-called 'hard-to-reach' adolescents, influencing their adjustment positively even into mid-life.''[105] Also in the 1960s, Ostrom and colleagues carried out a successful and inexpensive short-term project on modification of delinquent behavior.[106] The project was geared toward emphasizing specific behavioral activities instead of treating the whole personality of the participants. Leaders were selected on the basis of educational achievement and the belief that ''success in life could be achieved without engaging in criminal behavior,'' without requiring professional training in counseling or handling delinquents. The subjects' attendance at meetings was secured through minimum monetary incentives. Seven two-hour sessions extending over a two-month period were held after the recruitment meeting. Most activities and discussions dealt with specific delinquent acts, the consequences of such acts, and alternative activities to achieve the participants' personal goals. Role playing was the most extensively used activity. During the sessions a permissive atmosphere prevailed, which encouraged the participants to talk freely about their undiscovered past crimes and their future intentions. The four group leaders suggested legal ways to attain the same goals pursued through delinquent behavior.

A major alternative to traditional institutionalization in the last fifteen years has been wilderness training programs and outdoor education, such as VisionQuest, Associated Marine Institutes, the Eckerd Foundation, or Homeward Bound.[107] These programs encourage cooperative behavior for overcoming difficulties and physical challenges created by particular living conditions. A recent study judged VisionQuest, the largest of its type, as particularly successful. It is not clear, however, what makes such programs effective.[108] Their distinctive features are their ability to instill in participants a sense of achievement and responsibility, and the quality and intensity of staff involvement, favored by the high ratio of staff to youths. Affection, the creation of a family atmosphere within the program, and an emphasis on family therapy, with parent participation, are also significant ingredients of these outdoor programs.[109]

The Massachusetts Deinstitutionalization Experiment

The best example of a far-reaching juvenile rehabilitative policy is the reform effort carried out in Massachusetts between 1969 and 1976, which was the object of simultaneous and continuing research by the Center for Criminal Justice at the Harvard Law School. The Massachusetts experience provided "the broadest empirical base to date for examining the efficacy of the community-based model for delivering services to delinquent youths."[110] The Harvard research generated a series of reports, which are summarized and referenced in the culminating publication by Miller and Ohlin, which examines the theoretical and practical issues involved in the experiment.[111] Although focused on youth corrections, the studies contain rich insights into the problems of change and policy implementation in human services organizations in general.

In 1969, when Jerome Miller was appointed commissioner of the Massachusetts Department of Youth Services (DYS), the state's training schools for delinquent boys had become virtual warehouses, characterized by neglect and discipline based on authoritarian manipulation of the inmates. Originally introduced as a humane solution, they now embodied an oppressive and authoritarian model of rehabilitation. Miller, who had studied the workings of the therapeutic community in the British mental health system, attempted to introduce a treatment based on self-determination and respect for the inmate's individuality.

Miller began by eliminating traditional depersonalizing institutional practices such as dictating the inmates' hair length and requiring them to march in silent formation and to wear uniforms. He also made it easier for inmates to bring their complaints to the central office and liberalized parole procedures. To educate the public about his innovative policies, Miller exposed the atrocities of institutional life to the mass media and opened the institutions to public scrutiny. He also tried to spread the idea of the therapeutic community among the staff. The institutions within the jurisdiction of his department were made as democratic as possible, and he encouraged the maximum possible involvement of the juveniles in their own destiny.

Miller's approach, in consonance with the most progressive policies already applied in the California Community Treatment Project, included the creation of community resources to replace juvenile corrections in institutions. He tried to establish living groups within the institutions, foster home placements, vocational-training programs, volunteer tutoring programs, and special programs developed by special groups, such as ex-addicts or ex-offenders.

Miller's innovations were opposed by some politicians, the institutional staff, and others who felt their vested bureaucratic interests or power positions were threatened. Eventually, Miller recognized that his revolution was bound to be neutralized or bureaucratized by the opposing pressure. He then substituted radical change for his gradual approach to correctional reform. Conferring only with his closest staff members, he decided to close the institutions, beginning without warning in the late fall of 1971. His plan relied on the establishment of a network of regional decentralized community-based services.

By January 1972, Miller had closed all but one of the institutions and placed the residents in foster homes, privately run community-based programs, and group homes, while a considerable number were paroled. Only those who seemed dangerous were kept confined in small, therapeutically oriented facilities. In early 1973 Miller resigned as commissioner of DYS. Even after the thrust of the deinstitutionalization policy weakened, a recent study by Bullington and colleagues found that it enjoyed widespread support in Massachusetts.[112] The same study concluded that "the policies of the Miller era have been compromised, but not dismantled" and that "the current success of the juvenile justice system in Massachusetts must be attributed to the boldness of the Miller reform initiative coupled with the administrative sophistication with which his successors have brought both organizational stability and credibility to the system."[113]

One of the Harvard studies pointed out that Massachusetts's experience with deinstitutionalization transformed the youth corrections system. Research results "suggest strongly that the vast majority of committed delinquents can be handled in relatively noninstitutional settings." The study concluded that a community-based system is a viable alternative to a training-school system.[114] "Even youths requiring secure facilities can be handled in smaller, more humane settings than the traditional training school."[115] The study also concluded that the correctional staff should take risks to act on behalf of youths in establishing constructive relationships with community networks. Advocacy should proceed at three levels: individual, which requires an involvement with the youngster's total situation; community, which focuses on making existing community resources available or generating new ones; and public policy, which tends to modify guidelines for dealing with youths across the state.[116] The youth's family, peer group, and school and work opportunities must all be taken into account in any attempt at "a lasting redirection of his or her career patterns."[117] The study also urged caution in categorizing the youths, to avoid the stigmatizing consequences of organizational labels, which tend to become self-fulfilling prophecies.

REHABILITATION OF MENTALLY DISORDERED OFFENDERS

The conventional division between the sane and the insane has represented a bulwark against the invasion of experts and administrative authorities into areas reserved to privacy and individual freedom. Experience has shown the dangers of extending therapeutic criteria beyond the unequivocally mentally ill. A modern anthropocentric approach is especially cautious in this matter, recognizing that the label of mental illness can be used to mask incapacitative policies instead of encouraging real therapeutic initiatives. The anthropocentric model of rehabilitation fundamentally insists on respecting the constitutional limits to state intervention and avoiding the isolating stigma of mental illness as far as possible.

Despite the dangers and drawbacks in extending the therapeutic approach to what Maudsley called the grayish zone between normality and insanity,[118] some fruitful innovations have been made in this area. The most significant European rehabilitative experiments dealt with precisely this intermediate group, consisting primarily of people formerly called psychopaths or sociopaths and today known as antisocial personalities. There have been many abuses and false pretenses of treatment for this type of lawbreaker, but there have also been valuable programs, the results of which may illuminate the future development of the overall correctional system. Habitual offenders with personality disturbances clearly require some kind of special reaction more effective than mere punishment. The difficulty of defining the category does not lessen the practical need for special programs for its constituents.

The first mentally disordered offenders to be considered for intensive individualized treatment were those rejected by both prisons and mental hospitals because of their troublesome or unruly character. Only a few countries have attempted to rehabilitate these apparently incorrigible offenders. For the rest, harsh incapacitative policies prevailed, consistent with determinist solutions of the late nineteenth century, which advocated their indeterminate and prolonged segregation.

The difficulties in defining exactly who should be treated derive from the differences between legal and psychiatric viewpoints. The conventional boundary between the sane and the insane does not always coincide with the division between those who are amendable to treatment and those who are not. The first classification is linked to the criminal law rationale, which requires only minimal mental capacity to categorize a person as sane. In contrast, classification in terms of amenability to treatment is based on purely therapeutic considerations. Each subset—amenable and nonamenable—includes persons from both sides of the legal borderline of criminal responsibility. This dichotomy can be clearly seen in the 1971 reforms of the Swiss penal code, which made the determination of criminal responsibility and the choice of a nonpunitive sanction relatively independent.[119]

The difference between classifications based on the diagnosis of responsibility and those founded on therapeutic considerations is especially significant for insanity acquittees with highly deteriorated condition beyond any meaningful treatment. At the same time some convicted offenders who have met the standards of criminal responsibility may critically require psychiatric treatment for their rehabilitation. Similar problems are posed by prison inmates who suffer mental disturbances as a result of their correctional experience. Whether because of their particular disposition or the excessive pressures of imprisonment, they pay a psychological price beyond the pains inherent in imprisonment.[120] Treatment is then necessary even if their disturbances do not constitute insanity.

The rehabilitation of mentally disordered offenders encompasses psychiatric treatment and various supplementary efforts to reintegrate them into the community. The therapeutic model, whose applicability for the average criminal is highly controversial, is generally accepted for this type of offender.[121] The notion of rehabilitation as a right for mentally disordered offenders is closely related to the right of the mentally ill in general to treatment in the least restrictive setting.[122] This right favors the use of ambulatory (outpatient) treatment, all the more feasible since the diffusion of psychotropic drugs. The affirmation of a right to treatment for the mentally ill leads to the formulation of minimum standards of quality and efficiency.[123] A correlative right is the right to refuse treatment, also related to a rights model of rehabilitation.[124] The refusal of treatment should not automatically lead to other types of restrictions of freedom without independent evidence of dangerousness.

Mentally disordered offenders have special rehabilitative needs. These include, depending on the category of offender, psychotherapy, special education, and vocational training, but in all cases more intensive care and assistance than the normal adult offender requires. The notion of rehabilitation as a right opposes not only the merely nominal offering of these services, but also their use in an oppressive form. Predictions of dangerousness based on the police power of the state have to be carefully distinguished from the specific therapeutic function.[125] If treatment is part of a right to rehabilitation, it cannot be used as a manipulative brainwashing device or as a way to justify prolonging hospitalization or commitment.

Special Treatment of Sex Offenders

In early twentieth-century legislation, special consideration of mentally disordered offenders aimed particularly at the feebleminded. This legislation was influenced by Goddard's theories, which stressed the relationship between mental retardation and crime. Defective delinquent statutes tended to be applied to feebleminded troublemakers in need of more-secure institutions.[126] Although these early institutions did not achieve true rehabilitative programs, they developed significant forms of occupational training.[127]

In the 1930s efforts to identify and isolate dangerous offenders were refocused on sexual psychopaths. After World War II a series of highly publicized sexual crimes seemed to justify a wave of special statutes. The public experienced a true collective hysteria toward sex offenders, who were seen as "degenerate social fiends." The new legislation also sprang from what was later considered a criminological fallacy: an exaggerated estimate of the relationship between stubborn recidivism and sexual crimes.[128] The sexual emphasis of the new legislation has been seen as reflecting the Puritan tradition[129] and the 1950s revival of family values and the consequent strong rejection of deviant behavior.[130] In 1969, thirty-one states had developed special programs for the treatment of sexual criminals. The discredited expression "sexual psychopaths" was replaced in later statutes by such phrases as "dangerous sexual criminals" or "mentally disordered sexual criminals," which emphasized either dangerousness or general mental derangement. More recent statutes eliminate the reference to sexual abnormality altogether, encompassing various mental disorders instead.

In most of the special programs, rehabilitation played a small role. Candidates for special programs were confined under the label of civil commitment, thus avoiding constitutional safeguards and allowing abuses, such as indefinite detention for minor offenses.[131] In the late 1960s, a series of judicial decisions declaring certain special programs unconstitutional strengthened the rights of offenders assigned to them. Many of the statutes were drastically reformed or repealed. Constitutional challenges to the Patuxent Institution were particularly numerous. In 1976 its legal framework was totally transformed, and it became a leading rehabilitative experiment on a voluntary basis, fully respecting the individual rights of the inmates.

In recent years, growing attention has been given to sexual offenders, in part because of new sociological and criminological findings in the field of private violence in general and new perceptions of rape, largely resulting from the women's movement. Rape is no longer seen as a strictly sexual crime but as a violent assault that is acted out sexually.[132] The new emphasis on rape, incest, child molestation, and other forms of sexual abuse has led to improved mechanisms of detection and state intervention in general. As a consequence, the number of sex offenders in prison has increased dramatically. According to a 1986 survey the number of sex offenders has grown recently in more than two-thirds of the nation's prison systems. In a few states, sex offenders accounted for 25 to 30 percent of the inmate population. The increase was attributed to several factors: greater public awareness and better reporting, more prosecutions and convictions, changes in the statutes on sex offenses, the imposition of more and longer sentences (some of them mandatory), and reluctance and delay in paroling sex offenders. Connecticut is the only state in which the survey reports a decrease, which is explained as a result of "more diversion programs and jail sentences for less serious offenders."[133]

The rise in sexual offense rates has been paralleled by a new approach in treatment that aims to teach sex offenders how to control their sexually abusive or assaultive behavior.[134] The treatment candidates include those guilty of rape, child sexual assault, and incest, as well as minor offenses such as exhibitionism and voyeurism. The new approach has discarded old popular stereotypes of the sexual offender as mentally disordered, emphasizing that a fairly large, heterogeneous proportion of the population commits sexual offenses. Some sex offenders are actually psychotic or engage in antisocial behavior in general because of personality abnormalities. But many compulsive sex offenders "obey the law in other ways, may be responsible in their work, may have concern for other persons."[135] It is for this type of offender, suffering "paraphilia," that the new treatment endeavors are particularly significant. Treatment aims to "discover ways for sex offenders to learn how to intervene, control, and manage" their deviances and to "foster appropriate, nonaggressive lifestyles."[136]

Renowned specialists in the treatment of sex offenders affirm that their imprisonment, which is normally temporary, does not ensure the safety of the community. Quite the contrary it "increases sex-offenders' pathology so that they come out with worse fantasies than before their incarceration."[137] Punishment is considered to reinforce the shame and guilt from which the offenses come.[138] Treatment is considered the best protection for society, leading to a relative mastery of serious behavioral problems and thus reducing sexual deviances to a minimal level. A number of treatment programs are in effect, both community based and residential, in several states.[139] Chemical treatment using the drug Depo-Provera has been reported helpful in curbing sexual drive and facilitating the control of offensive sexual behavior. It is being currently applied by Dr. Fred Berlin at the Johns Hopkins Hospital in Baltimore, Maryland, to probationers, parolees, and inmates from the Maryland correctional system. Although administered only under conditions considered voluntary, it has a potential for abuse and poses delicate legal and ethical issues.[140]

The notion of rehabilitation as a right, developed earlier in this book, includes the right to prison conditions that do not make degeneration probable and self-rehabilitation impossible.[141] It is unlikely that paraphiliac sexual offenders will be able to control their impulses without the help of special treatments. For them, incarceration without treatment results in "the unnecessary and wanton pain caused by recidivism and future incarceration." Imprisonment under such conditions was considered unconstitutional in *Laaman v. Helgemoe*.[142] The violation of the Eighth Amendment lies in the suffering entailed in probable future incarceration. Conversely the right to Depo-Provera drug treatment was considered an application of a limited constitutional right of prisoners to psychological and medical treatment.[143]

European Social Therapeutic Experiments

Social therapy is the epitome of intensive rehabilitative treatment of mentally disordered offenders. It provides a model applicable to all institutionalized offenders, including those in regular correctional institutions. Thus programs engendered by the mental health movement may have a deep influence on corrections as a whole.[144]

The new psychiatric perspective focused on the social dimension of human beings, generating forms of collective treatment in which innovative techniques such as group therapy and psychodrama played an increasingly important role. This approach also reflects the general transformation of the medical model into a social learning one. The pioneer in this field was Georg Stürup, who directed Hersdtedvester in Denmark, the first social-therapeutic–oriented institution.[145] Social therapy has been carried out until now only on a small scale and in a few countries such as Denmark, Holland, the FRG, Austria, Norway, Switzerland, and the United States. Because of the considerable variations among institutions, a general appraisal is problematic.

Social therapy in its modern form began only after World War II. The impact of the war and Nazi occupation in Europe quickened its development. The most eventful consequence of the war in this regard was the therapeutic community established by Maxwell Jones in England. He drew his inspiration from the changes in psychiatric practice at the frontline, where the usual hierarchical and distant role of the psychiatrist was discarded and where individual treatment needs involved the cooperation of other patients. In this way, the therapeutic relationship at the frontline became horizontal, that is, the traditional elements of authority disappeared. Another effect of the war was to overcrowd psychiatric hospitals with casualties, creating a practical need for group therapy on a large scale. Through these transformations in the practice of psychiatry, Jones discovered the importance of the patient's peer group in promoting treatment. After 1947 he applied his conclusions in the social rehabilitation unit at the Belmont Hospital, later renamed the Henderson Hospital, where he worked for twelve years with one hundred sociopaths of both sexes in an open unit. There a genuine therapeutic environment was created, which included shared decision making, multiple leadership, and values such as honest communication that differed in many ways from those of the outside society.

The resistance against the Nazi invasion in France was another source of psychiatric change. Participation in active groups, where authority was relegated to a secondary place, brought an awareness of the therapeutic value of a close-knit community. The resistance thus opened a new perspective on the relation between psychiatrists, nurses, and patients. It also inspired a movement called "institutional psychotherapy," which aimed to restructure roles within the institution, much as in the British therapeutic community.[146]

The war further influenced emerging social-therapeutic concepts through the Nazis' imprisonment of influential Dutch government officials and scholars. Their direct contact with the grim realities of incarceration left them determined to change and humanize the penal system. After the war, this generous reformist impulse crystallized in the avant-garde Dutch social-therapeutic clinics.[147]

Social-therapeutic institutions for criminal offenders can be seen as the correctional counterpart of the innovations in the field of mental health brought about by the idea of the therapeutic community and new group treatment techniques. These institutions reflect enlightened criticism of conventional psychiatry, which was based on a predominantly custodial model, and of a purely incapacitative correctional system. They are based on modern sociological discoveries about the negative potential of penal institutions. They seek to make the institutional environment more humane, democratic, and effective, using the community as healing agent.

NOTES

1. Fyodor Dostoyevski, *Memoirs from the House of the Dead* (New York: Oxford University Press, 1983).

2. David J. Rothman, "Doing Time: Days, Months and Years in the Criminal Justice System," in *Sentencing*, ed. Hyman Gross and Andrew von Hirsch (New York: Oxford University Press, 1981), 378.

3. Leszek Lernell, "Réflexions sur l'essence de la peine privative de liberté. De certains aspects psychologiques et philosophiques de la peine de prison," in *Études en l'honneur de Jean Graven*, ed. Faculte de Droit de Genève (Geneva: Librairie de l'Université, Georg, 1969), 93.

4. Calvert R. Dodge, *A Nation without Prisons* (Lexington, Mass.: D. C. Heath, 1975), 235.

5. Hans-Heinrich Jescheck, "Die Krise der Kriminalpolitik," *Zeitschrift für die gesamte Strafrechtswissenschaft* 91 (1979): 1037–64.

6. See p. 8.

7. See "Report on the Panel on Research on Rehabilitative Techniques," in *New Directions in the Rehabilitation of Criminal Offenders*, ed. S. B. Martin, L. B. Sechrest, and R. Redner (Washington, D.C.: National Academy Press, 1981), 135–73.

8. The German Alternative Draft speaks of criminal punishment as "a bitter necessity of a community of imperfect nature." See *Alternativ-Entwurf eines Strafgesetzbuches—Allgemeiner Teil* (Tübingen: J.C.B. Mohr, 1969), 29.

9. See pp. 65–68.

10. See pp. 71–76.

11. See pp. 65–68.

12. "Erläuterungen zur Kriminalstatistik des Reichs für 1884," (Berlin 1886), quoted by Adolf Wach, *Die Reform der Freiheitstrafe* (Leipzig: Dunker & Humblot, 1890), 64.

13. Franz von Liszt, *Strafrechtliche Aufsätze und Vorträge* (Berlin: J. Guttentag, 1905), 1:345.

14. Ibid., 346.

15. See pp. 51–52.

16. German Penal Code, ¶47 (1).

17. Marc Ancel, *La défense sociale nouvelle* (Paris: Cujas, 1981), 197–98, 275–76.

18. Norman Bishop, "Beware of Treatment!" in *Some Development in Nordic Criminal Policy*, ed. E. Aspelin, N. Bishop, H. Thornstedt, and P. Tornudd (Stockholm: Scandinavian Research Council for Criminology, 1975), 19–27.

19. D. W. Steenhuis, L.C.M. Tigges, and J.J.A. Essers, "The Penal Climate in the Netherlands" *The British Journal of Criminology* 23 (Jan. 1983): 11.

20. Claus Roxin, "Strafzweck und Strafrechtsreform," in *Programm für eines neues Strafgesetzbuch*, ed. Jürgen Baumann (Frankfurt am Main: Fischer Bucherei, 1968), 84.

21. *Alternativ-Entwurf*, ¶¶36, 48.

22. Roxin, "Strafzweck und Strafrechtsreform," 85.

23. Ibid., 89.

24. Frieder Dünkel, "Die Öffnung des Vollzugs—Anspruch und Wirklichkeit," *Zeitschrift für die gesamte Strafrechtswissenschaft* 94 (1982): 669–710.

25. See pp. 150–53.

26. See pp. 31–33.

27. J. Thorsten Sellin, *Slavery and the Penal System* (New York: Elsevier, 1976).

28. José L. de la Cuesta Arzamendi, *El Trabajo Penitenciario Resocializador* (San Sebastián: Caja de Ahorros Provincial de Guipúzcoa, 1982), 175.

29. Ibid., 177.

30. Urs Heierli, *Gefangenenarbeit, Entlohnung und Sozialisation* (Zürich: Flamberg, 1973), 95, 97.

31. Ibid., 98.

32. de la Cuesta Arzamendi, *El Trabajo Penitenciario*, 185.

33. Spanish Constitution, Article 25 (2), ¶¶1, 2, 3.

34. Ibid., 271. On the principle of less eligibility see pp. 111–12.

35. Dünkel, *Die Öffnung des Vollzugs*, 671.

36. Erik Andersen, "Ringe: A New Maximum-Security Prison for Young Men and Women in Denmark," in *Confinement in Maximum Custody*, ed. David A. Ward and Kenneth F. Shoen (Lexington, Mass.: D. C. Heath, 1981), 160.

37. Ibid., 162.

38. Karl Peter Rotthaus, "Das Dänische Staatsgefängnis in Ringe—ein Gegenmodell zur Sozialtherapeutischen Anstalt?" in *Sozialtherapie und Behandlungsforschung*, special issue of *Zeitschrift für Strafvollzug und Straffälligenhilfe* 29 (1980): 101.

39. Andersen, "Ringe," 186.

40. Ibid., 167.

41. Ibid., 168.

42. Ibid., 167.

43. Ibid., 168.

44. Ibid.

45. Ibid., 172.

46. Rotthaus, "Das Dänische Staatsgefängnis in Ringe," 102.

47. Norval Morris, *The Future of Imprisonment* (Chicago: Chicago University Press, 1974).

48. Gilbert L. Ingram, "Butner, A Reality," *Federal Probation* 42 (1978): 36.

49. U.S. Department of Justice, *Federal Correctional Institution Butner*, foreword Norman Carlson (Washington, D.C.: U.S. Department of Justice, Federal Prison System, 1981), 2.

50. See Bernadette Pelissier and Kathy Smith, *The Effects of a Rapid Increase in a Prison Population: A Pre- and Post-Test Study, Preliminary Report* (Butner: FCI, Dec. 1986).

51. U.S. Department of Justice, *Federal Correctional Institution Butner*, 3.

52. C. T. Love, Jane G. Allgood, and F. P. Samples, "The Butner Research Projects: The First Ten Years," *Federal Probation* 48 (Dec. 1984): 38.

53. Ronald Corbett, Jr., and Gary T. Marx use this expression, pointing out that in practice what usually happens is target displacement and not target expansion, in "When a Man's Castle Is His Prison: The Potential Perils of Home Confinement," paper presented at the Annual Meeting of the American Society of Criminology, Montreal, Canada, Nov. 1987, p. 5.

54. Gerhardt Grebing, *The Fine in Comparative Law: A Survey of 21 Countries* (Cambridge: University of Cambridge, Institute of Criminology, 1982), vii.

55. See Sally T. Hillsman and Judith A. Greene, *Improving the Use and Administration of Criminal Fines* (New York: Vera Institute of Justice, 1987) and "Tailoring Criminal Fines to the Financial Means of the Offender," *Judicature* 72 (June–July 1988): 38–45.

56. Andrew Scull, "Community Corrections: Panacea, Progress or Pretence," in *The Power to Punish*, ed. D. Garland and P. Young (London: Heinemann, 1983), 111.

57. R. B. Coates, A. Miller, and L. E. Ohlin, *Diversity in a Youth Correctional System: Handling Delinquents in Massachusetts* (Cambridge, Mass.: Ballinger, 1978), 7.

58. Ibid., 6, 7.

59. Alden D. Miller and Lloyd E. Ohlin, *Delinquency and Community* (Beverly Hills, Calif.: Sage, 1985), 26.

60. David J. Rothman, *Conscience and Convenience: The Asylum and Its Alternatives in Progressive America* (Boston: Little, Brown, 1980), 61–66.

61. Ernst Rosenfeld, *Welche Strafmittel können an die Stelle der kurzeitigen Freiheitstrafe gesetzt werden?* (Berlin: J. Guttentag, 1890), 24.

62. Cleon H. Foust and D. Robert Webster, *An Anatomy of Criminal Justice* (Lexington, Mass.: D. C. Heath, 1980), 277.

63. James M. Byrne, "The Control Controversy: A Preliminary Examination of Intensive Probation Supervision Programs in the United States," *Federal Probation* 50 (June 1986): 12.

64. Donald Cochran, Ronald P. Corbett, Jr., and James M. Byrne, "Intensive Probation Supervision in Massachusetts: A Case Study in Change," *Federal Probation* 50 (June 1986), 32.

65. Marc Ancel, *Suspended Sentence* (London: Heinemann, 1971), 2, 3.

66. Leon Radcinowics, "Foreword," in ibid., vi.

67. Ancel, *Suspended Sentence*, 70.

68. Hans-Heinrich Jescheck, *Lehrbuch des Strafrechts* (Berlin: Duncker & Humblot, 1972), 625.

69. Günter Blau, "Die gemeinnützige Arbeit als Beispiel für einen grundlegenden Wandel des Sanktionenwesens," in *Gedächnisschrift für Hilde Kaufmann*, ed. Hans Joachim Hirsch, Günther Kaiser, and Helmut Marquardt (Berlin: De Gruyter, 1986).

70. Barbara Huber, "Community Service Order como alternativa a la pena privativa de libertad en Inglaterra," *Anuario de derecho penal y ciencias penales* 36 (1983): 39.

71. Anthony E. Bottoms, "Neglected Features of Contemporary Penal Systems," in *The Power to Punish*, ed. D. Garland and P. Young (London: Heinemann, 1983), 179.

72. Ibid., 169, 170.

73. Young, quoted by ibid., 170.

74. Peter P. Lejins, "Community Service as Special Sanction in the United States,"

in *Community Service as an Alternative to the Prison Sentence*, ed. International Penal and Penitentiary Foundation (Bonn, 1987), 12.

75. Susan Martin, "Restitution and Community Service Sentences: Promising Sentencing Alternative or Passing Fad?" in *New Directions in the Rehabilitation of Criminal Offenders*, ed. S. Martin, L. Sechrest, and R. Redner (Washington, D.C.: National Academy Press, 1981), 475.

76. Bottoms, "Neglected Features," 169.

77. See Peter J. P. Tak, "Community Service as an Alternative to the Prison Sentence in the Netherlands," in *Community Service as an Alternative to the Prison Sentence*, ed. International Penal and Penitentiary Foundation (Bonn, 1987), 115.

78. See Jean Pradel, "Community Service: The French Experience," in *Community Service as an Alternative to the Prison Sentence*, ed. International Penal and Penitentiary Foundation (Bonn, 1987), 27.

79. See Eduardo Correia, "Community Service and the New Portuguese Penal Code," in *Community Service as an Alternative to the Prison Sentence*, ed. International Penal and Penitentiary Foundation (Bonn, 1987), 81.

80. Martin, "Restitution and Community Service," 473.

81. Ibid., 474.

82. Ibid., 475.

83. Frederick E. Snyder, "Crime and Community Mediation—The Boston Experience: A Preliminary Report on the Dorchester Urban Court Program," *Wisconsin Law Review* 3 (1978): 739, 740.

84. Ibid., 777.

85. Ibid., 790.

86. Daniel McGillis, *Community Dispute Resolution Programs and Public Policy* (Washington, D.C.: National Institute of Justice, 1986), 83, 97.

87. Joan Petersilia, "Exploring the Option of House Arrest," *Federal Probation* 50 (June 1986): 50–55. See also Ronald Corbett and Ellsworth A. I. Fersch, "Home as Prison: The Use of House Arrest," *Federal Probation* 49 (Mar. 1985): 13–17.

88. Annesley K. Schmidt, "Electronic Monitors," *Federal Probation* 50 (June 1986): 56 and Petersilia, "Exploring the Option of House Arrest," 54. See also Gary T. Marx, *Undercover: Police Surveillance in America* (Berkeley: University of California Press, 1988), 214.

89. Rolando V. Del Carmen and Joseph B. Vaughn, "Legal Issues in the Use of Electronic Surveillance in Probation," *Federal Probation* 50 (June 1986): 60–69.

90. Schmidt, "Electronic Monitors," 57.

91. Charles M. Friel and Joseph B. Vaughn, "A Consumer's Guide to the Electronic Monitoring of Probationers," *Federal Probation* 50 (Sept. 1986): 9, 10.

92. Miller and Ohlin, *Delinquency and Community*, 12.

93. Ibid., 142.

94. See Marc Miller, "Changing Legal Paradigms in Juvenile Justice," in *Intervention Strategies for Chronic Juvenile Offenders*, ed. P. Greenwood (Westport, Conn.: Greenwood Press, 1986), 91–122.

95. M. Wolfgang, R. M. Figlio, and T. Sellin, *Delinquency in a Birth Cohort* (Chicago: University of Chicago Press, 1972).

96. Peter W. Greenwood and Allan Abrahamse, *Selective Incapacitation* (Santa Monica, Calif.: Rand Corporation, Aug. 1982), R–2815–NIJ.

97. Peter W. Greenwood and Franklin E. Zimring, *One More Chance: The Pursuit*

of *Promising Intervention Strategies for Chronic Juvenile Offenders* (Santa Monica, Calif.: Rand Corporation, May 1985), 14, R–3214–OJJDP.

98. Ibid., xii.

99. Ibid., 30.

100. Ibid., 31–35.

101. Robert Ross and Paul Gendreau, eds., *Effective Correctional Treatment* (Toronto: Butterworths, 1980), 161.

102. Ibid., 171.

103. Ibid., 182.

104. Ibid., 187.

105. Ibid., 216.

106. Ibid., 221.

107. Peter W. Greenwood, "Promising Approaches for the Rehabilitation or Prevention of Chronic Juvenile Offenders," in *Intervention Strategies for Chronic Juvenile Offenders*, ed. P. W. Greenwood (Westport, Conn.: Greenwood Press, 1986), 215.

108. Peter W. Greenwood and Susan Turner, *The VisionQuest Program: An Evaluation* (Santa Monica, Calif.: Rand Corporation, 1987), 45, R–3445–OJJDP.

109. Ibid., 16.

110. Coates, Miller, and Ohlin, *Diversity in a Youth Correctional System*, 175.

111. Miller and Ohlin, *Delinquency and Community*.

112. Bruce Bullington, James Sprowls, Daniel Katkin, and Harvey Lowell, "The Politics of Policy: De-institutionalization in Massachusetts 1970–1988," *Law and Policy* 8 (1986): 507–24, 510.

113. Ibid., 510.

114. Coates, Miller, and Ohlin, *Diversity in a Youth Correctional System*, 175.

115. Ibid., 176.

116. Ibid., 179, 180.

117. Ibid., 178.

118. Henry Maudsley, *The Pathology of the Mind* (London: Macmillan, 1895), 4.

119. Article 43 of the reformed Swiss Penal Code. See on this subject Christian Nils Robert, "Délinquants mentalment déficients, psychiatrie et justice penale en suisse." *Revue de droit pénal et criminologie* 30 (Oct. 1976): 12.

120. See Hans Toch, *The Pains of Imprisonment* (Beverly Hills, Calif.: Sage, 1982), 221 and Torsten Eriksson, *The Reformers: A Historical Survey of Pioneer Experiments in the Treatment of Criminals* (New York: Elsevier, 1976), 200.

121. Ancel, *La défense sociale nouvelle*, 264; Edgardo Rotman, "La politique du traitement a la lumière de la troisième édition de *La défense sociale nouvelle*," *Revue de science criminelle et de droit pénal compare* (1984): 577.

122. See Lessard v. Schmidt, 349 F.Supp. 1078 (E.D. Wis. 1972). See also Edgardo Rotman, "Rechtliche Voraussetzungen der Behandlung geistesgestörter Straftäter in den Vereinigten Staaten," in *Festschrift für Günter Blau*, ed. H. -D. Schwind (Berlin: De Gruyter, 1985), 562.

123. In this regard, the decision of Wyatt v. Stickney (344 F.Supp. 373 (1972)), is a unique example of detailed standard setting.

124. See Alan Stone, "The Right to Refuse Treatment," *Archives of General Psychiatry* 38 (1981): 358 and Alexander Brooks, "The Constitutional Right to Refuse Antipsychotic Medications," *Bulletin of the American Academy of Psychiatry and Law* 8 (1980): 179.

125. See Alan Stone, *Law, Psychiatry and Morality* (Washington, D.C.: American Psychiatric Press, 1984), 150.

126. Alan Stone, *Mental Health and Law: A System in Transition* (Rockville, Md.: National Institute for Mental Health, 1975), 182 and George E. Dix "Special Dispositional Alternatives for Abnormal Offenders," in *Mentally Disordered Offenders*, ed. J. Monahan and H. J. Steadman (New York: Plenum, 1983), 75.

127. Louis N. Robinson, "Institutions for Defective Delinquents," *Journal of the American Institute for Criminal Law and Criminology* 24 (1933–34): 383, in relation to the Institution for Defective Delinquents at Napanoch, New York, opened in 1921.

128. Edwin Sutherland, "The Sexual Psychopath Laws," *Journal of Criminal Law and Criminology* 40 (Jan.–Feb. 1950): 543–54.

129. See Alfred B. Vuocolo, *The Administration of the New Jersey Sex Offender Programs* (Ann Arbor, Mich.: University Microfilm, 1967), diss. New York University, No. 67-10, 994.

130. Arlene Skolnick, *The Intimate Environment* (Boston: Little, Brown, 1978).

131. See Alan M. Dershowitz, "Preventive Confinement: A Suggested Framework for Constitutional Analysis," *Texas Law Review* 51 (1973): 1295.

132. Fay Honey Knopp, *Retraining Adult Sex Offenders: Methods and Models* (New York: Safer Society Press, 1986), 27.

133. "Survey: 'Number of Sex Offenders in Prison Growing,' " *Corrections Compendium* 11 (May 1987): 5.

134. Knopp, *Retraining Adult Sex Offenders*, xiii.

135. Ibid., 9.

136. Ibid., 12.

137. Robert Freeman-Longo, quoted in ibid., 15.

138. Richard Seely, quoted in ibid., 16.

139. Ibid., 65–266.

140. Lauren J. Abrams, "Sexual Offenders and the Use of Depo-Provera," *San Diego Law Review* 22 (May–June 1985): 565–86.

141. See pp. 79–85.

142. 437 F.Supp. 269 (D. N.H. 1977).

143. An interesting application of this doctrine is contained in an action brought on by an Amended Petition for a Writ for Habeas Corpus filed by Yale Law School Clinical Program on behalf of an inmate seeking a Depo-Provera drug treatment to control his deviant sexual disorders. McDonald v. Bronson, No. 84–32654 (Conn. Sup. Ct., Tolland Jud. Dist., Rockville Nov. 30, 1984). The petitioner claimed that the denial of such treatment by Connecticut violated the Eighth Amendment as applied to the states through the Fourteenth Amendment. Petitioner's Memorandum at Law at 13–18, McDonald v. Bronson, No. 84–32654 (Conn. Sup. Ct., Tolland Jud. Dist., Rockville Nov. 30, 1984). A settlement was reached with the state, through which Depo-Provera was provided.

144. Ross and Gendreau, *Effective Correctional Treatment*, 38.

145. See Georg K. Stürup, *Treating the Untreatable* (Baltimore, Md.: Johns Hopkins University Press, 1968).

146. See Jean-Marc Dutrenit, "Le mouvement de psychothérapie institutionnelle: Analyse sociologique d'un courant psychiatrique," *L'année sociologique* 25 (1974): 165–235.

147. See Julie T.T.M. Feldbrugge, *Commitment to the Commited: Treatment as In-*

teraction in a Forensic Hospital (Lisse, Netherlands: Swets & Zeitlinger, 1986) and Edgardo Rotman, "El tratamiento socioterapéutico de delincuentes aquejados de perturbacionse mentales en la clínica del Dr. Henri van der Hoeven (Utrecht)." In *Congreso Panamericano de criminologia* (Buenos Aires: Universidad del Salvador, 1979).

6
Conclusions

I

Rehabilitation offers a constructive way to improve the criminal justice system. Its concern for offenders as whole human beings enriches the state's reaction to crime with a higher notion of justice and leads to a better law. Modern rehabilitative policies challenge the fantasy that the dark side of society can be forgotten and its deviants simply packed off to prisons. Without rehabilitative efforts before and after their discharge, offenders' grave social and individual problems will usually lead them to further crime. Rehabilitation thus increases the protection of those fundamental values guaranteed by criminal law. Moreover, rehabilitation improves the criminal justice system by connecting it to the public health, educational, and social welfare systems. Giving a social dimension to criminal justice, rehabilitation multiplies its resources and increases its quality and effectiveness.

Most of the well-meant criticism of rehabilitation fails to distinguish its two basic forms: one authoritarian, aiming to force normative compliance and institutional adjustment, and another humanistic, offering noncoercive dialogue and opportunity. The latter form of rehabilitation respects moral choice and individual values, and enhances self-determination and responsibility. In addition, it seeks to reorganize the community to which the offender returns, including the workplace, school, and family.

The liberty-centered perspective leads to the conception of rehabilitation as an offender's right, the culmination of a continuum of rights guaranteeing the dignity of human beings confronted with criminal conviction. The right to rehabilitation is defined as the right to an opportunity to return to society with a better chance of being a useful citizen and of staying out of prison. This right requires not only education and therapy but also a nondestructive prison environment and, when possible, less restrictive alternatives to incarceration. The right to rehabilitation is consistent with the drive toward the full restoration of prisoners' civil and political rights of citizenship after release.

Rehabilitation has undergone deep transformations over time, reflecting changing anthropological conceptions and broader social ideology. These transformations can be represented by four successive historical models: penitentiary, therapeutic, social learning, and rights oriented. The penitentiary model is centered on the basic elements of work, discipline, and moral education. The therapeutic model—criticized for viewing the criminal offender as sick—adds the valuable element of care, in the sense of help and assistance. The social-learning approach inspired the most remarkable rehabilitative experiments of this century. The rights-oriented model includes the viewpoint of the offender, recognizing rehabilitation as a substantive right independent from utilitarian considerations and transient penal strategies.

Rehabilitation has not been a unitary phenomenon, and its development through the penitentiary, therapeutic, social-learning, and rights-oriented models has not been a straightforward process. Instead, we see a pattern of relative progress, in which later models mix with earlier ones. The renewal of rehabilitative policies will require a careful evaluation of what has been done in the past to distinguish relevant and redeeming efforts from flawed experiments.

II

It is imperative to distinguish valid criticism of rehabilitation from the many misdirected attacks that are really aimed at different phenomena, such as prisons or indeterminate sentencing. Viewed as the culmination of a continuum of offenders' rights, rehabilitation can no longer provide a pretext for discretionary abuse on the part of sentencing and correctional authorities. Quite the contrary, a right to rehabilitation reinforces the legal status of the sentenced offender and requires sentencing and correctional policies compatible with rehabilitative prison conditions. Because of its deep connection with the essence of criminal punishment, the right to rehabilitation has a paramount constitutional significance. Countries that have decided to combat crime at the highest civilized level have fully recognized rehabilitation as a constitutional mandate.

Rehabilitation should no longer be made a scapegoat to explain the increase of crime rates and various flaws in the criminal justice system. This type of criticism aims to replace constructive correctional experiments with harsh sentences. But the effectiveness of punishment does not depend on its harshness but rather on its certainty and proportionality—as both eighteenth-century reformers and modern behavioral scientists agree. Rehabilitation does not oppose the measure of deterrence inherent in criminal punishment. It strives only to maintain punishment within the limits of a preexisting law, counteracting its unwarranted consequences.

It is wrong to argue that sociological theories of crime discredit rehabilitation. Only a rigid deterministic view of society or the individual is incompatible with the idea of rehabilitation. In fact, a sense of the role of society in the genesis of crime should deepen the rehabilitative concept beyond a mere readjustment to a criminogenic society. Constructive sociological criticism should not only help to improve the quality of rehabilitative programs but complement them with social policies that reach the community itself, improving the linkages of programs with families, schools, and the world of work.

Many critics took a dim view of rehabilitative effectiveness during the 1970s, embodied in the popularized apothegm "nothing works." In the 1980s a new era of cautious optimism has begun. Rehabilitation has been reaffirmed, and many instances of success proclaimed. This shift reflects not only correctional improvement, but also a refinement of evaluative methods and the identification of some fundamental flaws in the "nothing works" arguments, which exaggerated programs' failures and overlooked valuable results.

In any case, it is a mistake to focus exclusively on the issue of effectiveness. To do so is to take a one-sided view of rehabilitation, seeing it exclusively from the perspective of society, as part of governmental planning and social policy. When rehabilitation is also regarded as a right of the offender, its value independent of its outcome becomes evident. Although the effectiveness of rehabilitation is of vital importance, its rationale transcends its utility.

What about "incorrigible" offenders? This designation more often reflects correctional flaws, including the lack of rehabilitative support, than individual propensities. An offender who seems incorrigible within a particular rehabilitative context may be amenable to other, untried treatment approaches. Moreover, recidivism should not automatically lead to a conclusion of incorrigibility or justify incapacitation or overly extended incarceration. The incapacitation of dangerous offenders should be justified in its own right, strictly respecting constitutional safeguards and statutory limitations.

III

Imprisonment can never be rehabilitative in itself. Historically, a mistaken belief in the prison's rehabilitative efficacy was used to justify protracted incarceration and the excessive resort to imprisonment as a criminal sanction. In reality, the very fact of imprisonment creates the need to rehabilitate the inmate from the prison's own desocializing influence. The social and psychological effects of freedom deprivation demand a strong compensatory rehabilitative action. To subject the inmate to the harmful effects of imprisonment without allowing any possibility to counteract them is additional and unlawful punishment. Without opportunities for rehabilitation, at the educational, labor, and therapeutic levels, the warehoused offender inevitably deteriorates.

Because penal servitude and hard labor have been abolished by law, imprisonment in a modern civilized society should consist only of the deprivation of liberty. To administer such legal punishment without unwarranted side effects requires a positive rehabilitative action. This effort cannot be reduced to a discrete set of programs but should create a rehabilitative environment, by reorganizing the correctional institution and linking it with the community through various forms of furloughs and prerelease programs. A supportive intrainstitutional atmosphere should be geared toward enhancing the future life prospects of the individual offender.

A basic principle of modern corrections, directly linked with the rehabilitative aim, should be to make the conditions of prison life resemble those outside the prison as much as possible. The social bonds of the inmates should be maintained and visitation encouraged. The notion of an ''open prison'' should be a cornerstone of rehabilitation-oriented correctional reform, especially in the last stages of a prison sentence. The open prison should be oriented toward freedom and should support the inmate at the levels of education, work, and social welfare. The rehabilitative potential of prison work depends on its being integrated with the free labor market. Prison work should be meaningful, useful, productive, and realistic and should meet the requirements of the market.

Efforts to avoid the pernicious effects of incarceration find their ultimate expression in the creation of noncustodial alternatives to incarceration. At the sentencing level, the rehabilitative aim should lead to the use of alternatives to imprisonment whenever possible. Short prison sentences should be replaced by nonincarcerative alternatives, and excessively long sentences should be minimized to avoid destructive effects on inmates and their chances of future social reintegration.

The most effective way to carry out the rehabilitative task is to deal with offenders in the community. Genuine community corrections actually replaces imprisonment and can never be used to extend state intervention beyond its indispensable minimum. The community should not be considered a panacea in itself. The value of a concrete community for corrections depends on its cohesion, educational and moral resources, and its low criminogenic potential. As ideal conditions seldom prevail, a modern rehabilitative concept should be supplemented with action on the community to reorganize and transform it into an opportunity-providing social context.

A right to rehabilitation includes a right to be considered for probation, community service, or other available community-based programs. These rights should be exercised according to objective guidelines ensuring fair treatment. Probation—a fruitful field for improvement and creative innovation—should remain a centerpiece of a modern rehabilitative policy. Suspended sentences, which rely on offenders' responsibility and conscience, should be maintained as a way to impel them to assume themselves the task of integration into the community. Other nonincarcerative sanctions, such as fines, should also be used.

Traditional alternatives to imprisonment have been supplemented by community service sentences and restitution, which have achieved remarkable rehabilitative success, by creating a positive interaction with the community. Rehabilitation in the community, through various types of support centers, can be an alternative not only to arrest and pretrial detention, but also to prosecution. Mediation and arbitration of minor criminal cases by community representatives have become fruitful alternatives to adjudication in the courts, representing an important form of social learning and a powerful factor for attitude change. The field of juvenile delinquency has proved to be particularly promising for community corrections.

The broad intermediate category between the sane and the insane has represented a fertile ground for modern intensive rehabilitative experiments. The treatment of this category of mentally disturbed offenders inspired the main European social therapeutic programs after World War II, which included the creation of fields of intensive social interaction guided by an enlightened specialized staff as well as the active participation of inmates. These pilot programs have great significance for corrections as a whole, particularly because they can be administered within strict due process limitations, and the harmful label of mental illness can largely be avoided. Combined with a liberty-centered model of rehabilitation, these programs have curtailed past abuses, made treatment dependent on informed consent, and dramatically reduced the average length of institutionalization. Going beyond individual treatment, modern social therapy includes the transformation of the institutional structure, the introduction of new forms of collective treatment, and the creation of quasi-therapeutic communities within prison settings. These represent the correctional counterpart of major innovations in the field of mental health based on enlightened criticism of conventional psychiatry.

Appendix: The Dr. van der Hoeven Clinic in Utrecht, the Netherlands

This account of the van der Hoeven Clinic is intended to give a more detailed picture of an intensive rehabilitative experiment. Although the clinic does not always fully represent a liberty-centered concept of rehabilitation, it is one of the most important social-therapeutic attempts to go beyond custodial detention of mentally disordered offenders and to support their reintegration into the community. Thus it constitutes an outstanding precedent for the entire correctional system to shape a right to rehabilitative treatment in a less restrictive setting.

Its general guiding principles are based on a recognition of the negative effects of traditional prisons: social isolation, loss of personal initiative, and general impoverishment of the inmate's personality. While accepting institutional commitment as a necessary evil, the program attempts to counteract such effects through specific strategies.

To diminish social isolation, the clinic is located near the town center of Utrecht, a city of approximately 250,000. The location makes it easier to enlist potential employers and volunteer "contact families," who are visited regularly by the patients and help them in the process of reintegrating into society. Besides these social contacts with the external environment, the inmates' family members and friends are encouraged to visit them in the institution. In this way, social and family relationships are bolstered and effective links strengthened.

To combat the loss of initiative, a basic aim of treatment is to develop the patient's sense of responsibility. As far as possible staff members refrain from making decisions for the inmate. The institution takes only those initiatives that the patients themselves are not in a position to assume. To avoid the infantilizing atmosphere typical of total institutions, the nature of treatment and its financial aspects are explained to the patients from the very beginning. They must participate not only in planning and executing the treatment, but also rating their progress. It is also made clear to them that the clinic must be managed in the economically most rational way and that the patients will receive only those benefits they have earned through their work. Each "living group" of patients must determine its own budget and manage its assets; it is also responsible for broken windows or furniture and must repair any damages as well as replace missing tools. Under no circumstance is the patient to feel as if he were only a number or an impersonal entity. He is therefore partially responsible for the management of the clinic as a member of decision-making or consulting committees. He votes to elect a directing council and participates in both the election of a directing council and the daily running of the establishment.

The van der Hoeven Clinic's therapeutic system emphasizes the reintegration of the patient into normal life. Contact families actively help the institution in this task. By treating the patient as one of their own kin, they help him surmount his feelings of guilt and inferiority. Living conditions inside the clinic are kept as similar as possible to real life. Patients deal with real money, not credit coupons or similar documents. Contact between the two sexes is a daily occurrence, as in normal life. The staff consists of men and women in equal numbers, although the number of female patients is far too small for a similar ratio of inmates.

The number of patients is maintained at an optimal level, large enough to justify an amply variety of means and therapeutic options, but small enough to avoid the cold, impersonal atmosphere of large institutions. In August 1988 there were seventy-two inmates in the clinic, which has a total capacity of seventy-three persons. There were sixty-five men and seven women, divided into living groups of eight to twelve. The ages of the patients ranged from twenty to fifty years, but 75 percent were in the twenty to thirty-five age group. Juvenile patients have occasionally been admitted. The most frequent offenses causing detention are fraud, theft, violent crimes, sexual offenses, infanticides, and homicides.

Article 37a of the Dutch penal code of 1886, reformed by a 1929 statute, extends court orders placing irresponsible offenders under the care of the government to persons who at the time of the offense show an insufficient development or a pathological disorder of their mental faculties without reaching extreme irresponsibility. Placement at the pleasure of the government (*Ter Beschikking Stelling van de Regering*, usually referred to as TBR), is for a two-year term and can be extended by the court for another period not exceeding two additional years. The TBR should be imposed only in cases involving a serious offense or repeated offenses and only after the prison sentence has been served. The decision to order a TBR is based on reports from psychiatrists, psychologists, and other experts made during a required observation period.

ORIGINS OF THE CLINIC

The van der Hoeven Clinic originated in a psychiatric observation unit created in 1949 in the Department of Prisons at Utrecht. The medical superintendent and his closest collaborators searched for the means to carry out the treatment recommendations that they made in their reports to the courts. At the same time, the medical superintendent of the Willem Arntsz Foundation, a welfare corporation active in the field of mental health for more than five hundred years (founded in 1461), was trying to add a forensic psychiatric unit to that foundation's great psychiatric hospital. The Ministry of Justice lacked sufficient space to lodge the inmates of the existing institution, which was already overcrowded. These factors together led to the establishment of the van der Hoeven Clinic in 1955.

According to the contract between the Willem Arntsz Foundation and the Dutch government, the Ministry of Justice nominates candidates for treatment; the clinic's director can reject a proposed admission, but rarely exercises this power. The government helps fund the expenses of the establishment, but it is directly controlled and managed by a foundation commission. A great percentage of the patients are subjected to the TBR, while the rest are either being treated as an alternative to prison sentences, committed by the Juvenile Court or under suspended sentences. Every inmate suffers some kind of mental disturbance.

Initially, the clinic had twenty patients and a staff of thirty-five. The great novelty was the granting of responsibilities to the patients, most of whom had prior records in reformatories and prisons, where they had been strictly excluded from decision making and rigidly separated from the staff. In the new institution the patients helped draw up the rules that organized life in the establishment, were represented in consultative committees, and served with the staff on a great variety of other committees, which were concerned with finances, clothing, arbitration of conflicts, culture, leisure, and work.

At first, the therapeutic means were limited to psychotherapy and work therapy. The percentage of patients undergoing psychotherapy diminished over time, whereas work therapy was transformed into work training. Patients were not just kept occupied, but purposefully trained to develop a productive skill for use after their discharge.

THE NEW CLINIC

With development of new therapeutic criteria and means, the old clinic building became obsolete. In 1974 the clinic was relocated to a site near the center of Utrecht, surrounded by industrial establishments and offices. The sociologist Jessen participated in the architectural design of the new building, trying to avoid oppressive spatial sensations that led to compulsive escapes. The construction surrounds an ample interior garden, to which each group has access from its own section. The outer perimeter of the building has a minimum height of six meters, for reasons of security.

The building is divided into four quarters. One of them, with open doors, is reserved for the free circulation of patients. It is composed of four housing compounds, each of which is occupied by two living groups of eight to ten patients each. Each group occupies two living rooms with an exit to the garden, a kitchen, closet space, and toilets. On the first floor of each group section (or "house") are the individual rooms of the patients. Because inmates are given interior keys, groups can include both sexes. Patients also have a key that gives them access to their group's whole building section. The area of free circulation includes the garden, meeting halls, leisure halls, hairdresser's salon and grocery. It can be closed at various points in an emergency, however.

Treatment is carried out in another section of the building, which includes the sports complex, workshops, educational department, rooms devoted to religious worship and music, professional orientation, psychotherapy, group therapy (with the possibility of videotaping), the kitchen, and the surgery ward. On the first floor of this wing is the intensive treatment unit, including a small health care ward. This section is considered a transitional stage toward normal groups.

A third section of the clinic is reserved for the staff, while the fourth is an area of transition to the external world, housing staff members charged with maintaining and stimulating relations with the outer social environment. This section has guest rooms where patients' relatives may stay and rooms where they may meet with inmates privately. These spaces are used either for a prerelease period of family life in a semiliberty regime or for intensive treatment for the whole family group. The new building is very well equipped with complete sporting facilities as well as considerable space for expressive activities.

ORGANIZATION

The clinic staff consists of 150 persons working either full- or part-time, many of whom are not involved in treatment. There is also a group of psychotherapists and approximately ten teachers who are paid on an hourly basis for their group sessions and lessons. Security is considered to be of maximum importance, although no specialized personnel are provided for that purpose. To a great extent the issue is handled by granting a certain responsibility to the patients and maintaining close and constant contact with them. No keys are needed in the new building, which is equipped with an electronic security system; closed-circuit television monitors the doors (but not rooms, halls, or corridors).

The patients' living groups have a decidedly therapeutic character that promotes initiative and responsibility. Members participate not only in group management but also in the psychological care of the other members and even in the decisions taken on furloughs, leaves of absence, holidays, or other petitions. Each living group is supervised by four or five group leaders or group counselors, who are psychiatric nurses, social workers, and young psychologists and sociologists. Their mean age in 1987 was 32.9 years, and there are at least two women in each group, to maintain the maximum likeness with social contacts in the world outside. Group leaders closely participate in the life of patients including meals and leisure time. They express their opinions with great spontaneity and freedom, creating a flexible relationship and facing conflicts as they arise. Nevertheless they maintain proper limits with the group of patients. If the relationship between a group leader and the patients deteriorates and becomes manipulative, it is relatively easy to correct the problem because of the daily contact and shared efforts with the other group leaders. Groups are organized into pairs known as "blocks," and the two groups' supervisors constitute a "team," with a shared office. There is also a team coordinator.

The daily routine of the institution, such as watches and staff assignments, is handled by the five-member *Algemeen Coordinatieteam* ("general coordination group"), consisting of former group counselors. Another working group called *Overzichts-en Bege-leidingsfunktionarissen* ("treatment supervision and assistance") assists in structuring and developing the treatment plan of each patient and takes responsibility for other forms of assistance and supervision, participating in meetings and improving the existing therapeutic means.

Another important function is performed by councils consisting of two patients (who serve on a rotating basis) and the team coordinator of a block. The councils together, supplemented by representatives of the administrative commissions, form the clinic council, which meets twice a week to discuss all common events of the institution's life. The inmates' participation in the solution of the institution's problems, as well as in the treatment of each patient, entails a social-learning process of high therapeutic value. One patient chosen by the staff and other inmates prepares a statement summarizing the council's proceedings. In addition, various commissions composed of staff and patients are established to deal with such matters as clothing, money handling, or disciplinary conflicts arising, for example, from absence from work or slovenly housekeeping.

Five members of the staff are in charge of the external service, which is one of the most important facets of the clinic. They are responsible for communicating with relatives and friends of the patient, finding contact families, and organizing their relationships with the patient.

TREATMENT

The clinic originated in a critique of the traditional prison as an isolating, narrow and impoverished world. It was organized according to a therapeutic goal but also sought a radical change in attitude toward the offender, who is considered to be on a par with the therapist. As far as possible, treatment is tailored to the personality and needs of the patients, but it demands much of their efforts and cooperation. A wide array of therapy is available, although the prevailing direction is toward the model of the therapeutic community. Everyday action is pervaded by a concern to improve communication and cooperation between inmates and staff as well as among members of each group.

The guiding therapeutic idea is evident in the architecture of the clinic building, which looks more like a school or an office building than a traditional prison. The conference rooms, gymnasiums, and workshops for creative and expressive activities, study, work, and professional training give the impression of a learning institution. Reinforced glass panels in the new building substitute for iron bars and paradoxically offer better security than the old building. A closed television circuit, controlled from the entrance of the premises by special personnel, and night guards consisting of two unarmed group co-ordinators and a nurse further strengthen the security network. Although the system does not claim to be flawless—escapes have occurred—it can cope with extremely dangerous patients.

The treatment plan is carefully prepared and controlled. After a period of familiarization and evaluation, lasting no more than six weeks during which the patient is expected to participate actively, a plan is put together in agreement with him or her. All problems related to the plan are openly discussed. The treatment plan is reexamined monthly by the group counselors and the supervisor, as well as by the patients concerned, to determine whether changes are needed. Group counselors also write a monthly report, known as the "case history" or "status," concerning the evolution of the patient during the preceding month. This report is consulted when decisions are to be made on the patient's petitions regarding furloughs, holidays, etc. All reports and evaluations are recorded on a daily basis by a staff of five full-time typists.

Limited use is made of psychotherapy in its strict sense. In 1988, 50 to 60 percent of the patients were participating in some form of specific therapy, whereas in the clinic's early days all patients underwent psychotherapy. Because this practice did not produce significant changes, the clinic began prescribing psychotherapy only when specially indicated. Sessions take place once or twice a week. Psychotherapy can be closed or open. In the former case, three psychiatrists and two psychologists visit the establishment to meet with patients individually. The open psychotherapeutic team, permanently based in the clinic, is reserved for new patients or special problems. Therapeutic methods are overwhelmingly pragmatic and eclectic and adapted to the solution of concrete problems. Moving away from the initial bias toward psychoanalysis, the current trend favors the Rogers method of client-centered therapy. Therapy includes methods derived from systems theory (e.g., family, partners, and other relations therapies) and from learning theory (e.g., behavior therapy and social-skills training). Programs intend to be a blend of ordinary life, learning, and therapy in its strict sense. Sports, dance, and work are also part of the social-therapeutic concept. The main objective of work in the clinic is, however, the acquisition of behavior that, being less dangerous, allows for patients' reinstatement in the community after their discharge.

The normal work period of eight hours is reduced for most patients by their participation in other activities connected with their treatment, such as psychotherapy or education. In the new clinic there is a modern workshop for metalwork, where various finished and semifinished products are manufactured. There is also a carpentry workshop, and patients can choose from a wide variety of tasks such as those related to the kitchen, management, gardening, and maintenance, or the patients can be involved with the handling of the store where food for breakfast and lunch, cleaning products, sports shoes, toiletries, and some sundries are sold to the staff and patients. The clinic gives housekeeping money to each living group. An important aspect of the treatment is dealing with money, and the inmates are expected to pay even the government tax on the use of their television sets. They buy their own soap, coffee, newspapers, and bread and pay their own electric bills. Other treatment-oriented activities are creative games, music, drawing, sculpture, drama, and mime, led by qualified specialists.

Personal development, which includes study, is a cornerstone of the van der Hoeven Clinic. Participation is voluntary, but once a patient has committed himself to a study plan, he is no longer free to abandon it *ad libitum* (failure to meet work or study obligations may lead to a loss of privileges, such as furloughs or leaves, depending on treatment evaluation and other circumstances). The program includes professional orientation and vocational tests. Patients participate in the workshop's industrial process, from the beginning of the manufacture to the delivery of the finished product. Within the limits set by the number of patients, the clinic seeks to offer them the broadest possible scope of options. Staff members also help the patients in finding jobs, in joining clubs, and in all other aspects of their relationship with the world outside the clinic. The institution also encourages frequent visits with family and friends in order to strengthen the patients' social bonds.

In 1988, 78 percent of the patients were participating in an educational program—35 percent at the elementary school level and 43 percent at the secondary level. Schooling becomes vitally important when the patient works only half a day or not at all. The subjects taught in the clinic include art and sex education. Although some of the patients had been classified as apparently retarded, the actual intellectual level of the patients is normal or above average.

Several of the living groups are sexually mixed, reflecting a desire to make life in the institution as close to normal life as possible. Sexual relationships are discouraged, although as a rule not obstructed, and patients have the right to lock their rooms from the inside; only the social workers have master keys. A difficulty with the mixed group system is the considerably smaller proportion of women.

Patients' contact with volunteer families is a vitally important aspect of treatment. Roughly ten contact families receive and look after the patients on leave. With a few exceptions this system of support has worked smoothly.

Research on the effectiveness of treatment at the van der Hoeven Clinic has yielded satisfactory results. In 1980, the Scientific Research and Documentation Center of the Dutch Ministry of Justice carried out a follow-up study on former patients to evaluate the clinic's success in rehabilitation. Both the stopping of further dangerous behavior and the personal development of the patient were considered. The central issue was the relationship between the present-life situation of the patients and their previous treatment.

One of the most striking findings was the higher rate of recidivism (up to 70 percent) among patients who had been transferred to other institutions, as compared with those who had ended their treatment through the regular process of furlough programs (30 percent). (For this purpose recidivism was defined by at least one conviction for a crime or minor offense during a period of five years after leaving the clinic.) This research also verified that the number of patients undergoing long-term treatment at the institution had diminished considerably and the average length of stay had declined.

Select Bibliography

Allen, Francis A. *The Borderland of Criminal Justice*. Chicago: University of Chicago Press, 1964.

———. *The Decline of the Rehabilitative Ideal: Penal Policy and Social Purpose*. New Haven, Conn.: Yale University Press, 1981.

Allen, John. *Assault with Deadly Weapon: The Autobiography of a Street Criminal*. Edited by Dianne Hall Kelly and Philip Heymann. New York: Pantheon, 1977.

American Friends Service Committee. *Struggle for Justice*. New York: Hill & Wang, 1971.

Ancel, Marc. *The Indeterminate Sentence*. New York: United Nations, Department of Social Affairs, 1954.

———. "Peine et rééducation dans l'évolution du droit pénal." In Études et Documentations. Paris: Min. de la Justice, Direction de l'Adm. Pénitentiare, 1959.

———. "De la vengeance éxpiatoire au traîtement des délinquants." In *L'évolution du droit criminel contemporain (Hommage a J. Lebret)*. Paris: Presses Universitaires de France, 1968.

———. *Suspended Sentence*. London: Heinemann, 1971.

———. "La peine privative de liberté du point de vue de la politique criminelle moderne." In *Lebendiges Strafrecht (Festschrift für Hans Schultz)*, edited by H. Walder and S. Trechsel. Bern: Stampfli, 1977.

———. "Examen de conscience de défense sociale: Le problème du traitement des delinquants." *Revue de science criminelle et de droit pénal comparé* (1978): 949.

———. "Directions et directives de politique criminelle dans le mouvement de reforme pénale moderne." In *Festschrift für Hans-Heinrich Jescheck*, edited by Theo Vogler. Berlin: Duncker & Humblot, 1985.

———. *La défense sociale nouvelle*. Paris: Cujas, 1981. Translated by Thorsten Sellin. *Social Defense: The Future of Penal Reform*. Littleton, Colo.: Rothman, 1987.

Bartollas, Clemens. *Correctional Treatment: Theory and Practice*. Englewood Cliffs, N.J.: Prentice-Hall, 1985.

Bergalli, Roberto. *Readaptación social por medio de la ejecución penal?* Madrid: Pub-
    licaciones del Instituto de Criminología de la Universidad de Madrid, 1976.
Berman, Harold J. *The Interaction of Law and Religion.* Nashville, Tenn.: Abingdon
    Press, 1974.
———. *Law and Revolution: The Formation of the Western Legal Tradition.* Cambridge,
    Mass.: Harvard University Press, 1983.
Blau, Günter. "Kustodiale und antikustodiale Tendenzen in der amerikanischen Krimin-
    alpolitik." *Goldtdammer's Archiv für Strafrecht* (1976): 35.
———. "Die Kriminalpolitik der deutschen Strafrechtsreformgesetze." *Zeitschrift für
    die gesamte Strafrechtswissenschaft* 89 (1977): 511–46.
———. "Schuld und Gefährlichkeit des psychisch abnormen Täters. Strafrechtsge-
    schichtliche, kriminologische und rechtsvergleichende Aspekte." In *Straftäter in
    der Psychiatrie*, edited by G. Blau and H. Kammeier. Stuttgart: Enke, 1984.
———. "Die gemeinnützige Arbeit als Beispiel für einen grundlegenden Wandel des
    Sanktionenwesens." In *Gedächtnisschrift für Hilde Kaufmann*, edited by Hans
    Joachim Hirsch, Günther Kaiser, and Helmut Marquardt. Berlin: De Gruyter,
    1986.
———. "Diversion und Strafrecht." *Jura* 1 (1987): 25–34.
Blau, G., and E. Franke. "Diversion und Schlichtung." *Zeitschrift für die gesamte
    Strafrechtswissenschaft* 96 (1984): 485–501.
Bolle, P. -H. "La mise en oeuvre de la loi de 1971 et de solutions telles que le juge de
    l'application des peines." *Revue pénale suisse* 90, no. 4 (1974): 359–83.
Bueno Arus, Francisco. "La resocialización del delincuente adulto normal desde la
    perspectiva del derecho penitenciario." *Actualidad penal* 5 (Jan. 26–Feb. 1, 1987).
Carter, R. M., D. Glaser, and L. T. Wilkins. *Probation, Parole and Community Cor-
    rections.* New York: Wiley, 1984.
Cloward, R. A., and L. Ohlin. *Delinquency and Opportunity: A Theory of Delinquent
    Gangs.* New York: Free Press, 1960.
Coates, R. B., A. D. Miller, and L. E. Ohlin. *Diversity in a Youth Correctional System:
    Handling Delinquents in Massachusetts.* Cambridge, Mass.: Ballinger, 1978.
Conrad, John P. "A Lost Ideal, a New Hope: Toward Effective Correctional Treatment."
    Journal of Criminal Law and Criminology 72, no. 4 (1981): 1699–734.
Cormier, Bruno M. *The Watcher and the Watched.* Montreal: Tundra, 1975.
de la Cuesta Arzamendi, Jose Luis. *El Trabajo Penitenciario Resocializador.* San Se-
    bastián: Caja de Ahorros Provincial de Guipúzcoa, 1982.
Cullen, Francis T., and Karen E. Gilbert. *Reaffirming Rehabilitation.* Cincinnati, Ohio:
    Anderson, 1982.
Cullen, F. T., G. A. Clark, and J. F. Woznar. "Explaining the Get Tough Movement:
    Can the Public Be Blamed?" *Federal Probation* 49 (June 1985): 16–24.
Cullen, F. T., K. M. Golden, and J. B. Cullen. "Is Child Saving Dead? Attitudes towards
    Juvenile Rehabilitation in Illinois." *Journal of Criminal Justice* 11 (1983): 1–13.
Currie, Elliot. *Confronting Crime: An American Challenge.* New York: Pantheon, 1985.
Dershowitz, Allan M. "Indeterminate Confinement: Letting the Therapy Fit the Harm."
    University of Pennsylvania Law Review 123 (1974): 297–339.
DiIulio, John J., Jr. *Governing Prisons: A Comparative Study of Correctional Manage-
    ment.* New York: Free Press, 1987.
Dolcini, Emilio. "La rieducazione del condannato tra mito e realtà." *Rivista Italiana di
    diritto e procedura penale* (1979): 469.

Dünkel, Frieder. *Legalbewährung nach sozialtherapeutischer Behandlung*. Berlin: Duncker & Humblot, 1980.

———. "Die Öffnung des Vollzugs—Anspruch und Wirklichkeit." *Zeitschrift für die gesamte Strafrechtswissenschaft* 94 (1982): 669–710.

———. "Aspekte der Strafvollzugsreform in der Bundesrepublik Deutschland." In *German Research on Crime and Crime Control*, edited by H. J. Kerner, H. Kury, and K. Sessar. Cologne: Heymanns, 1983.

Dünkel, Frieder, and Elmer H. Johnson. "Introduction of Therapy into Tegel Prison: Evaluation of an Experiment." *International Journal of Comparative and Applied Criminal Justice* 4, no. 2 (1980): 233–47.

Dünkel, Frieder, and Gerhard Spiess, eds. *Alternativen zur Freiheitstrafe: Strafausetzung zur Bewährung and Bewährungshilfe im internationalen Vergleich*. Freiburg, West Germany: Max Planck Institut für ausländisches und internationales Strafrecht, 1983.

Egg, Rudolf. *Straffälligkeit und Sozialtherapie*. Cologne: Carl Heymanns Verlag, 1984.

Eriksson, Torsten. *The Reformers: A Historical Survey of Pioneer Experiments in the Treatment of Criminals*. New York: Elsevier, 1976.

Eser, Albin. "Resozialisierung in der Krise." In *Festschrift für Karl Peters*, edited by Jürgen Baumann and Klaus Tiedemann. Tübingen: J.C.B. Mohr, 1974.

Farrington, D. P., L. E. Ohlin, and J. Q. Wilson. *Understanding and Controlling Crime: Toward a New Research Strategy*. New York: Springer, 1986.

Feldbrugge, Julie T.T.M. *Commitment to the Committed: Treatment as Interaction in a Forensic Mental Hospital*. Lisse: Swets and Zeitlinger, 1986.

Feldbrugge, Julie T.T.M., and Y. A. Werdmuller von Elgg, eds. *Involuntary Institutionalization: Changing Concepts in the Treatment of Delinquency*. Amsterdam: Exerpta Medica, 1981.

Foucault, Michel. *Discipline and Punish: The Birth of the Prison*. New York: Vintage Books, 1979.

Garland, David. *Punishment and Welfare: A History of Penal Strategies*. London: Heinemann, 1985.

Gendreau, Paul, and Robert R. Ross. "Offender Rehabilitation: The Appeal of Success." *Federal Probation* 45 (Dec. 1981): 45–47.

———. "Revivification of Rehabilitation: Evidence from the 1980s." *Justice Quarterly* 4, no. 3 (Sept. 1987): 349–407.

Gibbons, Don C. "Correctional Treatment and Intervention Theory: Bringing Sociology and Criminology Back In." *International Journal of Offender Therapy and Comparative Criminology* 30 (1986): 255–71.

Glaser, Daniel. *The Effectiveness of a Prison and Parole System*. Indianapolis: Bobbs-Merrill, 1964.

———. "Concern with Theory in Correctional Evaluation Research." *Crime and Delinquency* 23 (April 1977): 173–79.

Gottfredson, Michael R. "The Social Scientist and Rehabilitative Crime Policy." *Criminology* (May 1982): 29–42.

Goudsmit, W., and J. W. Reicher, "Experience with Psychotherapeutic Treatment of Delinquents with a Serious Social Risk: Indication, Methods, Results." *International Journal of Law and Psychiatry* 1 (1978): 309.

Greenberg, David F., ed. *Corrections and Punishment*. Beverly Hills, Calif.: Sage, 1977.

Greenwood, Peter W., ed. *Intervention Strategies for Chronic Juvenile Offenders: Some New Perspectives.* Westport, Conn.: Greenwood Press, 1986.

Greenwood, Peter W., and Susan Turner. *The VisionQuest Program: An Evaluation.* Santa Monica, Calif.: Rand Corporation, 1987. R–3445–OJJDP.

Greenwood, Peter W., and Franklin E. Zimring. *One More Chance: The Pursuit of Promising Intervention Strategies for Chronic Juvenile Offenders.* Santa Monica, Calif.: Rand Corporation, 1985. R–3214–OJJDP.

Haffke, Bernhard. "Über den Widerspruch von Therapie und Herrschaft exemplifiziert an grundlegenden Bestimmungen des neuen Strafvollzugsgesetzes." *Zeitschrift für die gesamte Strafrechtswissenschaft* 88 (1976): 607–51.

Halleck, Seymour L., and Ann D. Witte. "Is Rehabilitation Dead?" *Crime and Delinquency* 23 (October 1977): 372–82.

Hardy, Richard E., and John G. Cull. *Introduction to Correctional Rehabilitation,* 2d ed. Springfield, Ill.: Charles Thomas, 1973.

Heymann, Philip B. *The Politics of Public Management.* New Haven, Conn.: Yale University Press, 1987.

Hicks, Stephen C. "The Jurisprudence of Comparative Legal Systems." *Loyola of Los Angeles International and Comparative Law Journal* 83 (1983): 93.

Huber, Barbara. *Die Freiheitstrafe in England und Wales.* Cologne: Carl Heymanns, 1983.

Hurtado Pozo, Jose. "La condena condicional." *Derecho* 31 (1973): 60–80.

Ignatieff, Michael. *A Just Measure of Pain.* New York: Pantheon, 1978.

International Penal and Penitentiary Foundation. *Criminal Records and Rehabilitation* (Proceedings of the Meeting of Neuchâtel, 1979). Neuchâtel, Switz.: Editions Ides et Calendes, 1982.

———. *New Trends in Criminal Policy* (Proceedings of the Fifth International Colloquium, Syracuse, 1982). Bonn: International Penal and Penitentiary Foundation, 1984.

———. *Community Service as an Alternative to the Prison Sentence* (Proceedings of the Meeting of Coimbra, Portugal, 1986). Bonn: International Penal and Penitentiary Foundation, 1987.

———. *Standard Minimum Rules for the Implementation of Non-Custodial Sanctions and Measures Involving Restriction of Liberty* (Groningen meeting, October 8–12, 1988). Deventer, Netherlands: Kluwer Publishers, 1989.

Irwin, John. *Prisons in Turmoil.* Boston: Little, Brown, 1980.

Jescheck, Hans-Heinrich. *Entwicklung, Aufgaben und Methoden der Strafrechtsvergleichung.* Tübingen: J.C.B. Mohr, 1955.

———. *Lehrbuch des Strafrechts. Allgemeiner Teil.* Berlin: Duncker & Humblot, 1978.

———. *Strafrecht im Dienste der Gemeinschaft.* Berlin: Duncker & Humblot, 1980.

Jessen, J. L., and A. M. Roosenburg. "Treatment Results at the Dr. Henri van der Hoeven Clinic, Utrecht, The Netherlands." *Excerpta Medica International Congress Series* 274 (1971): 723–33.

Johnson, Elmer H., and Frieder Dünkel. "Introducing Therapy into Tegel Prison: Implications from an Evaluation Perspective." *International Journal of Comparative and Applied Criminal Justice* 5, no. 1 (1985): 3–10.

Johnson, Robert. *Hard Time: Understanding and Reforming the Prison.* Monterey, Calif.: Brooks-Cole, 1987.

Kaiser, Günther. *Strategien und Prozesse strafrechtlicher Sozialkontrolle.* Frankfurt: Athenaum Verlag, 1972.

————. "Resozialisierung und Zeitgeist." In *Festschrift für Thomas Würtenberger,* edited by Rüdiger Herren, Diethelm Kienapfel, and Heinz Müller Dietz. Berlin: Duncker & Humblot, 1977.

————. "Krankheit, Behandlung und Strafrechtliche Schuld heute." *Universitas* 4 (Apr. 1978): 407.

————. "Was Wissen wir von der Strafe?" In *Festschrift für Paul Bockelmann,* edited by A. Kaufmann, G. Bemann, D. Krauss, and K. Volk. Munich: C. H. Beck, 1979.

Kaiser, G., H. -J. Kerner, and H. Schöch. *Strafvollzug: Eine Einführung in die Grundlangen.* Heidelberg: C. F. Müller, 1977.

Kaufmann, Arthur. "Dogmatische und kriminalpolitische Aspekte des Schuldgedankens im Strafrecht." *Juristenzeitung* 18 (1967): 553–60.

Kerner, H. J., H. Kury, and K. Sessar. *Deutsche Forshungen zur Kriminalitätsentstehung und Kriminalitätskontrolle.* Cologne: Heymanns, 1983.

Kittrie, Nicolas N. *The Right to Be Different: Deviance and Enforced Theory.* New York: Penguin Books, 1973.

Lejins, Peter P. "Massnahmen zur Behandlung abnormer Täter—Erfahrungsbericht aus den U.S.A." In *Sozialtherapie: Grenzfragen bei der Beurteilung psychischer Auffälligkeiten im Strafrecht,* edited by H. Göppinger and P. H. Bresser. Stuttgart: Enke, 1982.

Lipton, Douglas, Robert Martinson, and Judith Wilks. *The Effectiveness of Correctional Treatment: A Survey of Treatment Evaluation Studies.* New York: Praeger, 1975.

McGillis, Daniel. *Community Dispute Resolution Programs and Public Policy.* Washington, D.C.: National Institute of Justice, 1986.

Martin, Susan E., Lee B. Sechrest, and Robin Redner, eds. *New Directions in the Rehabilitation of Criminal Offenders: Final Report.* Washington, D.C.: National Research Council, National Academy of Sciences, 1981.

Martinson, Robert. "What Works? Questions and Answers about Prison Reform." *Public Interest* 35 (1974): 22–56.

Melzer, Michael. *Die neue Sozialverteidigung und die deutsche Strafrechtsreformdiskussion.* Tübingen: J. C. B. Mohr, 1970.

Miller, Alden D., and Lloyd E. Ohlin. *Delinquency and Community: Creating Opportunities and Controls.* Beverly Hills, Calif.: Sage, 1985.

Miller, A., L. E. Ohlin, and R. B. Coates. *A Theory of Social Reform: Correctional Change Processes in Two States.* Cambridge, Mass.: Ballinger, 1977.

Mitford, Jessica. *Kind & Usual Punishment.* New York: Vintage Books, 1974.

Moore, Mark, Susan Estrich, Daniel McGillis, and William Spellman. *Dangerous Offenders: The Elusive Target of Justice.* Cambridge, Mass.: Harvard University Press, 1985.

Morris, Norval. *The Future of Imprisonment.* Chicago: University of Chicago Press, 1974.

Müller-Dietz, Heinz. *Empirische Forschung und Strafvollzug.* Frankfurt: Klostermann, 1976.

Munagorri, Ignacio. *Sanción penal y política criminal: confrontación con la nueva defensa social.* Madrid: Editorial Reus, 1977.

Murton, Thomas O. *The Dilemma of Prison Reform.* New York: Holt, Rinehart & Winston, 1976.

Neuman, Elias. *Prisión abierta: una nueva experiencia penológica.* Buenos Aires: Ediciones Depalma, 1962.

Nietzel, Michael T. *Crime and Its Modification: A Social Learning Perspective.* New York: Pergamon, 1979.

Ohlin, Lloyd E., ed. *Prisoners in America.* Englewood Cliffs, N.J.: Prentice-Hall, 1973.

Parker, Craig L., Jr. *Parole and the Community Based Treatment of Offenders in Japan and the United States.* New Haven, Conn.: University of New Haven Press, 1986.

Peters, Karl. *Grundprobleme der Kriminalpädagogik.* Berlin: De Gruyter, 1960.

———. "Die ethischen Voraussetzungen des Resozialisierungs—und Erziehungsvollzuges." In *Festschrift für Ernst Heinitz,* edited by Hans Lütger. Berlin: De Gruyter, 1972.

Romkopf, Günter. "Sozialtherapeutische Anstalt Gelsenkirchen: Unterstützung der Wohngruppenarbeit durch Fachpersonal." *Sonderheft der Zeitschrift für Strafvollzug und Straffälligenhilfe* 29 (1980): 60–66.

Ross, Robert R., and Paul Gendreau, eds. *Effective Correctional Treatment.* Toronto: Butterworth, 1980.

Rothman, David J. *The Discovery of the Asylum: Social Order and Disorder in the New Republic.* Boston: Little, Brown, 1971.

———. "Behavior Modification in Total Institutions." *Hastings Center Report* 5 (Feb. 1975): 17–24.

———. *Conscience and Convenience: The Asylum and Its Alternatives in Progressive America.* Boston: Little, Brown, 1980.

Rotman, Edgardo. "Las técnicas de individualización judicial frente a un moderno concepto de resocialización." *Revista de derecho penal y criminología* (1972): 114–18.

———. "L'évolution de la pensée juridique sur le but de la sanction pénale." In *Aspects nouveaux de la pensée juridique (hommage à Marc Ancel).* Paris: Pedone, 1975.

———. "La protection des droits de l'homme en matière pénale dans le droit Argentin et Latino-Américain." *Revue internationale de droit pénal* (1976): 83–92.

———. "Le sens de l'individualisation judiciaire." *Revue de science criminelle et de droit pénal compare* (1977): 437–44.

———. "Resozialisierungstendenzen im argentinischen Strafgesetzbuch." *Zeitschrift für die gesamte Strafrechtswissenschaft* 91 (1979): 475–98.

———. "El tratamiento socioterapéutico de delincuentes aquejados de perturbaciones mentales en la Clínica Dr. Henri van der Hoeven (Utrecht)." In *Congreso Panamericano de criminologia.* Buenos Aires: Universidad del Salvador, 1979.

———. "La politique du traitement a la lumière de la troisième edition de *La défense sociale nouvelle.*" *Revue de science criminelle et de droit pénal compare* (1984): 573–77.

———. "Rechtliche Voraussetzungen der Behandlung geistiges gestörter Straftäter in den Vereinigten Staaten." In *Festschrift für Günter Blau,* edited by H. -D. Schwind. Berlin: De Gruyter, 1985.

———. "Do Criminal Offenders Have a Constitutional Right to Rehabilitation?" *Journal of Criminal Law and Criminology* 77 (1986): 1023–68.

Rotthaus, Karl Peter. "Sozialtherapie in der Dr. van der Hoeven Klinik in Utrecht." *MschrKrim* 58 (1975): 83–94.

————. "Die Neue Dr. van der Hoeven Klinik in Utrecht," *MschrKrim* 61 (1978): 126–34.

————. "Sozialtherapie in der Justizvollzugsanstalt Gelsenkirchen." *Zeitschrift für Strafvollzug und Straffälligenhilfe* 30 (1981): 323–33.

————. "Erfahrungen in der praktischen Sozialtherapie—Stellungnahme eines Juristen." In *Sozialtherapie: Grenzfragen bei der Beurteilung psychischer Auffälligkeiten im Strafrecht*, edited by H. Goppinger and J. P. Bresser, 79–99. Stuttgart: Enke, 1982.

Roxin, Claus. "Fin de la pena y reforma del derecho penal." *Revista de derecho penal, criminología y criminalística* (1973): 3–4.

Rudenstine, David. *The Rights of Ex-Offenders: The Basic ACLU Guide to an Ex-Offender's Rights*. New York: Avon Books, 1979.

Sánchez Galindo, Antonio. *El derecho a la readaptación social*. Buenos Aires: Ediciones Depalma, 1983.

Schuler-Springorum, Horst. *Strafvollzug im Übergang*. Göttingen: Verlag Otto Schwartz, 1969.

Schwind, H. -D., and Blau, G., eds. *Strafvollzug in der Praxis*, 2nd ed. Berlin: De Gruyter, 1988.

Sechrest, Lee, Susan O. White, and Elizabeth D. Brown, eds. *The Rehabilitation of Criminal Offenders: Problems and Prospects*. Washington, D.C.: National Academy of Sciences, 1979.

Serril, Michael S. "Is Rehabilitation Dead?" *Corrections Magazine* 1 (May–June 1975): 3–32.

Sherman, Michael, and Gordon Hawkins. *Imprisonment in America*. Chicago: University of Chicago Press, 1981.

Smith, Alexander B., and Louis Berlin. *Treating the Criminal Offender*. New York: Plenum Press, 1988.

Snyder, Frederick E. "Crime and Community Mediation—The Boston Experience: A Preliminary Report on the Dorchester Urban Court Program." *Wisconsin Law Review* 3 (1978): 739.

Stürup, Georg K. *Treating the Untreatable: Chronic Criminals at Herstedvester*. Baltimore, Md.: Johns Hopkins Press, 1968.

Toch, Hans, ed. *Therapeutic Communities in Corrections*. New York: Praeger, 1980.

van Emmerik, J. L. "Behandlung von Straffälligen in der van der Hoevenkliniek." *Monatschrift für Kriminologie und Strafrechtsreform* 65 (1982): 288.

van Kalmhout, Anton M., and Peter J. P. Tak. *Sanctions-Systems in the Member-States of the Council of Europe. Part I: Deprivation of Liberty, Community Service and Other Substitutes*. Deventer, Netherlands: Kluwer Publishers, 1988.

Vasalli, Giuliano. "Il dibatito sulla rieducazione." *Rassegna penitenziaria e criminologica* 1–2 (1982): 437–81.

von Liszt, Franz. *Strafrechtliche Aufsätze und Vorträge*. Berlin: J. Guttentag, 1905.

von Trotha, Trutz. *Strafvollzug und Ruckfälligkeit*. Heidelberg: Muller, 1983.

Wright, Kevin. *The Great American Crime Myth*. Westport, Conn.: Greenwood Press, 1985.

Würtenberger, Thomas. *Kriminalpolitik im sozialen Rechtsstaat*. Stuttgart: Ferdinand Enke, 1970.

Yackle, Larry W. *Reform and Regret: The Story of Federal Judicial Involvement in the Alabama Prison System*. New York: Oxford University Press, 1989.

Zaffaroni, Eugenio R. *Tratado de derecho penal*. Buenos Aires: Ediar, 1983.

Zimbardo, Philip. "Pathology of Imprisonment." *Society* 9 (1972): 6.

Index

Addictions. *See* Dependency
Alcohol, 4, 128–29. *See also* Dependency
Alexander, Franz, 62, 63
Allen, Francis A., 23, 26–27, 42, 76, 110
Alternative Draft for a Penal Code (1966), 51, 52, 65–66, 71, 109, 148, 149, 160–61
American Civil Liberties Union, 104
American Convention of Human Rights, 76, 89
American Psychoanalytic Association, 123
Ancel, Marc, 49–51, 160
Anectine (drug), 102
Anthropocentric models. *See* Humanistic model
Anti-institutional ideology, 157
Antiquity, 27
Antisociality, 114, 115, 116, 117–18
Arbitration, 165, 187
Architecture of prisons, 33, 34, 59
Argentina, 42, 62, 106
Asylums, 26, 27, 61
Atascadero State Hospital (California), 102
Auburn prison (New York), 33, 35–37, 49, 59

Australia, 35–36, 162
Austria, 36, 109, 175
Authoritarian model, 8–9, 29, 109, 120–21, 146–47, 169, 183
Aversion therapy, 102

Barnes v. Government of Virgin Islands, 12
Bavaria, 39, 105–6, 147
Beccaria, Cesare, 90, 111
Behavioral-Employment Intervention Program (Michigan), 168
Behavioral sciences, 26, 43, 44–45, 60–63, 107
Behavior modification, 69, 76–77, 102–5. *See also* Personalities of offenders
Belgium, 36, 42–43, 106, 159, 160, 164
Bentham, Jeremy, 34, 47, 112
Boston, Massachusetts, 36, 48, 157, 158, 165
Bowring v. Godwin (U.S.), 85
Brainwashing, 27, 50, 69, 74, 77, 90, 105, 116, 167, 172
Bresolin v. Morris (U.S.), 84
Bridewell prisons (Great Britain), 32, 35, 38
Brockway, Zebulon, 40–41, 106–7
Buddy System (Hawaii), 168
Butner prison (North Carolina), 153–54

California, 102, 125, 134, 170
California Community Treatment Project, 134, 170
Cambridge-Somerville Youth Study, 123
Chain gangs, 157
Christianity, 28–31, 33, 60
Clonce v. Richardson (U.S.), 104
Coercion, 6–7, 8–9, 22, 23, 29, 146, 162, 183
Coffin v. Reichard (U.S.), 86
Collective responsibility, 118–19
Community, 3, 48, 60, 119–20, 149, 183, 186
Community adjustment, 4, 128–29, 131
Community rehabilitation: advantages of, 155; and the authoritarian model, 169; and Butner prison, 154; and criticism of rehabilitation, 119–20, 124–25; and dangerousness, 156, 159, 167; definition of, 154–55, 157; and depersonalization, 155, 169; and drugs, 161, 172, 174; and education, 155, 167; and the effectiveness of rehabilitation, 124–25; and the environment of prisons, 154–71; essence of, 157; as the essence of rehabilitation, 147, 186; and the humanistic model, 155–56; and incorrigible offenders, 14; and isolation, 155; and juvenile delinquency, 119–20, 124–25, 166–71, 187; and labeling, 170–71; and the liberty-centered model, 155, 159–60, 167; and medical treatment, 166, 174; as a method for rehabilitation, 4; and overcrowding, 155, 158, 161, 165, 166; as a panacea, 156–57, 186; and parole, 169, 170; and personality/attitude change, 156, 165, 187; and probation, 155, 157–59, 160, 161, 162, 174; and psychiatric/psychological treatment, 155, 158, 166, 168, 172; and recidivism, 158, 167; and the rights model, 78–79; and the rights of offenders, 163, 167; and the right to rehabilitation, 155, 156, 167, 172, 186; and self-determination, 169, 170; and sentencing, 155, 156; and sex offenders, 174; and socialization, 156, 159, 161, 164, 167; and the

social learning model, 5–6; and social therapy, 174–76; and sociological theory/research, 119–20; and staff, 169; and stigma, 166, 170–71; and superfluous/impracticable rehabilitation, 14; and supervision, 156, 158–59, 160, 163, 164–65; and suspended sentences, 159–61; types of programs for, 167–68; and vocational training, 170; and work, 164, 165, 166, 168. *See also names of specific types of programs*
Community service, 13, 50, 72, 155, 156, 161–64, 166, 186–87
Community transformation, 119–20, 186
Congregate system, 59
Conjugal visitation, 152
Conrad, John P., 122, 125, 153
Constitutional mandates: in the Federal Republic of Germany, 73–75, 88; in Italy, 71–73; and the rights model, 71–90, 184; in Spain, 75–76; in the United States, 76–90
Conviction, 86
Corporal punishment, 41
Correctional system, aims of the, 145–46
Counseling, 75, 128–29
Covenant on Civil and Political Rights (United Nations), 76, 89
Crime: causes of, 34–35, 42, 48, 60–61, 65, 109–10; environmental theory of, 26, 65–68; hidden, 114–15; as an illness, 60, 62–63; prevention of, 1, 49–50; war theory of, 110
Criticism of rehabilitation. *See names of specific topics*
Crofton, Walter, 38, 39, 40
Cruel and unusual punishment, 79–85, 88–89, 90, 111
Cuesta Arzamendi, José Luis de la, 75, 76, 150
Cullen, Francis, 91, 116
Culpability, 51–52, 108

Dangerousness: and community rehabilitation, 156, 159, 167; and criticism of rehabilitation, 106; and the historical aspects of rehabilitation, 23, 42–45; and imprisonment, 144, 151; justification of, 185; and juvenile delinquency, 167; and the mentally disordered, 172, 173; and positivism, 42–45; and the rights model, 72, 74–75; and sentencing, 15, 106, 159; and the therapeutic model, 61

Death penalty, 28, 33–34, 44–45, 72

Democracy, 48–49, 64, 69, 112, 116

Denmark, 36, 148, 149, 150–53, 163, 175

Dependency, 4, 84–85, 128–29, 151

Depersonalization, 12, 66, 72, 83, 144–45, 149, 155, 169

Depo-Provera drug treatment, 174

Detention institutions, 46

Deterioration/deprivation of prisoners. See Environment of prisons

Determinism, 42, 43, 60, 61, 113–14, 171, 185

Deterrence: and criticism of rehabilitation, 111, 112, 126–27, 184; and the effectiveness of rehabilitation, 126–27; and the emergence of prisons, 37; and the historical aspects of rehabilitation, 31, 37, 38, 44, 47; and imprisonment, 147–48; and individualization, 47; and law and order, 111; and the less eligibility principle, 112; and the penitentiary model, 5, 60; and positivism, 44; and the right to rehabilitation, 12–13; and sentencing, 16, 147–48; and the significance of rehabilitation, 2; and the social learning model, 66; specific deterrence, 9–10, 111

Deviance, 24, 114, 118

Dignity, 25, 31, 78, 87, 149, 183

Discipline: and coercion, 146; and community rehabilitation, 166; and the historical aspects of rehabilitation, 23, 24, 25, 30, 32, 33, 34, 39; and the humanistic model, 155–56; and imprisonment, 146–47, 152; and the liberty-centered model, 146–47; and the penitentiary model, 5, 59–60, 184; and the rights model, 77, 79; and staff, 147; and the state, 146–47

Diversion program, 4, 164–65. See also names of specific types of programs

Dorchester (Massachusetts) Urban Court Program, 165

Double celling, 82–83

Drugs, 4, 76, 102–3, 128–29, 151, 161, 172, 174. See also Dependency

Ducpetiaux, Edmond, 36, 37

Due process, 9, 11–12, 78–79, 85–86, 104

Dünkel, Frieder, 151

Eastern Penitentiary (Cherry Hill, Pennsylvania), 35

Education: and community rehabilitation, 155, 167; and criticism of rehabilitation, 110, 128–29; and the definition of rehabilitation, 3; and the effectiveness of rehabilitation, 4, 128–29; and the environment of prisons, 186; and the historical aspects of rehabilitation, 33, 34, 39, 40, 41, 42, 46; as an incentive, 39, 40, 41; and individualization, 46; and juvenile delinquency, 167; and law and order, 110; and the liberty-centered model, 10, 149; and the mentally disordered, 172; and the moral content of rehabilitation, 7; and positivism, 42; and the rights model, 70, 71–73, 75–76, 78, 87; and the rights of offenders, 6; and the right to rehabilitation, 87, 184; and the significance of rehabilitation, 2; and the social learning model, 65

Effectiveness of rehabilitation: and criticism of rehabilitation, 101–2, 120–35; evaluative studies about the, 122–26; and Martinson's "What Works," 126–33; measurement of the, 4; and the "Nothing Works" conclusion, 127–28, 133–35, 185; problems in evaluating the, 130–35; relevance of the, 120–22. See also names of specific topics

Eighth Amendment, 79–80, 81–84, 85, 88, 90, 174

Elbowroom theory, 51–52

Electric shock, 102

Electronic surveillance, 165–66

Elmira Reformatory (New York), 40–41, 42, 59, 106–7

El Reno prison, 104
Enculturation, 64–65
England. *See* Great Britain
Enlightenment, 30, 111
Environmental theory, 26, 65–68
Environment of prisons: and community rehabilitation, 154–71; and criticism of rehabilitation, 111–12; and cruel and unusual punishment, 81–84; and the definition of rehabilitation, 3; and dehumanization,11; and education, 186; and the historical aspects of rehabilitation, 36, 37; and imprisonment, 143–45, 165–86; and the less eligibility principle, 111–12; and the liberty-centered model, 10; and the mentally disordered, 172; and prisons as problem-solving communities, 5–6; and psychiatric/psychological treatment, 172; and the rights model, 70, 78, 79, 81–84, 87; and the rights of offenders, 6, 70–71; and the right to rehabilitation, 87, 91, 174, 184; and sentencing, 16; and socialization, 185–86; and the social learning model, 5, 65–68; and therapeutic communities, 187; and the therapeutic model, 61; and work, 186
Equal protection clause, 86–88
Estelle v. Gamble (U.S.), 84
Eugenics, 45, 46–47, 60
Europe, 2, 5–6, 45–46, 122, 159, 161, 163, 171, 174–76, 187. *See also names of specific nations*
European Convention on Human Rights, 163
Executioners, 31

Fair warning, 11–12
Family therapy, 4, 169
Federal Bureau of Prisons (U.S.), 104–5, 154
Federal Republic of Germany (FRG), 51, 73–75, 88, 148, 160, 163–64, 175
Fifth Amendment, 11, 104
Fines, 43, 50, 124, 148, 156, 163, 186
First offenders, 26, 124, 129, 131
Forced labor, 163
Foster homes, 4, 164, 170

Foucault, Michel, 22–23, 24, 25–26, 30, 61
Fourteenth Amendment, 11, 85–86
France, 33, 36, 38, 45, 50, 106, 147, 159, 163
Freudianism, 48, 61–62
Furloughs, 66, 72, 73, 79, 131, 146, 154, 186

Gangs, 11, 145, 166
Garland, David, 25–26, 27, 46, 47, 116–17
Garofalo, Ricardo, 42, 117
Gendreau, Paul, 127, 133–34, 168
George Junior Republic (Freeville, New York), 48–49
Germany, 36, 42–43, 67, 68, 71, 108, 112, 147. *See also* Federal Republic of Germany
Ghent prison, 33, 36
Gilbert, Karen E., 91, 116
Gladstone Committee Report, 25, 47, 49
Gloucester prison (Great Britain), 35
Good behavior, 38–39, 40
Gottfredson, Michael R., 123, 134–35
Graduate-release program, 154
Great Britain: community service in, 161–62, 163; and criticism of rehabilitation, 106, 112; dangerousness in, 106; deterrence in, 47; discipline in, 25; education in, 46; first offenders in, 26; and the historical aspects of rehabilitation, 25–26, 32, 35–36, 42–43, 46–47; individualization in, 25, 46–47; juvenile delinquency in, 46; and the less eligibility principle, 112; positivist influence in, 42–43; retribution in, 47; right to rehabilitation in, 12; scientism in, 47; sentencing in, 106, 160; social engineering in, 47; and social therapy, 175; types of prisons in, 46. *See also names of specific persons or prisons*
Gregg v. Georgia (U.S.), 80
Group living, 164, 168, 170
Group therapy, 4, 68, 125–26, 128–29, 168–69, 175

Halfway houses, 128–29, 164
Hard labor, 12, 25, 34, 35, 44, 149, 185

Hartford (Connecticut) Community Correctional Center, 88
Harvard University Center for Criminal Justice, 119–20, 169–71
Hawkins, Gordon, 23, 37, 110
Heredity, 61
Hidden crime, 114–15
Holt v. Sarver (U.S.), 80, 83
Homicidal monomania theory, 61
Hood, Roger, 123, 124
House arrest, 165, 166
Houses of corrections, 31–33
Howard, John, 23–24, 34, 35, 83, 150
Humanistic model: characteristics of the, 8–9; and the community/community rehabilitation, 155–56, 183; and dialogue, 8; and discipline, 155–56; and due process, 9; and the environment of prisons, 11; as a form of rehabilitation, 8, 183; and the historical aspects of rehabilitation, 24, 27, 44, 49–52; and imprisonment, 10, 144; and moral character, 183; and positivism, 44; and power, 24; and psychiatric/psychological treatment, 9, 62; and the rights of individuals, 8–9, 24; and the rights model, 77–78; and the rights of offenders, 9; and self-determination, 9, 183; and self-discovery, 8–9; and the social defense movement, 49–52; and the state, 8–9; and the therapeutic model, 62–63
Human nature, 41–42, 45

Imprisonment, 10–11, 12, 15, 80, 82–83, 110, 143–50, 151–53, 185–86. *See also* Environment of prisons
In-and-out jail therapy, 131
Incentives, 5, 9–10, 38–41, 60, 107. *See also names of specific types of incentives*
Incorrigible offenders, 13–14, 42, 43, 44–45, 48–49, 171, 185
Indeterminate sentencing: abuses of, 107; and the behavioral sciences, 107; concealed, 106; and criticism of rehabilitation, 101, 105–7, 184; and deterrence, 148; and the historical aspects of reha-
bilitation, 38–41, 45–46, 47–48, 51, 105–6; and imprisonment, 151, 152; as an incentive, 38–41, 107; and individualization, 45–46, 47–48; and the mentally disordered, 85–86, 106; and parole, 107, 108; and the penitentiary model, 5, 59; and psychiatric/psychological treatment, 86, 108–9; and punishment, 14; purpose of, 107; and recidivism, 45–46; and the rights model, 69, 76–77, 86; and the rights of offenders, 108; and the right to rehabilitation, 86; and the social defense movement, 51; in the United States, 76–77, 86, 106–7
Individualization, 25, 44–49, 59, 86, 106, 159, 171
Individual transformation, 117–18
Institutional adjustment, 4, 128–29
Instituto de Criminología (Argentina), 62
International law, 76, 88–89, 103
International Penal and Penitentiary Congress, 12, 112
International Union of Criminal Law, 43, 46
Interstate Agreement on Detainers Act (U.S.), 91
Intrusive therapies, 101–5
Isolation, 30, 33, 34, 35, 36, 37, 59, 155
Italy, 33, 36, 42, 71–73, 163

Jones, Maxwell, 66, 175
Judges, 31, 43, 50, 106
Just deserts philosophy, 148
Justice, 2, 45, 183
Juvenile delinquency: and the authoritarian model, 169; and community rehabilitation, 119–20, 124–25, 162, 166–71, 187; and criticism of rehabilitation, 106, 114, 119–20, 122, 123, 124–25, 129; and dangerousness, 167; and depersonalization, 169; and education, 167; and the effectiveness of rehabilitation, 122, 124–25, 129; and families, 169; and foster care, 4; and the historical aspects of rehabilitation, 33, 44, 46, 48, 50; and individualization, 46, 48; and labeling, 170–71; and the lib-

erty-centered model, 167; and the Massachusetts Deinstitutionalization Experiment, 169–71; methods for rehabilitation of, 4; and overcrowding, 166; and parole, 169, 170; and positivism, 44; prevention of, 123; and psychiatric/ psychological treatment, 86, 123, 168; and recidivism, 167; and the rights model, 86; and the rights of offenders, 167; and the right to rehabilitation, 86, 167; and self-determination, 169, 170; sentencing of, 106; and the social defense movement, 50; and socialization, 167; and sociological theory/research, 114, 119–20; and staff, 169, 170; and stigma, 166, 170–71; and the therapeutic community, 169; types of programs to deal with, 167–68; and vocational training, 170; and work, 168

Kalamazoo State Hospital (Michigan), 102–3
Kassebaum, G., 125, 126

Laaman v. Helgemoe (U.S.), 81–82, 85, 174
Labeling, 114, 118, 134, 157, 170–71, 187
Lareau v. Manson (U.S.), 88
Law, 2, 42–45, 49–52, 76, 88–89, 103
Law and order, 109–11
Law Enforcement Assistance Administration (LEAA), 104, 162
Leavenworth prison, 104
Leave of absence, 66, 72
Legislation. *See* Law; *names of specific legislation*
Lehbach decision (FRG), 73, 75
Lerman, P., 124–25, 134
Less eligibility principle, 111–12, 150
Liberty-centered model: and community rehabilitation, 155, 159–60, 167; and criticism of rehabilitation, 109, 116, 117; and cruel and unusual punishment, 83; and depersonalization, 149; and discipline, 146–47; and education, 10, 149; and the environment of institutions, 10; and imprisonment, 146–47,

149–50; and incentives, 9–10; and incorrigible offenders, 14; and juvenile delinquency, 167; and the mentally disordered, 187; and psychiatric/psychological treatment, 10; and the rights model, 77–78, 79, 83; and the rights of offenders, 183; and the right to rehabilitation, 10, 183–84; and self-determination, 149; and self-realization, 10; and sentencing, 14, 159–60; and sociological theory/research, 116, 117; and superfluous/impracticable rehabilitation, 14; and visitations, 149; and vocational training, 10; and work, 149, 150
Life imprisonment, 52, 72, 73, 149
Lipton, Douglas, 4, 121, 124, 125, 126–33, 134
Liszt, Franz von, 43–44, 148
Lombroso, Cesare, 40, 61

Mabillon, Jean, 30, 37
Machonochie, Alexander, 26, 38–39, 40, 59
Mail, 77
Manhattan (New York) Court Employment Project, 165
Mannheim, Hermann, 112, 115
Marion (Illinois) prison, 104
Martinson, Robert, 4, 121, 124, 125, 126–33, 134
Massachusetts, 36, 48, 91, 119–20, 157, 158, 165, 169–71
Massachusetts Deinstitutionalization Experiment, 169–71
Mediation, 165, 187
Medical model. *See* Therapeutic model
Medical treatment, 3, 84–85, 116, 128–29, 166, 174
Mentally disordered, 14, 61, 65–68, 85–86, 102, 106, 144, 153, 171–76, 187
Merton, Robert K., 7, 114
Mesdag Kliniek (Groningen, Netherlands), 68
Milieu therapy, 127, 128–29
Miller, Jerome, 119–20, 169–70
Minimum Rules for the Treatment of

Prisoners (United Nations), 69, 76, 88–89

Monasticism, 5, 10, 28–30, 34, 35, 37, 144

Moral character/education, 5, 6–8, 13, 21–22, 24, 28–29, 31–33, 37, 42–45, 59, 183, 184

Morales v. Schmidt (U.S.), 86

Morris, Norval, 108, 153

National Academy of Sciences, 129–33

National Penitentiary Congress (Cincinnati, 1870), 39–40, 106–7

National Research Council, 120, 129–33

Netherlands: community service in, 162, 163, 164; and criticism of rehabilitation, 105, 106, 109; and the historical aspects of rehabilitation, 32–33, 38; houses of correction in, 32–33; and imprisonment, 148, 161; incentive strategies in, 38; increase in crime in, 161; mentally disordered in, 106; sentencing in, 105, 106, 109, 148; and the social learning model, 67; social therapy in, 175

Newgate prison (Great Britain), 26

Newman v. Alabama (U.S.), 84

New social defense movements, 49–51

Norfolk Island prison (Australia), 26, 38–39

Norway, 42, 106, 112, 148, 163, 175

"Nothing works" conclusion, 127–28, 133–35, 185

Nullum crimen, nulla poena, sine lege principle, 11–13

Offenders, types of, 39–40, 127, 134. *See also* Rights of offenders

Ohlin, Lloyd, 114, 119–20, 169–70

Open prisons, 147, 149, 154, 186

Overcrowding: at Butner prison, 154; and community rehabilitation, 155, 158, 161, 165, 166; and criticism of rehabilitation, 110; and cruel and unusual punishment, 82–83; and the historical aspects of rehabilitation, 31; and imprisonment, 11; and international law, 88; and juvenile delinquency, 166; and law and order, 110; and probation, 158; and the rights model, 78–79, 82–83, 88; and sentencing, 11, 15, 16

Overly intrusive methods, 102–5

Panel on Research on Rehabilitative Techniques (National Research Council), 129–33

Pardon, 106, 162–63, 164

Parole: and the Alternative Draft, 149; and community rehabilitation, 169, 170; contract system for, 91; and criticism of rehabilitation, 106, 107, 108, 109, 125, 128–29, 131; and drugs, 174; and the effectiveness of rehabilitation, 125, 128–29, 131; and first offenders, 131; function of, 107; and the historical aspects of rehabilitation, 38, 40, 43, 47–48; and individualization, 47–48; and juvenile delinquency, 169, 170; and positivism, 43; and the rights model, 72, 73, 76–77; and the right to rehabilitation, 91; and sentencing, 107, 108; and sex offenders, 173; shock, 131

Paternalism, 6, 27–28, 69, 77, 78, 118

Patuxent Institution, 173

Penal servitude, 12, 25, 185

Penal welfarism, 27–28

Penance, 29–30

Penitentiaries. *See* Prisons; *names of specific prisons*

Penitentiary model, 4–6, 27, 59–60, 101, 105, 107, 184

Pennsylvania, 33–37, 59, 165

Personalities of offenders, 4, 49–52, 76, 117–18, 121, 128–29, 156, 165, 187

Phrenology, 60–61

Pilot Intensive Counselling Project (PICO), 123–24

Pittsburgh Western Penitentiary, 34, 35

Poena medicinalis, 28–29, 60, 148

Positivism, 40, 41–45

Prins, Adolphe, 23, 43, 44–45

Prisons: architecture of, 33, 34, 59; as asylums, 26; as communities, 48, 149; and democracy, 48–49; emergence of, 26, 33–38; functions of, 46–47; models of, 150–54; purposes of, 26, 31, 32; realities of, 21–22; subcultures of, 11, 74–75; types of, 46; violence in, 11, 82–83, 110. *See also names of specific prisons*

Privacy, 72, 77, 90, 104, 171

Probation: and the Alternative Draft, 149; and community rehabilitation, 155, 157–59, 160, 161, 162, 174; and corporate offenders, 13; and criticism of rehabilitation, 124, 128–29; and drugs, 174; and the effectiveness of rehabilitation, 124, 128–29; and first offenders, 129; goals of, 158; and the historical aspects of rehabilitation, 48, 50, 51, 52; and individualization, 48; and overcrowding, 158; and psychiatric/ psychological treatment, 158; and recidivism, 158; and the rights model, 72; and the right to rehabilitation, 91, 186; shock, 158; and the social defense movement, 50, 51, 52; subsidies for, 158; and supervision, 158–59; and surveillance, 158–59; and suspended sentences, 160, 161; and white-collar criminals, 13

Probation officers, 158, 166

Procunier v. Martinez (U.S.), 77, 84

Progressive-stage system, 38–40, 59

Project CREST (Clinical Regional Support Teams), 168

Project Crossroads (Washington, D. C.), 164

Prolixin, 102–3

Psychiatric/psychological treatment: and community rehabilitation, 155, 158, 166, 168, 172; and criticism of rehabilitation, 102–5, 108–9, 115, 121, 123, 124, 125, 127–28; and the definition of rehabilitation, 3; and the effectiveness of rehabilitation, 121, 123, 124, 125, 127–28; and the environment of prisons, 172; and the equal protection clause, 86–87; and the humanistic model, 9; and juvenile delinquency, 86, 123, 168; and the liberty-centered model, 10; and the mentally disordered, 85–86, 172; as a method for re-

habilitation, 4; overly intrusive methods of, 102–5; and probation, 158; and the rights model, 76, 78, 79, 85–87; and the rights of offenders, 174; and the right to rehabilitation, 85–87, 184; and sentencing, 86, 108–9; sexual psychopaths' right to, 86; and the social learning model, 65–68; and the therapeutic model, 62–63; as voluntary or involuntary, 68, 76, 108–9, 153

Psychiatry, 60–63

Psychosurgery, 102–3

Pugh v. Locke (U.S.), 81

Punishment: in antiquity, 27; characteristics of modern, 185–86; in the Christian era, 28–31; and criticism of rehabilitation, 101–2, 109–13; cruel and unusual, 79–85, 88–89, 90, 111; definition of lawful, 87; demand for increased, 109–13; fair, 1–2; function of, 113–14; goals of, 22; and the historical aspects of rehabilitation, 42; and the less eligibility principle, 111–12; and the nature of punitive reactions, 112–13; and penal welfarism, 27; and positivism, 42–45; in the sixteenth century, 31–33

Punitive society, 62–63, 115

Quakers, 23, 24, 33–37

Quay, H. C., 126, 130

"Quick dip" sanction, 131

Racism, 11, 82–83, 116

Radicals, 115–17

Rasphuis prison (Netherlands), 38

Recidivism: causes of, 15; and community rehabilitation, 158, 167; and criticism of rehabilitation, 106, 109, 111, 121–22, 123, 124, 125, 126–35; and the effectiveness of rehabilitation, 4, 121–22, 123, 124, 125, 126–35; and first offenders, 129; and group counseling, 126; and the historical aspects of rehabilitation, 36, 45–46; and imprisonment, 15, 144; and incorrigible offenders, 185; and individualization,

45–46; and juvenile delinquency, 167; and the mentally disordered, 173; and the "Nothing Works" conclusion, 127–28, 133–35; and probation, 158; and the rights model, 79, 81, 82; and sentencing, 15, 45–46, 106, 109, 124, 147; and the significance of rehabilitation, 2; and the social learning model, 65, 66; and superfluous/impracticable rehabilitation, 13; and white-collar criminals, 13. *See also* Incorrigible offenders

Reform, 3, 6

Rehabilitation: components of, 3; definition of, 3–4, 70; goals of, 27; historical models of, 4–6; and prospective models, 8–9; and the purpose of imprisonment, 10–11; and the realities of prison, 21–22; and sentencing, 14–16; significance of, 1–2, 183; and specific deterrence, 9–10; superfluous/impracticable, 13–14. *See also names of specific models*

Reintegration: and criticism of rehabilitation, 118; and the definition of rehabilitation, 3; and the historical aspects of rehabilitation, 25, 51; of the mentally disordered, 172; and the rights model, 70, 73–74, 75–76; and the rights of offenders, 6, 25; and sentencing, 161, 186; and the social defense movement, 51; and sociological theory/research, 118; and work, 186

Religion, 28–31, 33, 35, 36, 37, 40–41, 59, 60

Repentance, 34

Restitution, 4, 131, 156, 164, 186–87

Retribution, 1, 2, 11, 14, 31, 43–44, 47, 49–51, 73, 106, 126–27

Revisionism, 22–26

Rewards. *See* Incentives

Rhodes v. Chapman (U.S.), 82–83

Rights model: characteristics of the, 4–6, 69–76, 184; and constitutional mandates, 71–90; and the definition of rehabilitation, 3; and the environment of prisons, 70, 78, 79, 81–84, 87; in the Federal Republic of Germany, 73–75,

88; in Italy, 71–73; and nonconstitutional sources of a right to rehabilitation, 90–91; in Spain, 75–76; and state constitutions (U.S.), 89–90; in Switzerland, 71; in the United States, 76–91. *See also* Rights of individuals; Rights of offenders; Right to rehabilitation; *names of specific topics*

Rights of individuals, 5–9, 24, 43, 44, 50, 69–71, 75–78, 102–5, 116, 171

Rights of offenders: and the aims of the correctional system, 146; and community rehabilitation, 163, 167; and criticism of rehabilitation, 102–5, 107, 108, 120–21, 122; and the definition of rehabilitation, 3; and education, 6; and the effectiveness of rehabilitation, 120–21, 122, 185; and the environment of prisons, 6, 70–71; and the historical aspects of rehabilitation, 24, 25, 31, 50; and the humanistic model, 9; and imprisonment, 6, 11, 144, 146; and juvenile delinquency, 167; and the liberty-centered model, 183; and medical treatment, 174; and the mentally disordered, 173; and overly intrusive methods, 102–5; and psychiatric/psychological treatment, 102–5, 174; and reintegration, 6, 25; and the rights models, 73–76, 184; and the rights of individuals, 69–71; and sentencing, 107, 108, 184; and the social defense movement, 50; and the state, 70; and stigma, 70; and vocational training, 6. *See also* Rights model; Rights of individuals; Right to rehabilitation

Right to rehabilitation: characteristics of the, 186; and community rehabilitation, 155, 156, 167, 172, 186; constitutional mandates for the, 71–90, 184; and criticism of rehabilitation, 120–21; definition of the, 183–84; and depersonalization, 12; and deterrence, 12–13; and dignity, 87; and due process, 11–12, 86; and education, 87, 184; and the effectiveness of rehabilitation, 120–21; and the environment of prisons, 87, 174, 184; and the equal

protection clause, 86–88; in Europe, 2, 88; and fair sentences, 15–16; and hard labor, 12; and the historical aspects of rehabilitation, 24, 27; and juvenile delinquency, 86, 167; and the liberty-centered model, 10, 183–84; and the mentally disordered, 172; nonconstitutional sources of a, 90–91; and the *nullum crimen, nulla poena, sine lege* principle, 11–13; and probation, 186; and psychiatric/psychological treatment, 85–87, 184; and sentencing, 12, 14–15, 86, 184; and sex offenders, 174; and socialization, 87; and state constitutions (U.S.), 89–90; and superfluous/impracticable rehabilitation, 13, 14; and vocational training, 87; and work, 87
Ringe prison (Denmark), 149, 150–53
Robinson, James, 124–26
Ross, Robert R., 103, 127, 133–34, 168
Rothman, David J., 22, 24, 25, 26, 34, 41, 107, 143
Rotthaus, Karl Peter, 152, 153

Saleilles, Raymond, 45, 159
San Filippo Neri Hospice (Florence, Italy), 33
Scientism, 27, 43–44, 47, 48
Searching of prisoners, 88–89, 104
Self-determination: and community rehabilitation, 169, 170; and constitutional mandates, 90; and criticism of rehabilitation, 117; and cruel and unusual punishment, 83; and humanitarianism, 9, 183; and imprisonment, 144, 149; and juvenile delinquency, 169, 170; and the liberty-centered model, 149; and the moral content of rehabilitation, 7; and the rights model, 83, 90; and the social learning model, 6, 67; and sociological theory/research, 117; and superfluous/impracticable rehabilitation, 13; and white-collar criminals, 13
Self-discipline, 5, 38, 60
Self-discovery/realization, 8–9, 10, 77, 119

Self-esteem/respect, 67, 144, 149
Self-government, 48–49
Self-rehabilitation, 81–82
Self-reliance/responsibility, 51, 152
Sellin, Thorsten, 27–28, 32, 150
Sentencing: abuse of, 184; and the behavioral sciences, 107; and community rehabilitation, 155, 156; and criticism of rehabilitation, 101–2, 105–9, 116, 124, 126, 131, 184; and culpability, 108; and dangerousness, 15, 106; and deterrence, 16, 147–48; and the effectiveness of rehabilitation, 124, 126, 131; and the environment of prisons, 16; fair, 15–16; and the historical aspects of rehabilitation, 25, 27, 43, 45, 48, 50, 51, 51–52; and imprisonment, 144, 145, 147–49, 186; and individualization, 48; and judges, 106; and juvenile delinquency, 106; and the length of sentences, 147–49; and the liberty-centered model, 14; and the mentally disordered, 106; and overcrowding, 11, 15, 16; and parole, 108; and penal welfarism, 27; and the penitentiary model, 59, 105, 107; and positivism, 42, 43; and psychiatric/psychological treatment, 108–9; and punishment, 14–16; purpose of, 89; and recidivism, 15, 106, 109, 124, 147; and reintegration, 186; and retribution, 14; and the rights model, 71, 72–73, 75–76, 78–79; and the rights of offenders, 107, 108, 184; and the right to rehabilitation, 12, 14–15, 184; and sex offenders, 173; and the social defense movement, 50, 51–52; and the social learning model, 66; and sociological theory/research, 116; and the therapeutic model, 105, 107; and white-collar criminals, 14. *See also names of specific types of sentencing*
Separate system, 35, 36, 59
Sex offenders, 86, 172–74
Sherman, Michael, 23, 37, 110
Shock parole, 131
Shock probation, 158

Short sentences, 43, 44–45, 147–48, 156, 159, 161, 162–63, 186

Silent system, 35, 36–37

Sing Sing prison, 49

Smith, Gerald, 124–26

Social class system, 23, 116

Social control/engineering, 23–24, 47, 116, 126–27, 134

Social defense movement, 44–45, 49–52

Social ideology, 26–28, 184

Socialization: and community rehabilitation, 156, 159, 161, 164, 167; and culpability, 108; definition of, 64; and the definition of rehabilitation, 3; and democracy, 64; and enculturation, 64–65; and the environment of prisons, 185–86; and imprisonment, 11, 144, 185–86; and juvenile delinquency, 167; and the moral content of the rehabilitation process, 6; and personalization, 64–65; and recidivism, 65; and the rights model, 70, 71–75, 87; and the right to rehabilitation, 87; and suspended sentences, 159, 161. *See also* Social learning model

Social learning model: and the Alternative Draft, 65–66; characteristics of the, 4–6, 63–68, 184; and community rehabilitation, 5–6; and criticism of rehabilitation, 113–20; and democracy, 64; and depersonalization, 66; and deterrence, 66; and education, 65; and environmental theory, 65–68; and the environment of prisons, 5; in Europe, 5–6; experimental aspects of the, 68; and furloughs, 66; and group therapy, 68; and the historical aspects of rehabilitation, 27; and imprisonment, 144–45; and institutional settings, 65–68; and leaves of absence, 66; and the mentally disordered, 65–68, 175; and psychotherapy, 65–68; and recidivism, 65, 66; and scientism, 64; and self-determination, 6, 67; and self-esteem, 67; and sentencing, 66; socialization as an aspect of the, 63, 64–65; and social psychiatry, 63; and social therapy, 175;

and sociological theory/research, 113–20; and staff, 67; and stigma, 66; and the therapeutic community, 66–67

Social psychiatry, 26, 63

Social reform, 115–16

Social responsibility, 73, 77

Social sciences, 43

Social therapy, 51, 52, 174–76, 187. *See also* Social learning model

Sociology, 43, 101–2, 113–20, 185

Solitary confinement, 30, 33, 34, 35, 36, 37, 59, 155

Spain, 39, 75–76, 150, 164

Sparks, Richard, 123, 124

Special Intensive Parole Unit (SIPU), 125

Staff, 67, 79, 144, 147, 152–53, 169, 170

START (Special Treatment and Rehabilitation Training Program), 104–5

State, 6–7, 8–9, 48, 49–50, 69–71, 73–75, 77, 121–22, 146–47. *See also* Constitutional mandates

State constitutions (U.S.), 89–90

Stigma, 5, 35, 66, 70, 118, 157, 166, 170–71

Succinylcholine (Anectine), 102

Supervision, 156, 158–59, 160, 163, 164–65, 166

Surveillance, 158–59

Suspended sentences, 50, 51, 52, 148, 159–61, 163, 164, 186

Sweden, 42, 106, 148, 160, 164

Switzerland, 42–43, 71, 106, 163, 171–72, 175

Therapeutic communities, 66–67, 169, 187

Therapeutic model: and the behavioral sciences, 60–61; characteristics of the, 4–6, 60–63, 184; and criticism of rehabilitation, 101, 107, 108, 109, 114–15, 184; and dangerousness, 61; and the historical aspects of rehabilitation, 27, 48, 50–51; and imprisonment, 151, 152, 153; inadequacies of the, 63; and mental illness, 61; and the mentally disordered, 171–76; and *poena medi-*

cinalis, 60; and psychiatry, 60–63; and public health, 61; and the punitive society, 62–63; and the rights of individuals, 5, 78; and sentencing, 105, 107; and the social defense movement, 50–51; and social therapy, 175; and sociological theory/research, 114–15; and stigma, 5
Therapists, types of, 127
Tort claims, 90–91
Torture, 30
Training-school system, 170
Transportation, 32, 35–36, 38
Tripartite prison system (Plato), 28

United Nations, 69, 76, 88–89
United States. *See names of specific persons, prisons, or topics*
Universal Declaration of Human Rights, 89

Vacaville State Hospital (California), 102
Vera Institute (New York), 156
Violence, 11, 82–83, 110
Visitation, 72, 82, 149, 152, 186
Vocational adjustment, 4, 128–29
Vocational training: and community rehabilitation, 170; and criticism of rehabilitation, 128–29, 131; and cruel and unusual punishment, 82; and the definition of rehabilitation, 3; and the effectiveness of rehabilitation, 128–29, 131; and the historical aspects of rehabilitation, 32–33, 41; and juvenile delinquency, 170; and the liberty-centered model, 10; and the mentally disordered, 172–73; and the rights model, 6, 70, 73, 75, 82, 87

Voluntary/involuntary treatment, 68, 76, 108–9, 153

Walnut Street Jail (Philadelphia, Pennsylvania), 23, 33–37
Weekend sentences, 165
"What Works" (Martinson), 126–33
White-collar crime, 13, 14, 115, 148
Wilderness training, 4, 168, 169
Wilkins, Leslie, 122, 123, 124
Wilks, Judith, 4, 121, 124, 125, 126–33, 134
Wolff v. McDonnell (U.S.), 77
Work: at Butner prison, 154; and community rehabilitation, 164, 165, 166, 168; and criticism of rehabilitation, 111, 131; and cruel and unusual punishment, 82; and the definition of rehabilitation, 3; and the effectiveness of rehabilitation, 130–31; and the environment of prisons, 186; exploitation of, 111, 150; and the historical aspects of rehabilitation, 30, 33, 34, 35, 36, 37, 38–39, 44; and imprisonment, 150, 151–52; as an incentive, 38–39; and juvenile delinquency, 168; and the liberty-centered model, 149, 150; and the penitentiary model, 5, 59, 60, 184; and positivism, 44; as punishment, 150; and reintegration, 186; remuneration for, 3, 87, 150, 151–52; and the rights model, 73, 75, 79, 82, 87
Work-release programs, 4, 165
World War II, 175, 187

Youth Authority Community Treatment Project, 124–25

About the Author

EDGARDO ROTMAN is a Staff Attorney at Massachusetts Correctional Legal Services. He has been a Visiting Scholar at Harvard Law School and a Visiting Professor at Boston University School of Law.